NORTH CAROLINA COAST

JASON FRYE

Contents

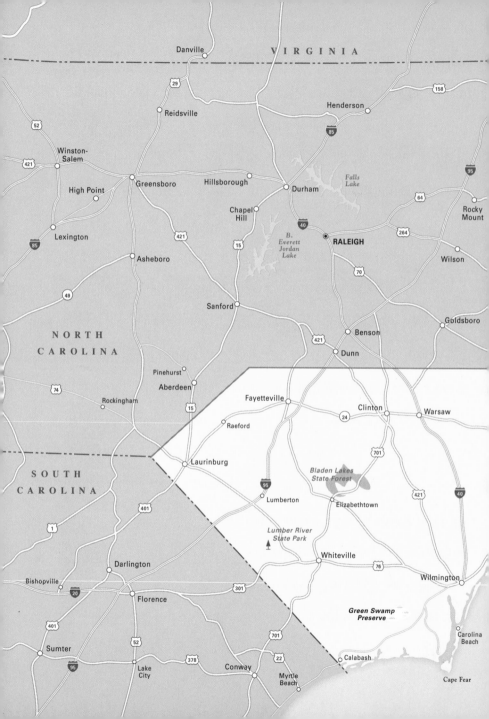

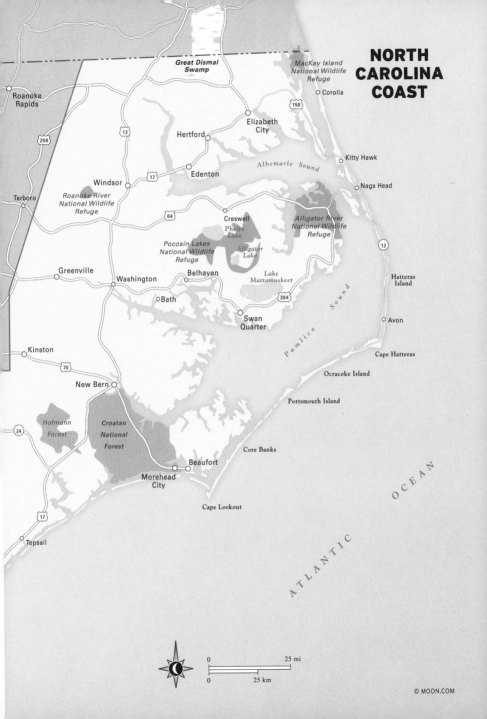

DISCOVER

North Carolina
Coast

I was a few steps behind my dad as he carried my 3-year-old nephew past the fig trees and the dune grass at Wrightsville Beach and paused at the crest of the walkway. My nephew, Silas, turned in his grandfather's arms, his eyes the widest I'd ever seen, his mouth open in a silent "O."

He turned back to the expanse of sand and surf and said one word:

"Whoa."

Then, "Whoaa. Whoaaaa."

He looked back at me and squealed.

My nephew had just seen the beach for the first time and in trying to process a horizon filled with waves and marked by a line of thunderheads hanging high over the curve of the earth, he laughed. His world had changed, and he laughed.

It was a moment I wanted to capture and cling to, not just out of love for my nephew, but also out of love of discovery.

This perfect moment — it's a singular thing, but we chase it. We crave it. We look for it every chance we get. And every once in a while, we're fortunate

Clockwise from top left: cruising the Intracoastal Waterway; the Elizabethan Gardens on Roanoke Island; spiral staircase in the Currituck Beach Lighthouse; surf shop near Wrightsville Beach; wild horse near Corolla; sunrise as seen from the sand dunes at the Outer Banks.

enough to feel it again. That feeling is why we come to places like this, to the shores of North Carolina.

There's a waking lullaby in the saline smell of the sea, in the cry of gulls and the beat of waves on the sand. Just a note or two of that song and we're lifted out of the moment, transported to our own instances of discovery, left grasping at the memory with all our senses and capturing pieces of it.

The call of songbirds in the marsh grass, lightning in a summer sky, ships' lights on the dark sea, golden evenings walking among the bent heads of sea oats — these can all take us there; so too can the taste of saltwater on our lips after we dive under that first wave, the heat of afternoon sun on our shoulders, the aroma of jasmine blossoms in the night.

Seeking these experiences is the first step and wherever you go on the coast of North Carolina, you'll find them. You'll find those things that allow you to see this world with fresh eyes and experience it anew.

Clockwise from top left: an egret at the Mattamuskeet National Wildlife Refuge; Bodie Island Lighthouse near the Cape Hatteras National Seashore; Pamlico Sound; fishing on Bald Head Island.

5 TOP
EXPERIENCES

1 **Meet Wild Horses:** Sign up for a wild horse tour to meet the majestic North Carolina residents who roam the beaches in the Outer Banks (page 38).

2 **Feast on Local Seafood:** Devour local seafood across the coast (page 21).

3 **Admire Historic Lighthouses:** Learn the stories behind these towering beacons and climb to the top to admire the sweeping views (page 55).

4 Make a Splash: Paddle, kayak, sail, and canoe your way to adventure (page 27).

5 **Wander the Cape Lookout National Seashore:** Get away from it all by wandering a stretch of this 56 miles of coastline (page 108).

Planning Your Trip

Where to Go

The Outer Banks

This strip of narrow islands is a haven for anglers, sun-seekers, and history-lovers; they come for the ecological wonder of the maritime forest, the dune habitats and the shallow sounds that separate the Outer Banks from mainland North Carolina. Surfers, kiteboarders, and hang gliders ride the waves and wind around **Nags Head** and the **Cape Hatteras National Seashore**. On **Roanoke Island**, one of the first English settlements appeared then disappeared under baffling circumstances—a mystery that pervades today. Pirates and privateers plied these waters, and Blackbeard lost his head near **Ocracoke**. The vast **Pamlico and Albemarle Sounds** are home to colonial towns and fishing villages centuries old. Inland, the **Great Dismal Swamp**, an eerie,

unforgettable place, and the **Alligator River National Wildlife Refuge** are home to twisting marsh creeks and arrow-straight, hand-dug canals perfect for kayaking and spotting the rare **red wolf**. Generations of families have called the rivers and sounds of the **Inner Banks** home, farming the land and fishing the waters decade after decade. Along the **Roanoke River** are mill towns, fishing villages, and the colonial crossroads river town of **Halifax**, birthplace of the documents that inspired the Declaration of Independence.

Beaufort and the Crystal Coast

The architecture of **New Bern** and **Beaufort**, two of North Carolina's most important colonial cities, are among the finest in the south, and their waterfronts are lined with stunning homes dating

Pamlico Sound

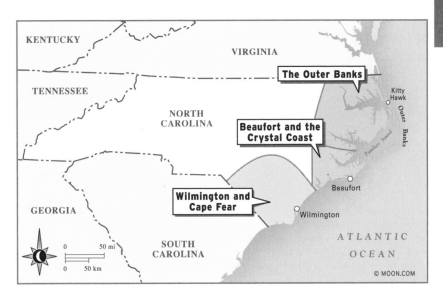

back to the state's earliest days. Scuba divers love **Morehead City,** a convenient home base for dives in crystal-clear waters of **"The Graveyard of the Atlantic"** — where they can explore the hundreds of wrecks that dot the North Carolina coast. At the southern tip of the **Cape Lookout National Seashore,** the **Cape Lookout Lighthouse** stands sentinel, keeping safe the ships that pass. Along that seashore, the ghosts in the abandoned town of **Portsmouth,** wild horses known as **Banker ponies,** and hundreds of migratory birds are the only denizens. The dread pirates **Blackbeard** and **Stede Bonnet,** both regulars in these parts, rubbed elbows with high society here by night, and by day prowled the waters looking for prey. And all along the Crystal Coast, the **fishing is fine** as hundreds of species call the oceans, sounds, rivers, and creeks home.

Wilmington and Cape Fear

The rich, podark waters of the **Cape Fear River** flow past **Wilmington,** a port city known for **antebellum homes and gardens,** lively shops and restaurants, and the annual **Azalea Festival,** which greets spring in high Southern style. Beach towns like **Topsail Island, Wrightsville Beach,** and **Kure and Carolina Beaches** are some of the most beautiful stretches of sand in the nation. Between Wilmington and the South Carolina line, you'll find the legendary **Calabash seafood,** dozens of outstanding golf courses, and the Brunswick Islands. The beaches of **Oak Island, Holden Beach,** and **Ocean Isle** are lovely, family-friendly spots, and **Bald Head Island,** home of **Old Baldy,** a lighthouse commissioned by Thomas Jefferson, offers solitude. Inland, the Waccamaw and Lumber rivers creep through beautiful blackwater swamps while the Cape Fear River leads upstream to **Fayetteville,** a military hub and destination for history, gardens, and various adrenaline-pumping sports, such as roller derby.

When to Go

Spring debuts in the southeast as early as late February, but reliably by mid-March. As it creeps up along the coast, temperatures are a pretty consistent 60-70 degrees by mid-April.

Summer means great weather and the **high season.** The beaches are packed, and you'll find festivals and events throughout the region. The heat can be brutal, especially when combined with humidity, but the coast stays cooler than inland destinations, and ocean breezes offer relief. Temperatures range from the upper 70s to the mid 90s, with water temperatures in the mid 70s to low 80s, making for ideal beach days.

Autumn reaches the coast by early November, after hurricane season has passed. Autumn weather stays in the high-60s-low-70s, punctuated by days that push into the 80s, making it ideal for outdoor activities. Along the coast, the water stays swimmably warm past Halloween most years.

Winter is milder here than in many parts of the country. Daytime temperatures are usually in the 40s and 50s between late December and February, with frequent dips below freezing as the season wears on. The coast only gets one or two snow showers a year. Fall and early winter attract anglers, but many coastal businesses reduce their hours or even close entirely during winter.

During the **shoulder seasons—late spring** and **early fall**—rental rates drop, beaches are a little less crowded, and visitors can find bargain getaways (although the eastern Sandhills and areas around Pinehurst and Southern Pines can be quite crowded in the spring and fall, when the weather is most beautiful for golfing).

Before You Go

There are some seasonal events that are so large that entire cities or corners of the state can be heavily booked. April is the cruelest month for making short-notice travel arrangements, especially in Wilmington, where the **Azalea Festival** draws 100,000 visitors annually. Around the 4th of July, **Oak Island, Bald Head Island,** and **Southport,** the epicenter of a massive Independence Day celebration, are jam-packed with visitors enjoying fireworks and celebrations. During festival times like these, it can be difficult to find a motel room, campground, or spot for your RV anywhere near the event. October sees Morehead City packed to the gills for the **North Carolina Seafood Festival.** If you'll be visiting the coast in winter, plan ahead for accommodations and dining, as businesses may be closed.

Coastal weather can change dramatically on a whim. Even on hot days, it can be breezy and cool on the water. Bring sun protection no matter when you visit. A water bottle is also handy. In spring and fall, it's not a bad idea to keep some long sleeves, even if they're light, on hand; and in winter you'll want something to break the chill of the ocean breeze.

Cell phone signals are pretty consistent throughout North Carolina, but there are pockets on the coast where cell service and 3G, 4G, and LTE connectivity is spotty.

The Best of the North Carolina Coast

North Carolina's coast spans some 300 miles from Virginia to South Carolina. There's tons of beach, marsh, history, food, and fun to be had, but you can make it to all the highlights in a week.

Wilmington and Cape Fear

DAY 1

Start your journey in, **Wilmington,** the hub of the southeastern coast, easily accessible by road or air and lovely in its own right. Visit **Wrightsville Beach** for a swim and some beach time. Around lunch, pack up and drive 10 minutes to downtown Wilmington for a gyro at **The Greeks,** a stroll along the **Riverwalk,** and shopping at **The Cotton Exchange.** Stay downtown for dinner. Try **PinPoint** for a delicious twist on Southern cuisine, or **The Fork n Cork** for a spin on burgers you'll remember, or dine on the river and savor the views. Not ready for bed? Pay a visit to one

of the best breweries in town – **Waterline, New Anthem and Flytrap** are all great choices – or a cocktail at **manna** before retreating to your downtown bed and breakfast or the riverside **Hotel Ballast.**

DAY 2

Make an early tee time at **Cape Fear National** or one of the **Big Cats** courses and give Brunswick County your day, or head to the charming fishing village of **Southport** for a morning of shopping. At lunch, go for Southport's **Yacht Basin Provision Company,** or head south to **Calabash** for a taste of the world-famous style of seafood at **Waterfront Seafood Shack.**

Backtrack to Southport (or head there for the first time) and take the **ferry** to **Fort Fisher** and walk off lunch at this historic Civil War fort. Next,

Wilmington Riverwalk

visit the nearby **North Carolina Aquarium** for a look at what lies beneath the waves.

Dinner takes you back to Wrightsville Beach. Dine dockside at **Dockside,** overlooking Banks Channel at **South Beach Grill,** or have an omakase sushi feast at **Bento Box.**

Beaufort and the Crystal Coast
DAY 3

Drive north on U.S. 17 and U.S. 70 to Beaufort and Morehead City. Beaufort's pirate history is on display via a **walking tour of downtown,** you can even pay your respects to Blackbeard at the **North Carolina Maritime Museum,** which contains artifacts recovered from his sunken pirate ship. Do lunch a little differently with a culinary bike tour from **Hungry Town Tours** before heading north on U.S. 70 to New Bern, the second oldest town in the state.

Spend the afternoon exploring **art galleries** and **antique shops** in downtown New Bern, and visit the beautiful gardens and home of **Tryon Palace.** On the way back to your bed and breakfast, drop in the **Birthplace of Pepsi** to learn about this iconic Southern drink. Dinner will be waterside at **Persimmons Restaurant,** where fresh seafood and sophisticated preparations are the norm.

DAY 4

Spend your morning at one of the **coffee shops and bakeries** in New Bern, then walk off your pastry on a tour of the elegant homes in the neighborhoods on the north side of town. Head inland to the famous **Skylight Inn,** a whole hog barbecue joint that serves barbecue sandwiches, plates and platters that exemplify the Eastern North Carolina style – smoky, vinegary, delicious.

For the afternoon, head to **Kinston** for a look at the remains of a Civil War Ironclad at the **CSS *Neuse* Interpretive Center** and the full-scale replica of this fearsome ship just a couple of blocks away. Enjoy a beer at **Mother Earth Brewing**'s tap room, then appetizers at **The Boiler Room,** and finally dinner at **Chef & the Farmer.** Spend the night in Kinston at **Mother Earth Motor Lodge,** a boutique motel that's the exact right amount of retro chic.

Tryon Palace

Eat Seafood Like A Local

Fishing villages dot the coast of North Carolina, and many restaurants still use fresh-caught seafood on their menus. To dine like a local, pick restaurants like the favorites listed below, which use local seafood, meat, and produce while paying homage to the culinary traditions that make each coastal culture distinct. Check out **Outer Banks Catch** (www.outerbankscatch.com), **Carteret Catch** (http://carteretcatch.org), and **Brunswick Catch** (http://brunswickcatch.com) for more restaurants serving local seafood in each region.

THE OUTER BANKS

- **Basnight's Lone Cedar Café** serves the freshest seafood from a dining room surrounded by water.

- Enjoy an oyster stout with your dinner at the **Outer Banks Brewing Station**, where fresh seafood plays a prominent role in the menu.

- **Sam & Omie's** opened in 1937 to feed hungry fishermen, and the concept stuck. Try a platter of broiled or fried seafood the way the first patrons ate it—hot and fresh.

- In Duck, **AQUA Restaurant** serves a small menu of exquisitely prepared dishes that take advantage of the abundant seafood harvested right on the Outer Banks.

BEAUFORT AND THE CRYSTAL COAST

- **Clawson's 1905 Restaurant** serves a number of dishes featuring fresh-caught shrimp, a local delicacy.

- **Big Oak Drive-In and Bar-B-Q** serves shrimpburgers, a Crystal Coast classic, in as informal and lovely a setting as you'll find.

- At **Amos Mosquito's Restaurant & Bar** you can't go wrong with the fresh catch or the Skeeter Fried Seafood.

The shrimp burger from Big Oak Drive-In and Bar-B-Q is a regional favorite.

- You expect fresh seafood when dining dockside, and Morehead City's **Ruddy Duck Tavern** delivers, with incredibly fresh, immaculately prepared fish.

WILMINGTON AND THE CAPE FEAR REGION

- **Catch** is all about infusing local seafood with Asian, creole and even Gullah flavors and there's not a dish on the menu that disappoints.

- **Yacht Basin Provision Company** puts you dockside for a feast of peel and eat shrimp, grouper sandwiches and as much fresh seafood as you can stand.

- **Waterfront Seafood Shack** serves fresh fish, shrimp and more—purchased from the fishmonger next door—done in the traditional Calabash style.

The Outer Banks

DAY 5

Queen Street Deli has breakfast and eye-opening coffee to fuel you for the three hour push to **Roanoke Island** on the **Outer Banks.** Drive northeast to Jamesville and join U.S. 64, which will take you through the rural **Inner Banks** into Manteo. Along the way, soak up the scenery and stop to stretch your legs at **Pettigrew State Park.**

You'll arrive on Roanoke Island around lunchtime. Grab a bite to eat at **Poor Richard's Sandwich Shop** in **Manteo** and visit the **Elizabethan Gardens** and **Fort Raleigh National Historic Site** before you enjoy the longest-running outdoor drama in the U.S., **The Lost Colony.** Spend the night at the **Tranquil House Inn** and enjoy dinner in-house at **1587.**

DAY 6

Pack up and head across the sound toward the beach. Grab breakfast at **Sam & Omie's,** and Outer Banks classic, in Nags Head, then walk across the street to **Jennette's Pier** for some beach time. Drive south on Hwy. 12 to the **Bodie Island Lighthouse** and climb to the top for a breathtaking view of the Outer Banks.

Take Hwy. 12 north toward **Duck.** Stop at the **Wright Brothers National Memorial** and see a replica of the brothers' famed flying machine and the site where those historic first flights took place. Continue north to the village of Duck for lunch at **AQUA Restaurant and Spa** before checking in to luxe accommodations at the oceanfront **Sanderling Resort.** Spend the afternoon on the beach or relaxing at the **spa,** or take an excursion to Corolla, the next town up from Duck, to climb the **Currituck Beach Lighthouse** or take a **wild horse tour** on the beach to spot some of the famous **Banker ponies.**

Dinner and drinks tonight are just up the road at **The Blue Point,** a waterside restaurant that makes the most of local seafood and stunning sunset views

DAY 7

It's about three hours from Duck to **Ocracoke,** your last stop before heading home, so strike out early and get breakfast at **Duck Donuts,** before following Hwy. 12 south through **Cape Hatteras National Seashore.** This stretch of beach is wild, and you'll find just a handful of small towns. Close to the southern tip is the **Cape Hatteras Lighthouse** with its iconic black and white spiral paint job. Snap a photo or to climb to the top. A few miles to the southeast in **Hatteras,** board the ferry to **Ocracoke Island.**

On Ocracoke, arrange for a **fishing charter** or spend the day relaxing on the shell-strewn beach. Take your lunch at **Eduardo's Taco Stand,** a taco food truck that's a must-dine for locals and visitors. In the evening, head to the harbor for oysters on the half shell at **Howard's Pub & Raw Bar Restaurant.** Spend the night here (taking time for stargazing, which is especially good outside of town) and begin to make your way home in the morning. A three-hour ferry ride puts you back on the Inner Banks near **Beaufort,** where you're not far from the airports in Wilmington or Raleigh, as well as I-40 and I-95.

Outdoor Adventure

There's no shortage of outdoor activities along North Carolina's coast. **Surfers** come in droves; **kayakers and standup paddleboarders** rave about the marshes, sounds, rivers, and swamps; **divers** dig the wrecks and reefs offshore; and **hikers and campers** find a surprisingly diverse set of environs to explore. Most surprising are the **hang gliders** who come to **Jockey's Ridge** on the Outer Banks. This massive sand dune is the perfect launch and landing point for hang gliders of all skill levels.

Kayaking

I've paddled all along the North Carolina coast, and although some prefer to take their kayaks oceanside, I'm happiest on the sounds, marshes, creeks, rivers, and swamps inland and on the back side of the barrier islands. No matter where you are along the coast, outfitters rent kayaks and standup paddleboards and quite often lead visitors on tours.

Along the Virginia border, the **Great Dismal Swamp** offers miles of paddling through what is a beautiful swamp, despite its name. Put ins are plentiful, but outfitters are a little ways away. It's best to bring your own gear or make arrangements for day-long or longer rentals.

The same holds true for the **Alligator River National Wildlife Refuge,** where you stand a good chance of seeing an alligator (be careful if you do and do not approach), black bear, or even the elusive and endangered red wolf. If you take a moonlight paddling tour, listen for the howls of red wolves.

Perhaps the greatest paddle on the coast is exploring the 56 miles of shoreline along the sound at **Cape Lookout National Seashore,** a long island inhabited only by wildlife, including birds, crabs, and wild horses. The ocean side of Cape Lookout is just ocean, but the sound side is rife with marshes and creeks. Paddle over from

Cape Lookout National Seashore

surfing at Wrightsville Beach

Harkers Island and spend a night or two to have enough time for discovering this place.

Near Wilmington, **Town Creek** winds for many miles from Brunswick County's Green Swamp to the Cape Fear River, ranging from a tight, heavily wooded swamp creek to a wide coastal marsh. The brackish water, stained a rich coffee color by tannins from rotting vegetation, looks like something from *Creature From the Black Lagoon.* Twists and turns and plenty of wildlife, including circling osprey and the occasional snake, keep trips interesting. On **Bald Head Island**, the marsh creeks wind around for miles and the birdwatching—osprey, golden and bald eagles, painted bunting, egret and ibis—is top notch.

Surfing

From powerful storm swells to gentle, easy-to-learn-on beach break, the North Carolina coastline welcomes surfers of all skill levels from all over the world.

The **Outer Banks** is perpetually popular. The deserted **Cape Hatteras National Seashore** and the villages of **Waves, Buxton,** and **Salvo** are popular basecamps for surf safaris. Bring your boards and drop in along the National Seashore, or head north into the more populated **Nags Head** and **Kill Devil Hills** area for good waves closer to numerous surf shops, restaurants, and bars. You won't just find surfers here, you'll also see some daredevils kiteboarding. Strapped to a wakeboard and giant kite, they use the winds to propel them and the waves to launch them into the air all along the beaches and sound around Cape Hatteras.

For south-facing beaches known for catching swells, head to **Emerald Isle** on the Crystal Coast and **Oak Island,** one of the Brunswick beaches. This pair is especially popular when there are storms offshore.

Wrightsville Beach and **Topsail Island,** near Wilmington, are hot spots along the Cape Fear coast. At Wrightsville, wide beaches and consistent breaks satisfy experienced and learning surfers. Topsail, a smaller, slightly steeper beach, makes for great sessions for experienced surfers, especially those looking to show off a little.

Hiking

There aren't mountains along the North Carolina coast, so any hiking you do will be relatively flat. And sandy. You can get a little elevation at **Jockey's Ridge**, the largest sand dune on the east coast, which stands more than 100 feet high and offers amazing views of the sunrise, sunset, shores, and sounds. Wander through this dune system and watch hang gliders, kite flyers, and sand boarders (think snowboarding on a sand dune, sans parka). Notice the changes in vegetation and wildlife as you near the sound, then go for a swim, or just watch the boats and wind surfers go by. Be prepared for lots of sand in your boots.

From dunes and patches of forest to beach, there's plenty to explore at **Cape Lookout National Seashore**. Get up close and personal to the diamond-patterned **Cape Lookout Lighthouse**, but keep your distance from the wild **Banker ponies**.

Croatan National Forest on the Inner Banks has more than 40 miles of trails, ranging from half a mile to the 20-plus mile **Neusiok Trail**. Passing through swamp, hummock, and an inland forest, you'll feel like you've been transported into the past.

More than 10 miles of trails circle through **Ev-Henwood Nature Preserve**, a former farm and turpentine supply point that's now a nature preserve and study center for the University of North Carolina Wilmington. It's easy to link these trails and explore piney forests, a few stands of hardwoods, and the black headwaters of Town Creek.

The truly adventurous can hike the 11-mile spit of land that connects **Bald Head Island** to the mainland. The long, hot hike from Fort Fisher along the shore and dunes to the island is best made in the shoulder seasons. Bring water, food, sun protection, and a plan for when you reach the end, because Bald Head Island is closed to cars and accessible only by ferry (or hiking). It's a five-mile trek across the island to the ferry once you arrive, but friendly residents and vacationers offer rides. You may also want to explore the shorter trails that dive into Bald Head Island's maritime forest.

Camping

You can rent a tent or RV site at plenty of campgrounds, but many of North Carolina's best spots put you in reach of true wilderness.

Kayak or take a ferry from Harkers Island to **Cape Lookout National Seashore** and camp there or to the west at **Shackleford Banks**. Both islands are inhabited by wild horses and are beautiful places for nights under the stars.

In the **Croatan National Forest** you'll find several great camping spots, especially along the Neusiok Trail. Select a high and dry spot to camp or you just may wake up wet.

Hammocks Beach State Park on Bear Island offers paddling campers and ferry-takers alike a place to spend a few nights in the wild. Just north of Topsail Island and just south of Emerald Isle, the beaches here are gorgeous, shell-littered things that few visitors see.

Near Wilmington, **Carolina Beach State Park** is a popular spot to set up your tent. Hiking trails through pine forests and along the Cape Fear River give you plenty to do, but the campground's close enough to town—just five minutes from a restaurant—to get something to eat or drink in the evenings.

Inland, camp beside one of the strange Carolina Bays at **Lake Waccamaw State Park**, where you'll find odd plants like the Venus flytrap and a shallow, circular lake of unknown, possibly cosmic, origin.

Best Beaches

The Outer Banks

COROLLA
Best for Wildlife
Visit Corolla to view the **Banker ponies,** wild horses that have lived along the Outer Banks for hundreds of years.

DUCK
Best for Sunbathing, Sunsets
The beach at Duck is at a slight incline that provides maximum sun exposure and great ocean views. The wide wash of sound and marsh behind the thin strip of beach makes Duck a favorite for sunsets.

NAGS HEAD AND KILL DEVIL HILLS
Best for Family Fun
Family vacations to the Outer Banks include seafood buffets, golf carts, mini golf, sunburns, and the occasional carnival ride. Recreate my childhood at Nags Head and Kill Devil Hills, beaches I haunted as a kid.

PEA ISLAND NATIONAL WILDLIFE REFUGE
Best for Birding
This refuge on Hatteras Island is an incredible spot for watching migratory waterfowl.

HATTERAS
Best for Beachcombing, Water Sports
The village of Hatteras on Hatteras Island is a popular surfing destination and also good for shelling.

OTHER HATTERAS ISLAND BEACHES
Best for Solitude
The villages of **Salvo, Buxton, Rodanthe, Waves,** and **Avon** provide privacy along with modern conveniences.

OCRACOKE
Best for Beachcombing, Solitude, Sunrises
Ocracoke Island has the benefits of a vacation town, but you'll find shell-strewn beaches you have almost all to yourself. Watch the sunrise over what seems like endless miles of ocean.

Beaufort and the Crystal Coast

CAPE LOOKOUT NATIONAL SEASHORE
Best for Long Walks, Solitude, Shells
With 56 miles of coastline, you can quickly find yourself alone in nature at Cape Lookout National Seashore. It's hard to beat these unbroken stretches of beach for long walks.

SHACKLEFORD BANKS
Best for Wildlife
Shackleford Banks in Cape Lookout National Seashore is a fantastic place to spot wild **Banker Ponies.**

ATLANTIC BEACH
Best for Water Sports
For great diving, including the chance to explore offshore wrecks in the **Graveyard of the Atlantic,** go to Atlantic Beach on the Bogue Banks and arrange for a dive charter to pick you up in nearby Morehead City.

EMERALD ISLE
Best for Family Fun, Water Sports
This Bogue Banks town, popular with surfers for its south-facing beach, is a laid-back, family-friendly getaway.

Wilmington and Cape Fear

TOPSAIL ISLAND
Best for Water Sports
Experienced surfers should head to this island, where the surf is consistent year-round and the

Make a Splash!

kayaking around the marsh of Bald Head Island

Along the coast, water is part of the fabric of life and every season of the year sailboats, powerboats, canoes, kayaks and standup paddleboards carry residents and visitors on adventures, explorations, fishing trips and pleasure cruises.

- **Cape Lookout National Seashore:** paddle to this long uninhabited strip of land and see what you find in the marshes—which may even include wild horses—the explore Cape Lookout lighthouse; or have a ferry bring you over, camp, and explore the waters at your leisure.

- **Bald Head Island:** the marsh creeks behind Bald Head Island offer dozens of miles of paddling where you can watch osprey and eagle hunt from the sky and occasionally spot dolphins hunting baitfish deep in the creeks.

- **Croatan National Forest:** paddling through the blackwater creeks and waterways of this waterlogged forest will transport you to another age.

- **Saltwater Adventure Trail:** this paddle trail is long—nearly 100 miles—and takes you through a variety of marsh, river and sound ecosystems.

- **Hammocks Beach State Park:** you'll need to paddle out or take a ferry to this island state park where you can camp, explore the islets and marsh creeks, and escape from the mainland for a while.

- **Great Dismal Swamp:** this vast swamp on the North Carolina-Virginia state line is filled with wildlife.

- **Roanoke River:** near Halifax, you can explore the Roanoke River by paddling upstream or down, and with fishing, camping and birding opportunities, it's a prime spot.

- **Lumber River State Park:** more than 115 miles of creek, river and waterway in the state park give you plenty to explore in a coastal river environment like none other.

Wrightsville Beach

wind shapes waves into steep peaks, allowing for aerial maneuvers and sharp cutbacks.

WRIGHTSVILLE BEACH
Best for Sunbathing, Water Sports
This wide, flat beach has sand that's not too packed, not too powdery—perfect for catching some sun. It's also popular with new and experienced surfers.

CAROLINA BEACH
Best for Family Fun
Carolina Beach State Park offers an abundance of hotels, a pier for fishing, a boardwalk crowded with shops and arcades, and a small carnival ground—all great for when kids need a break from sea and sand.

BALD HEAD ISLAND
Best for Long Walks, Sunrises, Wildlife
My favorite spot for long walks is the 14 miles of beach on Bald Head Island. On south-facing South Beach and east-facing East Beach, there's ocean on one side and a high dune ridge or maritime forest on the other. More than 225 species of birds have been spotted here. The sunrise over the tumultuous **Frying Pan Shoals,** which extend toward the ocean from the island's easternmost tip, is a sight to behold.

HOLDEN BEACH, OCEAN ISLE, AND SUNSET BEACH
Best for Beachcombing, Sunsets
These Brunswick beaches are rich with delicate sand dollars. The aptly named Sunset Beach comes to life when the day's last rays stretch over the marsh.

The Outer Banks

This series of islands traces a path along the northeastern coast some 125 miles long. You'll find lighthouses and pirate lore, wild horses, stretches of untamed shore, and enough beach to go around.

From the Virginia border in the north to Ocracoke Island in the south, The Outer Banks stand guard against the incessant grind of wind and wave and the powerful force of a single storm. As barrier islands, it's their job to protect the mainland, marshlands, and towns of the Inner Banks from a storm's brunt. As they do so, a centuries-old inlet may be filled in a night and a new channel opened a hundred yards away. In 2012, Hatteras Island was cut off from the rest of the Outer Banks as Hurricane Sandy washed out Highway 12—the only road to

Highlights

Look for ★ to find recommended sights, activities, dining, and lodging.

★ **Wright Brothers National Memorial:** See where North Carolina earned the slogan "First in Flight" and view a replica of the famed *Wright Flyer* (page 34).

★ **Wild Horse Tours:** See wild horses in the dunes, along the shore, and even swimming in the surf along the northernmost portion of the Outer Banks (page 38).

★ **Fort Raleigh National Historic Site:** See where the Lost Colony, the first English settlement in the New World, mysteriously disappeared in the 1580s (page 47).

★ **Cape Hatteras Lighthouse:** Climb to the top of this iconic lighthouse (page 57).

★ **Ocracoke Island:** On this remote island, you'll find a historic village home to one of the country's most unique communities, along with the waters where Blackbeard met his fate and one of the oldest lighthouses in the nation (page 61).

★ **Somerset Place Historic Site:** The graceful architecture and exotic setting of this early plantation contrast with the tragic history of its involvement in slavery (page 73).

★ **Pettigrew State Park:** Lake Phelps, the park's centerpiece, is an attractive enigma, a body of shallow water with a deep history (page 73).

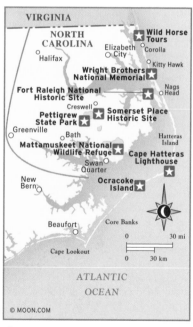

★ **Mattamuskeet National Wildlife Refuge:** This dramatic waterscape that attracts tens of thousands of migratory birds (page 75).

follow the length of the Banks—and damaged bridges, filling roadways with several feet of sand and changing, once more, the face of the Outer Banks.

Between the Outer Banks and the mainland in the Inner Banks is a collection of sounds known as the Albemarle-Pamlico Estuary. Many travelers ignore the sounds, giving them little more than a glance as they cross on a bridge or a ferry, but they play a crucial role in the region. The Albemarle-Pamlico Estuary is the second-largest estuarine system in the country after Chesapeake Bay to the north, and it includes Albemarle, Pamlico, Core, Croatan, Roanoke, and Currituck Sounds. Covering more than 3,000 square miles, the sounds drain more than 30,000 square miles and provide diverse marine and terrestrial environments that shelter essential plant and animal life. The vast and beautiful marshlands and wide, shallow sounds protect the mainland from storm surges and the Atlantic Ocean from toxins and sediment, all the while providing nursery grounds to countless fish and bird species.

Sheltered from the Atlantic, the Inner Banks are a much more accommodating (ecologically speaking) and familiar landscape than the Outer Banks. Along the marshes and wetlands, hundreds of thousands of migratory birds shelter and rest on their annual journeys, while pocosins (a kind of bog) and maritime forests have nurtured innumerable generations of animals and people. This is where you'll find North Carolina's oldest towns—Bath, New Bern, and Edenton. Settlers established their roots here, and the towns have survived for more than 300 years. In Washington County, a rural expanse of farms and wetlands, 4,000-year-old canoes pulled out of Lake Phelps stand witness to the region's unplumbed depths of history. Rivers flow from farther inland, with towns like Roanoke Rapids and Halifax that played

a vital role in North Carolina's history and development from colony to state.

PLANNING YOUR TIME

Most visitors plan to come to the coast during late spring and summer, and the reasons are obvious: the beaches, restaurants and attractions that are only open in season, as well as numerous warm-weather festivals and goings-on. However, don't overlook mid-spring and early fall. During the fall, the water is still warm, most of the restaurants and attractions are still open, and the crowds are smaller. Perhaps surprisingly, winter is picking up in popularity, too. To many, the solitude offered by a winter beach is hard to beat.

Agriculture affects eastern North Carolina in a unique way. In fall, the area's second-busiest season, the tobacco harvest fills the nostrils of visitors. In rural areas, trucks laden with huge yellow-green tobacco leaves head for the curing barns. The smell of curing tobacco, and later the tight bales of golden leaves, is like none other, and once you smell it, you'll have a taste for fall in this part of the state. Early autumn also brings intermittent clouds of smoke as farmers and backyard-garden hobbyists clear their summer gardens and prepare the ground for cool-weather crops. Beds of lettuce and onions and patches of mustard greens and collards begin to appear alongside houses. Cotton comes in late in the year; as the bolls ripen, the fields appear snow-covered and quite beautiful.

Water sports should also be considered when planning your trip. Spring and fall, and even the occasional winter warm spell, offer many ideal days for exploring eastern North Carolina's rivers, creeks, and swamps in a kayak, canoe, or stand-up paddleboard. In the fall, mild temperatures are comfortable enough for a day of paddling, and though the foliage is still green, the absence of summer's leafiness means you can see deeper into the landscape and spy on wildlife from a safe

Pronunciation Primer

North Carolina is full of oddly pronounced place-names, and the far northeast corner is a good place to pause for a lesson in talking like a native. The Outer Banks are a garland of peculiar names as well as names that look straightforward but are in fact pronounced in unexpectedly quirky ways. If you make reference publicly to the town of **Corolla** and pronounce it like the Toyota, you'll be recognized right away as someone "from off." It's pronounced "ker-AH-luh." Similarly, **Bodie Island**, site of the striped lighthouse, is pronounced "body." That same pattern of pronouncing *o* as *ah* is repeated farther down the coast at **Chicamacomico**, which comes out "chick-uh-muh-CAH-muh-co." But just to keep you on your toes, the rule doesn't apply to **Ocracoke**, which is pronounced like the Southern vegetable and the soft drink: "O-kra-coke."

Farther south along the banks is the town of **Rodanthe**, pronounced "ro-DAN-thee." On Roanoke Island, **Manteo** might resemble a Spanish word but is in fact front-loaded, like so many Carolina words and names. It's pronounced "MAN-tee-oh" or "MAN-nee-oh." Next door is the town of **Wanchese**, pronounced like a pallid dairy product, "WAN-cheese." Inland, the Cashie River is pronounced "cuh-SHY," **Bertie County** is "ber-TEE," and Chowan County is "chuh-WAHN."

distance. Keep in mind, though, that you can see alligators or even snakes in late fall and throughout the winter.

While fall can be ideal to visit the coast, remember that autumn is peak hurricane season in North Carolina. Surfers may love the waves before and after storms, but even people with lots of experience avoid hurricanes. These storms can be beautiful in their ferocity and violence, but anyone who's been through even a weak hurricane will tell you they're no joke. About a week before a fall visit, check the long-term forecasts and call to confirm the weather where you're staying. If authorities issue evacuation orders during your visit, don't hesitate; just pack up and head to safety on the mainland.

INFORMATION AND SERVICES

The **Aycock Brown Welcome Center** (Milepost 1, Kitty Hawk, 877/629-4386, www.outerbanks.org, 9am-5pm daily Nov.-Feb., 9am-5:30pm Mar.-Oct., closed Thanksgiving and Dec. 25) at Kitty Hawk and the **Outer Banks Welcome Center on Roanoke Island** (1 Visitors Center Circle, Manteo, 252/473-2138 or 877/629-4386, www.outerbanks.org, 9am-5pm daily Nov.-Feb., 9am-5:30pm Mar.-Oct., closed Thanksgiving and Dec. 25) are the main welcome centers in the Outer Banks, with smaller welcome centers at Hatteras and Whalebone Junction.

Major hospitals include **The Outer Banks Hospital** (4800 S. Croatan Hwy., Milepost 14, Nags Head, 252/449-4500, www.theouterbankshospital.com) in Nags Head, **Sentara Albemarle Medical Center** (1144 North Road St., Elizabeth City, 252/335-0531, www.sentara.com) in Elizabeth City, **Vidant Roanoke-Chowan Hospital** (500 S. Academy St., Ahoskie, 252/209-3000, www.vidanthealth.com) in Ahoskie, **Vidant Chowan Hospital** (211 Virginia Rd., Edenton, 252/482-8451, www.vidanthealth.com) in Edenton, **Vidant Beaufort Hospital** (628 E. 12th St., Washington, 252/975-4100, www.vidanthealth.com) in Washington, **Vidant Bertie Hospital** (1403 S. King St., Windsor, 252/794-6600, www.vidanthealth.com) in Windsor, and **Halifax Regional Hospital** (250 Smith Church Rd., Roanoke Rapids, 252/535-8011, www.halifaxmedicalcenter.org) in Roanoke Rapids. On Ocracoke, which is only accessible by air or water, nonemergency medical situations can be addressed by **Ocracoke Health Center** (305 Back Rd., 252/928-1511, after hours 252/928-7425, www.ocracokeisland.com). Note that 911 emergency service is available on Ocracoke, as it is throughout the state.

The Outer Banks

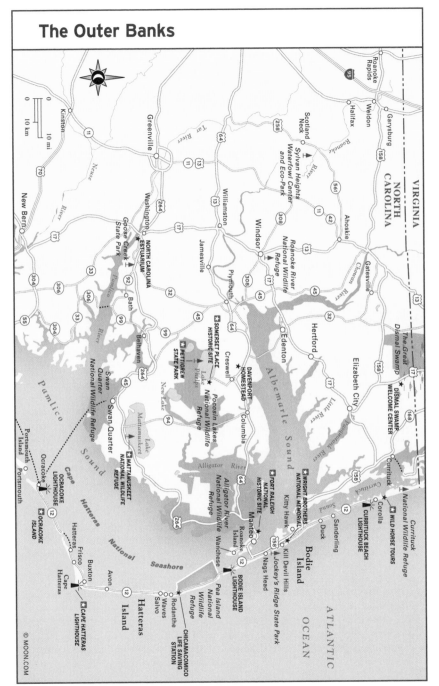

Nags Head and Vicinity

Coral reefs anchor most barrier islands, lending them a bit of strength and permanence; not so on North Carolina's Outer Banks. Here, no reef helps shape the islands, and they're more like enormous sandbars, susceptible to the whims of the wind, the sea, and storms. But that's part of their beauty. These natural forces shape the land as well as its history and culture.

Jockey's Ridge, a 100-foot-high dune visible far out to sea, has been used as a navigational aide for hundreds of years. Legend has it that Nags Head earned its name because of these dunes and the passing ships. Islanders known as proggers (a shipwreck scavenger or land pirate) would lead a nag or mule along the beach and dune ridge with a lantern hung around its neck, luring ships into the shallows and shoals where they'd wreck, making their cargo easy pickings. Likewise, the shoals, shallows, and currents gave birth to the heroic members of the United States Lifesaving Service, predecessor to the Coast Guard, who braved many storms to save those shipwrecked.

The relentless wind on the Outer Banks lured Orville and Wilbur Wright to Kill Devil Hills, where they became the first people in history to take flight. It also drew Francis Rogallo, a NASA engineer and inventor of hang gliding. Today, thousands flock to the Wright Brothers Memorial to see where history was made, and even more visit Jockey's Ridge to watch hang gliders or even to take to the sky themselves. With kite-flying, kiteboarding, skydiving, parasailing, and even paragliding, flight enthusiasts love the Outer Banks. Add to this sailing, diving, surfing, paddling, hiking, bird-watching, and, of course, visits to beaches like Duck, which is lovely at sunset, and Corolla, where you can spot wild ponies, and it's obvious that the northern Outer Banks are among the most promising areas in North Carolina for outdoor adventure.

SIGHTS

★ Wright Brothers National Memorial

In 1903, Orville and Wilbur Wright changed the world in just 12 seconds. Their first flight was short, but it was the culmination of more than three years of failed designs, tests, and travels between their Dayton, Ohio, home and Kitty Hawk, North Carolina, where they tested their gliders on Kill Devil Hill, then the tallest dune on the Outer Banks. A number of Banker families fed and housed them, built them hangars, and assisted with countless trial runs. On the morning of December 17, 1903, several local people were on hand to help that famous first powered flight get into the air. John Daniels, a lifesaver from a nearby station, took the iconic photo of the airplane lifting off. It was the only photograph he ever took. He was later quoted in a newspaper saying of the flight, "I didn't think it amounted to much." Even though he was unimpressed, the feat is honored at the **Wright Brothers National Memorial** (Milepost 7.5, U.S. 158, 1000 N. Croatan Hwy, Kill Devil Hills, 252/473-2111, www. nps.gov, park and visitors center 9am-5pm daily year-round, $10 adults 16 and up, free 15 and under). Replica gliders, artifacts from the original flight, and tools the Wright brothers used are on display. In the adjacent field a wooden runner and stone markers show their runway, takeoff point, and the spots where their first four flights landed. Climb nearby Kill Devil Hill to see the 60-foot monument honoring their achievement and marking the spot where they launched hundreds of gliders that preceded that first powered flight. At the foot of the hill, a life-size bronze sculpture of the *Wright Flyer* seconds after liftoff lets you get a sense of the excitement of the moment.

Nags Head and Vicinity

To Duck, Corolla, and Currituck
National Wildlife Refuge

WRIGHT MEMORIAL BRIDGE

Currituck Sound

AYCOCK BROWN
WELCOME CENTER

OCEAN BOULEVARD

SEA SCAPE GOLF LINKS

ATLANTIC
OCEAN

BYP 158

Kitty Hawk

BEACH HAVEN MOTEL

MILE POST 4

*Kitty Hawk Woods
Coastal Reserve*

W. KITTY HAWK RD

Kitty Hawk Bay

TRIO

CHIP'S WINE
AND BEER
MARKET

MILE POST 6

Kill
Devil
Hills

COLINGTON
CREEK INN

WRIGHT BROTHERS
NATIONAL MEMORIAL

COLINGTON RD

Colington

COLINGTON
CAFE

MILE POST 8

CYPRESS
HOUSE INN

OUTER BANKS
BREWING STATION

MILE POST 9

*Albemarle
Sound*

Nags Head
Woods
Ecological
Preserve

ATLANTIC
STREET INN

BYP 158

MILE POST 10

MAMA KWAN'S
GRILL & TIKI BAR

Nags Head

KELLY'S OUTER
BANKS RESTAURANT

0   1 mi

0   1 km

US 158/S. CROATAN HWY
(THE BYPASS)

NC 12/VIRGINIA DARE TR
(BEACH ROAD)

MILE POST 12

LUCKY 12

*Jockey's Ridge
State Park*

OUTER BANKS
DIVE CENTER/
KITTY HAWK KITES

© MOON.COM

Jockey's Ridge State Park

Jockey's Ridge State Park (Milepost 12, U.S. 158, 300 W. Carolista Dr., Nags Head, 252/441-7132, http://ncparks.gov, park 8am-6pm daily Nov.-Feb., 8am-8pm daily Mar., Apr., and Oct., 8am-9pm daily May-Sept., visitors center 9am-5pm daily Nov.-Feb., 9am-6pm daily Mar.-Oct.), contains 420 acres of recreational opportunities in an array of environments. With the big dune, which shifts between 80 and 100 feet high, the smaller dunes

surrounding it, the maritime forest, and the sound, you can sand-board (think snow-boarding at the beach), fly kites, hike, go for a swim, or even learn to hang glide. Another resource is www.jockeysridgestatepark.com, a site operated by Friends of Jockey's Ridge State Park, where you'll find a few additional notices of outings and activities.

Nags Head Woods Ecological Preserve

Adjacent to Jockey's Ridge, the Nature Conservancy maintains the 1,111-acre **Nags Head Woods Ecological Preserve** (701 W. Ocean Acres Dr., 1 mile from Milepost 9.5 on U.S. 158, 252/441-2525, www.nature.org, dawn-dusk daily year-round). The landscape includes deciduous maritime forest, dunes, wetlands, and inter-dune ponds, providing a compact look at the diverse environments found on the Outer Banks. It's a bird-watcher's paradise, as more than 50 species nest here in season. Ruby-throated hummingbirds, green herons, and red-shouldered hawks are among the easiest to spot, but don't just look for winged wildlife; a number of land animals and reptiles, and even some unusual plants call this place home. Five miles of public trails wind through the property, starting at the visitors center. Dogs are welcome on several trails, provided they are on leash.

Kitty Hawk Woods Coastal Reserve

Kitty Hawk Woods Coastal Reserve (trail access from Woods Rd. and Birch Lane, off Treasure St., south of U.S. 158, Kitty Hawk, 252/261-8891, http://nccoastalreserve.net, dawn-dusk daily year-round), a 1,824-acre nature preserve maintained by the North Carolina Coastal Reserve, contains one of the largest remaining maritime forests in the Outer Banks. Maritime forests help barrier islands absorb the brunt of powerful storms, and Kitty Hawk Woods contains unusual examples of maritime swale ecosystems, swampy forest sheltered between coastal ridges. Hiking and birding opportunities are abundant, and exploring it from the water via canoe, kayak, or stand-up paddleboard is easy thanks to a put-in. Hunting is permitted in Kitty Hawk Woods, so exercise caution while hiking or paddling during the spring and fall hunting seasons.

Jennette's Pier

My family vacationed on the Outer Banks for years, and **Jennette's Pier** (Milepost 16.5, 7223 S. Virginia Dare Tr., Nags Head, 252/255-1501, www.ncaquariums.com, 9am-5pm daily Dec.-Mar., 7am-9pm Apr. and Nov., 6am-midnight May-Oct., fishing $14 adults, $7 child, walk on, $2 adult, $1 child 12 and under) was a fixture on each trip. The then-wooden pier, originally built in 1939, was picturesque but fragile; the owners repaired it after each storm until 2003, when the North Carolina Aquariums bought the pier and Hurricane Isabel demolished 540 feet of the pier structure. Many thought it was the end of the beachside institution, but a friend of mine—Chip Hemingway of Bowman Murray Hemingway Architects— designed a new 1,000-foot concrete pier. The LEED Platinum-certified facility is beautiful and will stand to serve countless vacationing families. The North Carolina Aquarium manages Jennette's Pier as an educational and recreational platform, and activities in peak season include summer day camps and nighttime seashore expeditions that teach kids and adults about the ecology of the area.

Currituck Heritage Park

We've come to expect grand, ostentatious beachside homes, but on the shore of Currituck Sound, you'll find what may be the original one on the Outer Banks: the **Whalehead Club** (1100 Club Rd., Corolla, 252/453-9040, www.whaleheadclub.org, tours 10am-4pm Mon.-Sat. year-round, $7 adults, $5 seniors and children ages 6-12, free under age 5). This art deco home was built in the 1920s as a summer cottage for Edward Collings Knight Jr., an industrialist whose wealth was made in railroads and sugar. The beautiful, simple yellow house is the centerpiece of **Currituck Heritage Park,** where visitors can picnic, wade, launch from the boat ramp, or learn about the ghosts (yes, it's rumored to be haunted, and it's no wonder, with so many shipwrecks just off shore).

Next to the Whalehead Club is the **Outer Banks Center for Wildlife Education** (1160 Village Lane, Corolla, 252/453-0221, www.ncwildlife.org, 9am-4:30pm Mon.-Sat., Apr.-Oct., 9am-4:30pm Mon.-Fri. Nov.-Mar.). Exhibits focus on native birds, fish, and other creatures in Currituck Sound as well as a huge collection of antique decoys. These decoys represent an important folk-art tradition and way of life for many along the Carolina coast. They're beautiful not just for their design but also for their utility. Naturalists put on a number of nature and art programs throughout the year; check the calendar on the website before you go.

A favorite spot here is the **Currituck Beach Lighthouse** (1101 Corolla Village Rd., 252/453-4939, www.currituckbeachlight.com, 9am-5pm daily Mar.-Nov., 9am-8pm Wed. and Thurs. Memorial Day-Labor Day, $10, under age 8 free) and its grounds. Built in 1875, this 158-foot-tall redbrick lighthouse is open to ascend much of the year. As you climb the 214 steps to the top, think about the lighthouse keepers, who for years carried pails of lard and then later kerosene to the top to fuel the light. Once at the observation deck, take a moment to catch your breath and take in the scenery (and hold on to your hat; it can be windy). The Currituck light is a twin to the Bodie Island Lighthouse, 32 miles south. Upon its completion it lit the last "dark spot" on the North Carolina coast, making for safer navigation.

Corolla Wild Horse Museum

In the town of Corolla you'll find a museum dedicated to some of the more unexpected residents of the Outer Banks. The **Corolla Wild Horse Museum** (520 B Old Stoney Rd., Corolla, 252/453-8002, www. corollawildhorses.com, 10am-4pm Mon.-Fri. and 10am-4pm Sat.-Sun.) tells the history of

Kitty Hawk to Corolla

COROLLA
LIGHTHOUSE ★ WILD HORSE TOURS
★ COROLLA
Corolla ○ WILD HORSE
WHALEHEAD MUSEUM
CLUB CURRITUCK
HERITAGE
PARK

Whalehead
Bay

OCEAN TRAIL

0   2 mi

0   2 km

Sanders
Bay

Wells
Bay

ATLANTIC OCEAN

12

Currituck
Sound

Beasley
Bay

Goat Island
Bay

Pine Island
Bay

Dowdy
Bay

SANDERLING
RESORT AND SPA/
KIMBALL'S KITCHEN

Currituck Sound

OUTER BANKS
STAND-UP PADDLE

NOR'BANKS SAILING
& WATERSPORTS

TOWN OF DUCK
BOARDWALK   THE BLUE POINT
Town of Duck

DUCK DONUTS
AQUA RESTAURANT   SCARBOROUGH FAIRE/
AND SPA   SCARBOROUGH LANE

DUCK RD

158

CARATOKE HWY

DUCK WOODS
COUNTRY CLUB
To Nags Head
and Roanoke
Island

© MOON.COM

WRIGHT MEMORIAL
BRIDGE   Kitty Hawk

the herd of horses that has lived on the Outer Banks from Corolla to Cape Lookout since the 1600s. The Corolla herd now lives in a preserve north of the town, and several guides offer tours to see the horses in their native habitat.

SPORTS AND RECREATION

Beaches

Beaches along the Outer Banks are easily accessible. Highway 12, which many call the

"Road to Nowhere," is the main, and usually the only, route to travel, though in a few places where the barrier islands widen enough to warrant it, you'll find a beachfront road as well as one skirting the sound. The Outer Banks is divided up into several smaller beach towns and communities. From the north the towns are Corolla, Duck, Southern Shores, Kitty Hawk, Kill Devil Hills, and Nags Head. South of Nags Head you have Whalebone Junction and the Oregon Inlet, then Hatteras Island and its collection of towns. Just west of Nags Head and Whalebone Junction is Roanoke Island, where two towns—Manteo and Wanchese—make up the population centers.

Though these towns abut one another in a seamless transition of beachiness, each has a different character. Corolla is still a little wild, which is fitting as Highway 12 terminates here (though you can drive to the Virginia border in a four-wheel-drive vehicle, provided you have some knowledge of driving in sand and have a plan of what to do once you arrive at our northern neighbor), and a herd of wild horses known as Banker ponies calls the marshes, dunes, and scrubby forests here home. Duck's grown up since my family stayed here, and now it's become a shopping destination. Kitty Hawk, Kill Devil Hills, and Nags Head have row upon row of homes marching from the sea to the sound; it's here that you'll find much of the commercial activity—shops for beach towels, fudge, and taffy; bars and restaurants; and grocery stores.

The beaches can be separated into three categories: wild, sparse, and blanket-to-blanket. Corolla's the wild beach where you'll get a real sense of isolation (save the occasional wild horse tour). Along Duck, Southern Shores, and the southern reaches of Nags Head (minus the area around Jennette's Pier), the crowds are thinner, and you can spread out for a leisurely day on the shore. Starting in Kitty Hawk and running south through Kill Devil Hills to Nags Head, you find the blanket-to-blanket area. The beaches here are significantly more populated than those at Duck, and you'll find pockets of beachgoers near public access points, piers, and the like.

Kayaking and Stand-Up Paddleboarding

The Outer Banks combines two very different paddle-sport opportunities, kayaking and stand-up paddleboarding (SUP), in two very different environments—the challenge of ocean paddling and even surfing, and the leisurely drifting tours of salt marshes and creeks. **Kitty Hawk Kites** (Milepost 12.5, 3925 S. Croatan Hwy./U.S. 158, Nags Head, 877/395-8447, www.kittyhawk.com, kayak tours $35-55, SUP lessons $59) has 10 locations up and down the Outer Banks offering kayak tours, SUP lessons and rentals, and a range of other recreational activities—like mermaid school ($59), as well as water-powered flyboard ($85) and JetPak lessons ($150) lessons—and equipment. *National Geographic Adventure* magazine called them one of the "best adventure travel companies on earth," and they have been in business since the early 1990s.

Kitty Hawk Kayak & Surf School (Milepost 1, 6150 N. Croatan Hwy./U.S. 158, Kitty Hawk, 252/261-0145, www.khkss. com, tours $40-60, kayak rentals from $69/week, SUP rentals from $150/week) teaches kayaking and SUP, rents equipment for paddling and surfing, and leads group and private tours, including overnighters. Many of the tours take you to seldom-seen marsh habitats and gorgeous creeks, or even back to the mainland to explore the waterways of the Alligator River National Wildlife Refuge.

Coastal Kayak Touring Company (reservations at North Beach Outfitters, 1240 Duck Rd., Duck, 252/441-3393, www. outerbankskayaktours.com, kayak tours $40-70, SUP tours $75) leads groups through some of the beautiful nature reserves on the Outer Banks, namely Kitty Hawk Woods Coastal Reserve and the Pine Island Audubon Sanctuary. Tours range 1.5 to 3 hours.

Outer Banks Stand-Up Paddle (1446 Duck Rd., Duck, 252/305-3639, www. outerbankssup.com, lessons from $75, rentals

from $120/week) teaches SUP techniques. Introductory lessons on the sound give first-timers a feel for the board in shallow, wave-free water, where they can build confidence to try ocean-side SUPing on their own with a rented board or with an advanced lesson. The most advanced paddlers will definitely want to take advantage of the SUP surfing lessons.

Hiking and Tours

At **Jockey's Ridge State Park** (Milepost 12, U.S. 158, 252/441-7132, http://ncparks. gov, park 8am-6pm Nov.-Feb., 8am-8pm Mar.-Apr. and Sept., 8am-7pm Oct., 8am-9pm May-Aug., visitors center 9am-5pm daily Nov.-Feb., 9am-6pm daily Mar.-Oct.), explore the dunes freely or follow one of the trails. The Soundside Nature Trail is about one mile long and takes you through maritime thickets and grassy dunes on a walk through a seldom-seen part of the park. Follow the Tracks in the Sand trail on its 1.5-mile course early in the morning to see animal tracks left during the night. Remember, the sand can be downright hot, especially during the summer. Bring sunscreen, shoes, and plenty of water if you're trekking around this park.

The **Currituck Banks National Estuarine Preserve** (N.C. 12, 877/623-6748, www.nccoastalreserve.net) protects some 1,000 acres of woods and water, extending far out into Currituck Sound. A short boardwalk runs from the parking lot to the sound, and a primitive trail runs 1.5 miles through the maritime forest.

TOP EXPERIENCE

★ WILD HORSE TOURS

You can hike in any park and most of the preserves on the Outer Banks, but nothing compares to seeing the wild horses in Corolla. The **Corolla Wild Horse Fund** (1129 Corolla Village Rd., Corolla, 252/453-8002, www. corollawildhorses.com, $45, $20 children) is a nonprofit group dedicated to preserving the herd and its environment, and they lead tours (3 times daily Mon.-Sat.). You'll ride along with herd managers and conservationists and get a glimpse into how they help keep the horses and their environment safe and healthy.

Back Country Outfitters and Guides (1159 Austin St., Corolla, 252/453-0877, http://outerbankstours.com, 8am-8pm daily year-round, wild horse tours $51, $31 ages 3-12, $20 ages 2 and younger, Segway safari $149 age 13 and up, Segway history tours $64 age 13 and up) leads wild horse tours as well as backcountry Segway tours, kayak trips, and other off-road tours. One cool offering is combined nature tours, where you kayak and explore in a 4x4 ($84 ages 13 and up, $51 ages 5-12); these tours are small, and they take you back into some interesting, and often unseen, spots on the Outer Banks.

Surfing

North Carolina has a reputation for having some of the best waves on the East Coast, making this a top destination for experienced surfers and those new to the sport.

Kitty Hawk Kites (Milepost 12.5, S. Croatan Hwy./U.S. 158, Nags Head, 252/449-2210, www.kittyhawk.com) provides lessons and board rentals. At **Island Revolution** (1159 Austin St., Corolla, 252/453-9484, www.islandrevolution.com, group lessons $75, private lessons $120), you can take private or group surf lessons, and more experienced surfers can opt to join the Surf Safari ($135), where local surfers teach the finer points of reading local waves and breaks and show you some of the best surf spots on the island. They also offer stand-up paddleboarding lessons and tours (lessons from $80, tour $65). **Farmdog Surf School** (2500 S. Virginia Dare Tr., Nags Head, 252/255-2233, http://farmdogsurfschool.com, lessons from $65, surfboard and paddleboard rentals from $15/day) and **Corolla Surf Shop** (807 Ocean Tr., Corolla, 252/453-9283, www.corollasurfshop.com, lessons from $68, rentals from $25/day) also offer lessons, rentals, and advice.

If you're a veteran surfer and you're bringing your own board, several online resources will help you find the best conditions and the perfect breaks. The websites of OBXLiveSurf (www.obxlivesurf.com), OBXSurfInfo (www.obxsurfinfo.com), Surfline (www.surfline.com), and SwellInfo (www.swellinfo.com) describe the best places to suit up and drop in.

Hang Gliding

With all the wind on the Outer Banks, everyone thinks about flying a kite, but how about flying a hang glider? **Kitty Hawk Kites** (Milepost 12.5, S. Croatan Hwy./U.S. 158, Nags Head, 252/449-2210, www.kittyhawk.com, $99) offers hang gliding lessons that will give you a taste of the thrill of flight as you lift off over the face of dunes on Jockey's Ridge. More than 300,000 people have learned to hang glide here since the company's Hang Gliding Training Center opened in 1974. You can also up the thrill factor and try a tandem flight that will have you and an instructor towed up to a mile high before being released to fly back to earth. If you want to pursue advanced certification through the United States Hang Gliding Association, you can do that on the dunes or on a tandem flight; you can even buy a glider and all the accessories you need to get started at the Kitty Hawk Kites retail store across the road from the school.

Golf

There are plenty of mini golf courses on the Outer Banks, but for the full-scale experience, only a handful of courses are open to the public. **Sea Scape Golf Links** (300 Eckner St., Kitty Hawk, 252/261-2158, www.seascapegolf.com, greens fees $50-105) offers 18-hole, par-70 links-style play only a block from the ocean. The wind can be a major factor when you play here; keep your ball low. At another links-style course, the 18-hole, par-71 **Nags Head Golf Links** (5615 S. Seachase Dr., Nags Head, 252/441-8073, www.clubcorp.com, greens fees $59-129), the wind is definitely in play; in fact, *Golf Digest* once said this course was "the longest 6,126 yards you'll ever play."

Water Park

H2OBX Waterpark (8526 Caratoke Hwy., Powells Point, 252/491-3000, www. hwobxwaterpark.com, 10am-7pm daily, late-May-early-Sept., $42 adults, $30 seniors and children under 42 inches tall, discounts for online ticket purchases) is on the mainland just 12 minutes from Kitty Hawk, and it's packed with more than 30 watery attractions—splash pads, water slides, a Flowrider, wave pool, and more—for the daring and those who just want to bob around in the pool. Family rides using giant rafts, lighting-quick racing slides, even a watery obstacle course deliver a day's worth of fun.

ENTERTAINMENT AND EVENTS

My favorite spot for wine and beer on the Outer Banks is **Trio** (Milepost 4.5, 3708 N. Croatan Hwy., 252/261-0277, www. triowinebeercheese.com, 10am-11pm Mon.-Sat., 11am-11pm Sun., $6-25), a name which refers to wine, beer, and cheese, the passions of the four owners. The selection here encompasses a wide range of wine and beer styles, nations and regions, and grape varietals. Tastings include the Trio Passport (focusing on wine from different nations) as well as varietal- and style-specific tastings. Nearly two dozen beers are on tap, and self-serve wine vending stations give you the chance to try tasting-size samples or even full glasses of expensive, hard-to-find, or interesting wines. Trio serves a selection of small plates, including paninis, salads, cheese plates, and other nibbles that go well with a glass of whatever you're drinking.

Chip's Wine and Beer Market (Milepost 6, U.S. 158, 2200 N. Croatan Hwy., Kill Devil Hills, 252/449-8229, www.chipswinemarket. com, 10am-8pm Mon.-Sat., 11am-8pm Sun.) is exactly what its name says. More than 450 craft beers from regional, national, and international breweries along with 2,000-plus wines line the shelves—but don't worry, the knowledgeable staff can find a brew or a bottle that suits your taste. Chip's is also home of the Outer Banks Wine University, offering everything from beginner classes to private tastings.

Food Festivals

As food-centered travel has gained momentum, four festivals taking advantage of this trend have emerged on the Outer Banks. Each draws visitors during the shoulder seasons and showcases something different about the area and its cuisine.

In March, **Taste of the Beach** (www. obxtasteofthebeach.com) features wine tastings, cooking classes by local chefs, cook-offs, dine-arounds, and more, hosted by more than 50 restaurants, breweries, wine shops, and food purveyors on the Banks. The four-day festival culminates with the OBX Grand Tasting, where restaurants compete for the best overall dish, best local seafood dish, Chefs Award, and People's Choice Award. *Coastal Living* magazine named Taste of the Beach one of the top seafood and wine festivals in the country in 2008, and it has been on the list ever since.

The **Duck and Wine Festival** (www. duckandwine.com), a one-day cook-off held in mid-late April, brings foodies together in the town of Duck to sample dishes that local chefs have created using, you guessed it, duck. The town shines again in mid-October for the one-day **Duck Jazz Festival** (www. townofduck.com), which features talented national jazz artists and alfresco dining from some of Duck's best restaurants.

Mid-October is also the time for the **Outer Banks Seafood Festival** (www. outerbanksseafoodfestival.org). Although oyster roasts, shrimparoos, and other informal seafood celebrations have been the norm on the Outer Banks for more than a century, 2012 was the first year for this formal seafood festival. More than a dozen restaurants

---

1: trail at Jockey's Ridge State Park; **2:** the Currituck Beach Lighthouse in Corolla; **3:** hang gliding off Jockey's Ridge; **4:** Sanderling Resort and Spa

participate in the one-day event, and organizers plan to grow the festival into a marquee event.

Nightlife

Part beach dive bar, part sports bar, **Lucky 12** (Milepost 12, 3308 S. Virginia Dare Tr./ N.C. 12, Nags Head, 252/255-5825, www. lucky12tavern.com, 11:30am-2am daily) is a hit with locals and visitors alike. With 20 beers on tap, another 90 in bottles or cans, a staggering 40-martini drink menu, and more than a dozen TVs, it's perfect to watch a game, hang out with friends, and order a pizza (served until 2am).

Fish Heads Bar & Grill (Milepost 18.5, 8901 S. Old Oregon Inlet Rd., Nags Head, 252/441-5740, www.fishheadsobx.com, open 24 hours, breakfast $3-5, lunch and dinner $4-12) never closes and since it's at the Outer Banks Fishing Pier, it makes sense, after all, a snack and a cold beer go well with all-night fishing. They have a small food menu—sandwiches, tacos, a few salads, some good appetizers—and an incredible beer selection of around 30 brews, many from North Carolina. Throw in live music just about every night during summer and most nights in the off season, the crash of waves and a pier to explore and you've got a recipe for a fun evening.

Ocean Boulevard Bistro & Martini Bar (Milepost 2.5, 4700 N. Virginia Dare Tr., Kitty Hawk, 252/261-2546, www.obbistro.com, 5pm-late daily, entrées $21-32), an upscale but casual martini bar and bistro, features live music on Friday and Saturday during the season, and with the impressive drink menu, it's easy to see why the place is popular with locals and visitors. If you're looking for an excellent spot to stop by after a late round of golf, this is it.

A weird in the best way place to grab a drink and listen to some music is **Bonzer Shack Bar & Grill** (1200 S. Virginia Dare Tr., Kill Devil Hills, 252/480-1010, www. bonzershack.com, 11:30am-2am daily, lunch $7-12, dinner $9-17). They call themselves a surf shack hangout and that's just about right.

Music nearly every night (two shows: afternoon and late night), a decent beer selection, and some boozy cocktails add to the atmosphere, but it's the people—a collection of characters you'll tell stories about later—that make it special.

At **The Comedy Club** (1601 S. Virginia Dare Tr., Kill Devil Hills, 252/207-9950, www. comedyclubobx.com), local, up-and-coming, and established comedians perform three to four nights a week in summer. The venue may be small, but they regularly have a good slate of comedians.

SHOPPING

Much of the shopping on the Outer Banks is focused on souvenir T-shirts or beach supplies such as towels, boogie boards, and rash guards. These mass-market beachwear clearing houses are so prolific that they're easy to find. There are also some boutiques carrying bathing suits, art, and jewelry, though most of the shopping (not of the overly touristy variety) is found in towns like Duck, to the north, and Hatteras, to the south.

Birthday Suits (Milepost 10, 2000 S. Croatan Hwy., Kill Devil Hills, 252/441-5338, http://birthday-suits.com, 10am-9pm daily summer, 10am-6pm daily spring, 10am-5pm daily fall) has been in the business of outfitting Bankers and visitors in the best bathing suits for more than 25 years. They have two other locations on the Outer Banks: in Duck (1171 Duck Rd., Duck, 252/261-7297) at Scarborough Lane Shops, and in Corolla (801 Ocean Trail, Monterey Plaza, Corolla, 252/453-4862). **Kitty Hawk Kites** (Milepost 12.5, 3925 S. Croatan Hwy./U.S. 158, Nags Head, 252/449-2210, www.kittyhawk.com, call for hours) carries swimwear and beach supplies as well as kites, toys, and an assortment of beach games and sports equipment.

In Duck, **The Town of Duck Boardwalk** (www.townofduck.com) follows the Albemarle Sound for nearly a mile, passing countless scenic spots and cool shops. At www.DoDuckNC.com you'll find a map and list of shops provided by the Duck Merchants

Association. Shops along this stretch run quite a range. You can grab your fresh seafood at a **Dockside 'N Duck Seafood Market** (1216 Duck Rd., in Wee Winks Square, 252/261-8687, www.docksidenduckseafood.com, 10am-6:30pm Mon.-Sat., 10am-6pm Sun.), pick up donuts at the fantastic **Duck Donuts** (1190 Duck Rd., in the Osprey Landing Shops, 252/480-3304, www.duckdonuts.com, 6:30am-9pm daily), and pick up a hand-crafted gift at **SeaDragon Gallery** (1240 Duck Rd., in the Waterfront Shops, 252/261-4224, www.seadragongallery.com, 10am-9pm Mon.-Fri., 10am-7pm Sat., 10am-5pm Sun in summer, hours vary in shoulder seasons and winter).

One of those spots on the map is **Scarborough Faire** (1177 Duck Rd., Duck, 540/272-0975, www.scarboroughfaireinducknc.com, hours vary, generally from 10am daily), which has served the boutique shopping needs of visitors and residents for more than 30 years. More than a dozen shops call Scarborough Faire home, including **Island Bookstore** (252/261-8981, www.islandbooksobx.com, 9am-7pm Mon.-Fri., 9am-6pm Sat.-Sun.), which carries a decent selection of best-sellers and books for kids and teens; a **Corolla Wild Horse Store** (252/453-8002, www.corollawildhorses.com); and **Ruff Haus** (Suite 14), a canine outfitter where you'll get everything from treats to beach toys.

Next door is **Scarborough Lane** (1171 Duck Rd., 757/222-9411, www.scarboroughlaneshoppesucknc.com, hours vary by store), a collection of shops and eateries including **Flip Flop Shops** (252/441-1757, www.flipflopshops.com, 11am-5pm Sun. and Tues., 10am-6pm Wed.-Sat.), which sells summer footwear; **Outer Barks** (252/261-6279, www.outerbarks.com, 10am-5pm Mon.-Sat., 11am-4pm Sun.), with dog clothes (for them and you), toys, and even Yappy Hour for the canine crowds; **The Mystic Jewel** (252/255-5515, http://themysticjewel.com, 10am-5pm Mon.-Sat., 11am-4pm Sun.), a jewelry store specializing in unusual stones and limited-edition jewelry pieces by artists from around the world (prices range $20 to around $400); and **Duck Pizza Company** (252/255-0099, www.duckpizza.com, 11:30am-8pm Mon.-Sat., noon-8pm Sun., $9-22), which sells pizzas, calzones, and other crowd pleasers.

FOOD

When I first started visiting the Outer Banks, it seemed that every other restaurant was a seafood buffet. Today, buffets still abound, but a number of notable independent restaurants have taken root. The selection varies from gourmet to down-home, including pizza and burgers along with barbecue, fine dining, and a decent representation of international cuisines.

Sam & Omie's (7728 S. Virginia Dare Tr., Nags Head, 252/441-7366, www.samandomies.net, 7am-9pm Mon.-Sat., 7am-4pm Sun., breakfast $2-8, dinner $6-26) opened in the summer of 1937 as a place for charter fishing customers and guides to catch breakfast before heading out to sea. They still serve a hearty breakfast heavy on the classics—two eggs your way, pancakes, grits, and the like—but take a look at the specialties, such as crab Benedict or the chef's special. Sam & Omie's also serves lunch and dinner, and, as you may expect, both menus emphasize seafood. Sure, you can get a burger, steak, or chicken breast, but why would you when you can get a clam dog, fried oysters, or the massive Whale of a Seafood Platter (which really is more food than one person should eat)?

The ★ **Outer Banks Brewing Station** (Milepost 8.5, 600 S. Croatan Hwy., Kill Devil Hills, 252/449-2739, www.obbrewing.com, 11:30am-2am Mon.-Fri., 11am-2pm Sat., 11am-midnight Sun.., entrées $15-31) is an innovative and interesting spot to eat, not just because the food presses beyond expected seafood dishes (you'll find seared tuna with Asian-inspired hoppin' john, tuna tartare towers, and spicy crab claws) and the beers are adventurous, but because they're wind-powered. A group of friends who met in the Peace Corps combined their love of food, beer, and sustainability to create a hot spot on the Outer Banks' dining and nightlife scenes.

Pigman's Bar-B-Que (Milepost 9.5, 1606 S. Croatan Hwy., Kill Devil Hills, 252/441-6803, www.pigman.com, 11am-8:30pm daily, $5-25) is the spot for barbecue on the Outer Banks. Done right—over wood coals, low and slow—the barbecue here is succulent even without sauce, but add a dash of the house-made sauce to it and a sandwich, plate, platter or ribs are that much better. Not in the mood for pork? No problem; there's fried shrimp, a tuna-que sandwich, smoked turkey, and more.

AQUA Restaurant and Spa (1174 Duck Rd., Duck, 252/261-9700, www.aquaobx.com, 11:30am-9pm daily, $18-32) has an interesting concept, with a day spa upstairs and an excellent restaurant downstairs, creating flavorful food using community-sourced organic ingredients that will, as the owner puts it, "nourish your body and spirit." Grab a table by the windows or on the deck (weather permitting) and enjoy views of the sound while you dine. The food is a fusion of regional dishes and international flavors and techniques. Their *fruits de mer* pasta is Italian in nature but uses all fresh and local seafood. Their seared duck breast uses local ducks (when possible) and seasonal produce. Dishes like the fish-and-chips, shrimp or fish tacos, and crab cakes are—you guessed it—caught in the waters nearby. AQUA also has an exceptionally well-curated wine menu and knowledgeable staff able to steer you toward a glass or bottle that will complement your meal perfectly.

In the Waterfront Shops in Duck you'll find **The Blue Point** (1240 Duck Rd., 252/261-8090, www.thebluepoint.com, 11:30am-2:30pm Tues.-Fri. and Sun., 5pm-9:30pm daily, lunch $7-17, dinner $25-40). This isn't the restaurant you'd expect to find in a collection of waterside shops in a tourist town; it's fine food at its finest. The location is ideal—the dining room sits looking out over the Currituck Sound—and the menu more so. Blue Point is a hit with Outer Banks foodies because the menu makes the best of locally caught seafood and incredible produce in

every dish. Make a reservation or expect to wait for a while.

Colington Café (1029 Colington Rd., Kill Devil Hills, 252/480-1123, www.colingtoncafe.com, 5pm-9pm daily, $17-32), tucked back in the maritime forest in Kill Devil Hills and nestled under the live oak trees, feels like a secret spot. The restaurant was formerly someone's home, so the dining rooms are a little tight, but the food more than makes up for any lack of space. Steaks here are melt-in-your-mouth good, and the seafood is nearly flawless. Whether you dine from the land or sea portion of the menu, you can't go wrong.

Dune Burger (Milepost 16.5, 7304 S. Virginia Dare Tr., 252/441-2441, $2.50-7.50) may just be the oldest drive-up burger place on the Outer Banks. That throwback charm, plus a burger that's so good it's destined to become a tradition, is why you come here. Grab a couple of burgers and an order of onion rings, then head over to the beach and enjoy, it's right across the street from Jennette's Pier.

Pizza Stop (5385 N. Virginia Dare Tr., Southern Shores, 252/261-7867, www.pizzastopobx.com, 11am-9pm Wed.-Sun.) specializes in New York-style pizza by the slice ($2) and the pie ($11-20). Pizzas are of the standard "cheese plus toppings" variety and they have a half-dozen specialty pies from which to choose. You can also get salads, pastas, and hot sandwiches ($6-11), if that's your thing. They deliver, but not to everywhere on the Outer Banks, so inquire before you get your heart set on pizza arriving at your door.

Mama Kwan's Grill and Tiki Bar (1701 S. Croatan Hwy., Kill Devil Hills, 252/441-7889, www.mamakwans.com, 11:30am-10pm Tues.-Sun., lunch $9-13, dinner $10-22) serves killer fish tacos (especially the jerk-seasoned ones), but their sashimi tuna appetizer is fantastic. A little divey, always delicious, Mama Kwan's is a fun spot to stop for a bite.

Basnight's Lone Cedar Café (7623 S. Virginia Dare Tr. on the Nags Head-Manteo Causeway, 252/441-5405, www.lonecedarcafe.

com, dinner from 4:30pm-9pm daily, brunch 11am-3pm Sun., dinner $14-32, brunch $8-14) is a water-view bistro that specializes in local food—oysters from Hyde and Dare Counties, fresh-caught local fish, and North Carolina chicken, pork, and vegetables. It's one of the most popular restaurants on the Outer Banks, and they don't take reservations, so be sure to arrive early. The full bar is open until midnight.

To satisfy your sweet tooth, visit one of the many locations of **Duck Donuts** (1190 Duck Rd., in the Osprey Landing Shops, 252/480-3304, www.duckdonuts.com, 6:30am-9pm daily). My friend who lives on the Outer Banks calls eating them "a rite of passage," and I have to agree; these things are tasty, like carnival fritters, but made more delicious by the salt air. If you want something cold and sweet, try **Surfin' Spoon** (2408 S. Virginia Dare Tr., Nags Head, 252/441-7873, www.surfinspoon.com, noon-11pm Mon.-Sat.), a frozen yogurt bar where you fill a bowl with your chosen flavor and then pile it high with toppings (cookies, candy, sprinkles, fruit, gummy bears—you get the picture). The owners—pro surfer Jesse Hines and his wife, Whitney—go out of their way to make Surfin' Spoon an experience through surf movies, a game room, and tons of surf photos on the walls.

ACCOMMODATIONS

The ★ **First Colony Inn** (6715 S. Croatan Hwy., Nags Head, 855/207-2262, www.firstcolonyinn.com, $99-279) is a beautiful little 1932 beachfront hotel. This regional landmark has won historic preservation and landscaping awards for its 1988 renovation, which involved moving the entire building, in three pieces, three miles south of its original location. Of the 27 rooms here, all are exceedingly comfortable and give guests a taste of luxury accommodations at an affordable rate.

In Duck, the ★ **Sanderling Resort and Spa** (1461 Duck Rd., Duck, 855/412-7866, www.sanderling-resort.com, $299-729) is a mainstay for luxury travel on the Outer Banks. A 2013 renovation—totaling more than $6 million—added more guest rooms and an adults-only pool, upgraded public spaces, and gave the resort's dining options a real boost. In 2015, they continued their quest for the ultimate guest experience and added 28 new rooms ranging from suites with unobstructed ocean and sound views to queen rooms with ocean views. Sanderling has a renowned spa and one of the best restaurants on the Outer Banks, ★ **Kimball's Kitchen** (entrées $24-40). Kimball's serves a menu centered around local seafood and grass-fed steaks, but the view of the sound from the dining room is unparalleled. The view, when combined with the food and level of service, makes Kimball's Kitchen a spectacular dining experience.

There are many bed-and-breakfasts, including the **Cypress Moon Inn** (1206 Harbor Court, Kitty Hawk, 252/262-2731, www.cypressmooninn.com, no children, $135-210), a small but beautiful sound-side home featuring three guest rooms. The owners also have three cottages nearby that are perfect for secluded getaways.

The **Cypress House Inn** (Milepost 8, Beach Rd., 500 N. Virginia Dare Tr., Kill Devil Hills, 252/441-6127, www.cypresshouseinn.com, $99-219) is only 125 yards from the ocean, and that, combined with its central location and undeniable charm, makes it a desirable B&B. Guests staying in each of the six guest rooms at the 1940s-style inn are treated to complimentary beach chairs and towels. **The Atlantic Street Inn** (Milepost 9.5, Kill Devil Hills, 252/305-0246, www.atlanticstreetinn.com, $69-159) offers similar treatment, with bicycles available for guest use; reserve its six guest rooms individually or, if you book far enough ahead, reserve the entire inn or the nearby beach house. One thing you'll find at Atlantic Street that most other accommodations are lacking: a lawn. Their backyard is a lovely spot to relax and spend some time outside, but in the shade.

The **Colington Creek Inn** (1293

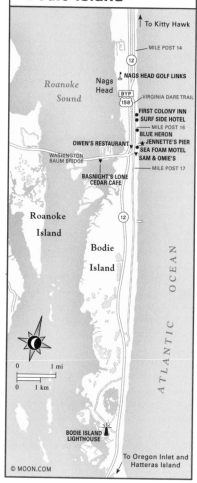

Nags Head to Bodie Island

To Kitty Hawk

MILE POST 14

12

Roanoke Sound

Nags Head

NAGS HEAD GOLF LINKS

BYP
158

VIRGINIA DARE TRAIL

FIRST COLONY INN
SURF SIDE HOTEL
MILE POST 16
BLUE HERON
JENNETTE'S PIER
SEA FOAM MOTEL
SAM & OMIE'S

OWEN'S RESTAURANT

WASHINGTON
BAUM BRIDGE

MILE POST 17

BASNIGHT'S LONE
CEDAR CAFE

Roanoke
Island

12

Bodie

Island

A T L A N T I C   O C E A N

0   1 mi
0   1 km

BODIE ISLAND
LIGHTHOUSE

To Oregon Inlet and
Hatteras Island

© MOON.COM

Nags Head, 800/552-7873, www.surfsideobx. com, $79-299) has simple, comfortable, standard guest rooms and efficiencies in a location that is only steps from the beach. At the **Blue Heron** (6811 Virginia Dare Tr., Nags Head, 252/441-7447, www.blueheronnc.com, $60-166), every guest room faces the ocean, and for rainy days or off-season visits there is an indoor heated pool.

At the **Nags Head Beach Inn** (303 E. Admiral St., Nags Head, 866/316-1843, www. keeshotels.com, $194-300), a converted beach club dating to the 1930s that's only steps from the beach, all the accoutrements that guests need—chairs, bicycles, body boards, and the like—are available for use. Quaint and comfortable, the Nags Head Beach Inn is one of several cottages known as the "Unpainted Aristocracy." Some of these cottages date back to the 1830s, but they all have common features—weatherworn shake siding and a yesteryear charm.

If you're looking for that classic beach-motel feel, three spots come to mind. The wood-paneled walls at **Outer Banks Motor Lodge** (1509 S. Virginia Dare Tr., Milepost 9.5, Kill Devil Hills, 877/625-6343, www.obxmotorlodge.com, $53-249) are tacky enough to add to the place's appeal. **Beach Haven Motel** (4104 N. Virginia Dare Tr., Kitty Hawk, 252/261-4785, www. beachhavenmotel.com, $105-199) offers a little kitsch in the accommodations and even a grill and outdoor picnic area where you can cook your own fresh catch. The bargain **Sea Foam Motel** (7111 S. Virginia Dare Tr., Nags Head, 252/441-7320, www. seafoam.com, $68-149) is a no-frills motel with a lot of wood paneling and a lot of retro charm.

Vacation Rentals

Many groups—families, bridal parties, bachelor parties, anglers, surfers—who need a place with plenty of space turn to rental homes, and on the Outer Banks there are a number of rental agencies to choose from. **Seaside Vacations** (3620 N. Croatan

---

Colington Rd., Kill Devil Hills, 252/449-4124, www.colingtoncreekinn.com, no children or pets, $178-298) has four guest rooms with water views of the sound and its namesake creek, along with porches perfect for morning coffee or an evening drink.

Throughout Kitty Hawk and Nags Head, you'll find a number of motels, ranging from chains to classic 1950s mom-and-pops. The **Surf Side Hotel** (6701 Virginia Dare Tr.,

Hwy., Kitty Hawk, 866/884-0267, www. outerbanksvacations.com) rents houses in every little town from Corolla to Nags Head and has a large selection of sizes, styles, locations (oceanfront, ocean view, soundside), and prices in their catalog of homes. **Sun Realty** (888/853-7770, www.sunrealtync. com) has a huge selection of homes, many with amenities—pools, hot tubs, game rooms, theater rooms—travelers are seeking. **Outer Banks Rentals by Southern Shores Realty** (5 Ocean Blvd., Southern Shores, 800/334-1000, www.southernshores. com) has more than 700 units in their rental catalogue, and they've been helping visitors find the perfect beach house since 1974, so you know they know the Outer Banks.

GETTING THERE AND AROUND

The closest major airport is **Norfolk International Airport** (ORF, 2200 Norview Ave., Norfolk, VA, 757/857-3351, www. norfolkairport.com), approximately an hour from the northern Outer Banks. **Raleigh-Durham International Airport** (RDU, 2600 W. Terminal Blvd., Morrisville, 919/840-2123, www.rdu.com) is three to five hours' drive from most Outer Banks destinations.

Only two bridges exist between the mainland and the northern Outer Banks. U.S. 64/264 crosses over Roanoke Island to Whalebone, just south of Nags Head. Not too far north of there, U.S. 158 crosses from Point Harbor to Southern Shores. Highway 12 is the main road all along the Outer Banks.

Roanoke Island

In the 1580s, the first nonnative residents of the Outer Banks, and perhaps their most famous denizens, moved in. These intrepid English colonists found Roanoke Island—protected from the brunt of storms by the Albemarle, Roanoke, and Croatan Sounds and the mass of Bodie Island—a fine place to call home. They established Fort Raleigh, and there, Virginia Dare, the first European born on the new continent, came into the world. Shortly thereafter, the community vanished, earning the name many now know them by: The Lost Colony. Where they went and the specifics of how and when they met their collective fate is unknown to this day, but one that's explored in the aptly named outdoor drama, *The Lost Colony.*

Visitors to Roanoke Island today will find what the colonists found: a beautiful, welcoming island ripe for exploration. The relative abundance of bed-and-breakfasts, restaurants, and shops make staying on Roanoke Island much easier than it was four centuries ago. At the northern end of Roanoke Island, Fort Raleigh National Historic Site marks the last known location of the Lost Colony, and the nearby town of Manteo offers a day or two of dining and distractions. Most of the island's offerings for visitors are concentrated here. It's a short drive across the causeway in Nags Head to Manteo—only 15 minutes—and beautiful.

★ FORT RALEIGH NATIONAL HISTORIC SITE

Fort Raleigh National Historic Site (1401 National Park Dr., Manteo, 252/473-2111, www.nps.gov, 9am-5pm daily, closed Dec. 25, free) includes much of the original site of the first English settlement in the New World. Archaeologists still conduct digs here, regularly unearthing new artifacts and assembling clues about the Lost Colony's fate, but sections of the earthworks associated with the original 1580s fort remain and have been preserved, making it easy to imagine the site as a working fort on the frontier of an unknown land. In the visitors center, artifacts and interactive displays tell the story of the fort, the missing

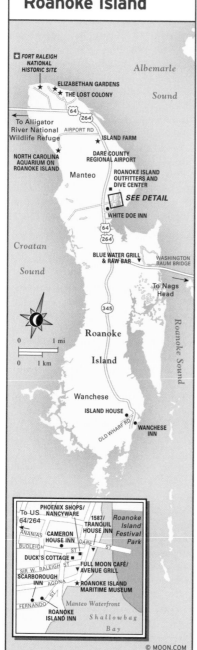

Roanoke Island

colonists, and the freedman's colony—a colony of freed and displaced slaves established on the island during the Civil War. Two nature trails in the park allow you to explore the natural landscape and the site of a Civil War battle.

Within the National Historic Site, two of Manteo's most famous attractions operate autonomously. Nearly 60 years ago, **Elizabethan Gardens** (1411 National Park Dr., Manteo, 252/473-3234, http://elizabethangardens.org, 10am-3pm Jan., 9am-5pm March. and Oct., 9am-6pm Apr.-Sept., 9am-4pm Nov.-Dec., closed Feb., $9, $6 ages 6-17, $2 ages 5 and under, $3 pets) was conceived by the Garden Club of North Carolina as a permanent memorial to the settlers of Roanoke Island. As a tribute, they planted the types of gardens and plants that would have been common in the colonists' native England in the 16th century. There are many corners to explore in this 10.5-acre garden and many treasures, both natural and artificial, to discover: an ancient live oak so huge that many believe it has been standing since the colonists' days; a sunken garden containing Renaissance-era statuary; an impressive display of camellias and azaleas; and a 19th-century statue of Virginia Dare. The statue was underwater off the coast of Spain for two years, was salvaged, and made it to Massachusetts, where it was nearly lost in a fire. It finally arrived in North Carolina in the 1920s, where modest residents, shocked by the statue's nudity, passed it around the state for years until it found a permanent home in Elizabethan Gardens.

Also within the park is the Waterside Theatre. North Carolina has a long history of outdoor performances celebrating regional heritage and history, and the best-known of these is Roanoke Island's *The Lost Colony* (1409 National Park Dr., Manteo, 252/473-6000, http://thelostcolony.org, from $20 adults, from $18 ages 13-18, from $10 ages 6-12, free ages 5 and under). Playwright Paul Green was commissioned to write a drama about the colony in 1937 to celebrate the 350th anniversary of the birth of Virginia Dare. What he thought would be a single-season production has turned into a fixture, with performances every year since, except when extraordinary circumstances, like German U-boats prowling off the coast during World War II, interrupted the production schedule. An impressive list of actors has performed in the play, including Andy Griffith and current director Ira David Woods.

OTHER SIGHTS

The **Roanoke Island Maritime Museum** (104 Fernando St., Manteo, 252/475-1750, www.townofmanteo.com, hours vary, free) is a unique working boat shop and repository for artifacts that offers a look at local and regional maritime heritage. Traditional boat builders offer classes in boat building and handling at the George Washington Creef Boathouse, but visitors not enrolled in the classes are still welcome to come and observe. Also on the grounds is the **Roanoke Marshes Lighthouse.** The large lighthouses protecting the outer Atlantic coast are well known, but a number of smaller river and marsh lighthouses also once dotted the coast. This structure is a reconstruction of the square cottage-style lighthouse that was decommissioned in 1955.

Both the Maritime Museum and the Marshes Lighthouse are part of **Roanoke Island Festival Park** (1 Festival Park, Manteo, 252/475-1500, www.roanokeisland.com, 9am-5pm daily March-Dec., $10 adults, $7 ages 6-17, free ages 5 and under, tickets good for two days), which has a lot to offer. There are plays and puppet shows for kids (call or check the website for performances and dates, tickets $5, free ages 5 and under) at an indoor theatre, the occasional concert, and the Roanoke Adventure Museum, where kids can don 16th-century costumes and learn a bit about life on the Outer Banks from the time of the Lost Colony on. The highlight for many is the *Elizabeth II*, a ship built to represent one of the seven English merchant vessels from the voyage of 1585. A staff of sailors is onboard in costume to show visitors a bit about living and working on such a ship.

Island Farm (1140 U.S. 64, Manteo, 252/473-6500, www.theislandfarm.com, 10am-4pm Tues.-Fri. Apr.-late-Nov., closed Thanksgiving Day, $8 adults, free under age 5) is a living-history site that transports you back to a Roanoke Island farm circa 1850. Reproduction outbuildings include the smokehouse, cookhouse, and slave house alongside the original farmhouse, built between 1845 and 1850. Period interpreters lead tours and talks that focus on gardening, cooking, and other day-to-day doings on a farm in the pre-Civil War Outer Banks.

The **North Carolina Aquarium on Roanoke Island** (374 Airport Rd., Manteo, 252/475-2300, www.ncaquariums.com, 9am-5pm daily year-round, closed Thanksgiving Day and Dec. 25, $13 adults, $12 seniors and military, $11 ages 3-12, free under age 3) is one of three state aquariums on the North Carolina coast. A great place for kids, the aquarium is home to all sorts of marine fauna and tells the aquatic story of North Carolina from the deep sea to freshwater tributaries. See river otters, alligators, freshwater fish, sharks, and more in traditional and touch-tank aquariums. Don't miss the daily dive shows in the huge 285,000-gallon Graveyard of the Atlantic tank. Displays in the aquarium detail the U.S. Lifesaving Service, and outside is the grave of Richard Etheridge, the first African American to captain a Lifesaving Station on Pea Island, just south of the Bodie Island Lighthouse.

SPORTS AND RECREATION

Roanoke Island Outfitters and Dive Center (627 US Hwy. 64, Manteo, 252/473-1356 or 252/423-1257, www.roanokeislandoutfittersanddivecenter.com, 9am-5:30pm Mon.-Fri., 9am-3pm Sat., call for Sun. hours) offers scuba diving classes (from $100), spearfishing and freediving classes (from $150), charters to wreck dives ($130) as well as beach dives ($40) and spearfishing excursions ($130). All levels of divers are welcome.

Spearfishing is just one way to catch a big one on the Outer Banks. On Roanoke Island it's easy to catch fish with a rod and a reel, thanks to a number of inshore and offshore charters that are available year-round. **The Outer Banks Visitors Bureau** (www.outerbanks.org) has a comprehensive list of charter operators and rates.

Daring travelers can take in the sights of Roanoke Island and the Outer Banks from 9,000 feet with **Skydive OBX** (410 Airport Rd., Manteo, 252/678-5867, www.skydiveobx.com, $249). Each tandem jump provides 30 seconds of free fall at 120 mph and plenty of time to admire the view. Discounts are offered on same-day second jumps.

TOURS

The *Downeast Rover* (sails from Manteo waterfront, 252/473-4866, www.downeastrover.com, daytime cruises $35 adults, $32 seniors and military, $25 ages 2-12, sunset cruises $45) is a 55-foot reproduction of a 19th-century schooner. Cruises last two hours and depart three times daily at 1:15pm, 3:45pm, and sunset. **OBX Air Charters** (410 Airport Rd., Manteo, 252/256-2322, www.outerbanksaircharters.com, $250 for up to 5 people, custom tours $465/hour up to 5 passengers) will take you on a standard or custom sightseeing flight tour, but they also arrange charter flights from a number of regional and east-coast airports. Charters range from $500-4,200 and they serve airports as near as Norfolk, Virginia, and as far away as Teterboro, New York.

The gardens and quaint waterfronts on Roanoke Island are charming for adult visitors, but not so much for kids; thankfully, two tours fulfill the fun quotient for the young ones. On **Captain Johnny's Outer Banks Dolphin Tours** (Manteo Waterfront, 252/473-1475, www.outerbankscruises.com, from $30 adults, $20 ages 2-12, $10 under 18 months, tours at 10am, 1pm and sunset\), you'll get up close to bottlenose dolphins in

their native habitat and watch as they swim, leap, and sometimes even inspect the boat on each two-hour tour. Kids get the chance to transform themselves into pirates with **Pirate Adventures of the Outer Banks** (408 Queen Elizabeth Ave., Manteo, 252/473-2007, www.pirateadventuresobx.com, tours 9:30am, 11am, 12:30pm, 2pm, 3:30pm, and 5pm daily, $25 ages 3 and up, $12 ages 2 and younger). Aboard the *Sea Gypsy*, a 40-foot pirate ship replete with a water cannon and a costumed pirate crew, kids get the chance to dress like pirates, hunt down an enemy pirate, engage in a water-cannon battle, find sunken treasure, and have a pirate party. These 1.25-hour tours sail six times daily, seven days a week, giving parents opportunities to take an hour to explore the Manteo waterfront.

If you don't mind a scare, take a 90-minute stroll through Manteo with **Ghost Tours of the OBX** (399 Queen Elizabeth Ave. and Budleigh St., Manteo, 252/573-1450, www.ghosttoursoftheobx.com, $13, $8 ages 10 and under). Visit the village cemetery, look for the ghosts of pirates and lost sailors along the shore and waterfront, and learn about supernatural creatures in the surrounding woods on one of three chilling, but kid-friendly, tours.

ENTERTAINMENT AND EVENTS

Roanoke Island is a pretty tame place, with most of the events and activities of a family-oriented nature. To that end, on the first Friday of the month from April to November, the town of Manteo celebrates **First Friday**, a free downtown festival that brings locals and visitors out for live music, street performers and more. In addition to live music on the streets, many restaurants and shops feature their own musical acts, sales, and refreshments. The **Dare County Arts Council Gallery** (300 Queen Elizabeth Ave., Manteo, 252/473-5558, www.darearts.org, 10am-6pm

---

1: statue of Virginia Dare in the Elizabethan Gardens; **2:** Island Farm

Mon.-Fri., 10am-8pm first Fri., noon-6pm Sat. May-Sept., 10am-5pm Tues.-Fri. and noon-4pm Sat. Oct.-Apr.) has lovely exhibits by local artists and hosts a reception during First Friday that showcases a new exhibit by a local or regional artist.

Poor Richard's Sandwich Shop (303 Queen Elizabeth St., Manteo, 252/473-3333, www.poorrichardsmanteo.com, 11am-3pm Mon.-Sat., bar 5pm-2am Mon.-Sat., $4-8) is more than a great place to eat (and it is—their burgers and sandwiches are legendary around here). During the summer season they have trivia on Wednesdays and live entertainment in the bar most other nights.

In May, the **Outer Banks Bluegrass Island Festival** (www.bluegrassisland.com, single day tickets $45, three-day pass $125) sees Roanoke Island Festival Park transformed into a bluegrass bonanza. Three days of music from acts like Rhonda Vincent & the Rage, Seldom Scene, and The SteelDrivers as well as a fantastic location have made this into a premier event on the Outer Banks.

SHOPPING

Roanoke Island is a haven for artists, with many calling Manteo home. Downtown are several studios and galleries featuring local artists' paintings, drawings, pottery, and jewelry. A favorite is the pottery studio of Nancy Huse, **Nancyware Pottery** (402 Queen Elizabeth Ave., Manteo, 252/473-9400, www.nancywareobx.com, call for hours), where she shapes, glazes, and fires beautiful and functional pots, trivets, decorative pieces, ornaments, and earrings. At **Silver Bonsai Jewelry & Art Gallery** (905 Hwy. 64, Manteo, 252/475-1413, www.silverbonsai. com, call for hours) has a gorgeous selection of jewelry and a great collection of fine and functional artwork.

The **Phoenix Shops** (Budleigh St. and Queen Elizabeth Ave., 252/473-2133) are home to an eclectic mix of boutiques, galleries, and home-goods stores. **Downtown Books** (105 Sir Walter Raleigh St., Manteo, 252/473-1056, www.duckscottage.com, 10am-5pm

Mon.-Thurs. and Sat., 10am-8pm Fri. and 11am-3pm Sun. summer, 11am-4pm daily Jan.-Mar.) is a small but well-stocked bookstore, with more than just the best-sellers; there is quite a selection of books by local and regional authors. The staff are friendly and knowledgeable and can point out easy summer reads.

FOOD

Located in the Tranquil House Inn with a great view of Shallowbag Bay, ★ **1587** (405 Queen Elizabeth Ave., 252/473-1587, www.1587.com, days and hours vary by season, dinner $17-42) is widely regarded as one of the best restaurants in this part of the state. The menu has hearty chops and seafood, with local and seasonal ingredients; a full vegetarian menu is available, and the wine list is a mile long. Surprises include curries, the buttermilk crab hush puppies, and their seasonal salad (especially when it's topped with Pamlico Sound shrimp).

The **Lost Colony Brewery & Cafe** (208 Queen Elizabeth St., 252/473-6666, www. lostcolonybrewery.com, 11am-9pm daily, $10-30) dishes up crab cakes, fish and chips, fried oysters, and a fried seafood platter that you may need a friend to help you eat. In addition, they have burgers, po' boys and barbecue sandwiches. Their beers—they brew eight—include an imperial stout, a red ale and an IPA; order a flight and find your favorite.

Blue Water Grill & Raw Bar (2000 Sailfish Dr., Manteo, 252/473-1955, www. bluewatergrillobx.com, 11:30am-10pm daily, lunch $11-15, dinner $11-28) has the selection of cooked and raw seafood you'd expect, but they go the extra mile and will cook your catch if you bring it in (cleaned and ready to go) and give them an hour.

Shaddai Peruvian & Mexican Grill (112 Hwy. 64, Manteo, 252/423-3013, 11am-9pm Mon.-Sat., $9-22) is a departure from the seafood-rich menus at restaurants around, and that's one of the reasons it's so popular with locals. The Peruvian half of their menu is a taste of Lima on the Outer Banks, and if you doubt it one bite of their *lomo saltado* (Peruvian stir-fry) or their *pollo a la brasa* (rotisserie chicken) served with Inca Kola will convince you. There is seafood here in the form of ceviche (Peruvians invented the dish, so it's fitting) and the *jalea mixta* (a South American spin on the fried fish you find along the North Carolina coast).

ACCOMMODATIONS

The ★ **White Doe Inn** (319 Sir Walter Raleigh St., Manteo, 252/489-2453, www.whitedoeinn. com, from $225 off-season, $250 summer) is one of North Carolina's premier inns. The 1910 Queen Anne is the largest house on the island and is listed on the National Register of Historic Places. Guest rooms are exquisitely furnished in turn-of-the-20th-century finery. Guests enjoy a four-course breakfast, evening sherry, espresso and cappuccino anytime, and a 24-hour wine cellar. Spa services are available on site, and you need only step out to the lawn to play croquet or bocce.

The **Roanoke Island Inn** (305 Fernando St., 252/473-5511, www.roanokeislandinn. com, $228-380) has been in the owner's family since the 1860s. It's a beautiful old place, with a big porch that overlooks the marsh. They also rent out a single cottage on a private island, five minutes away by boat, and a nice cypress-shingled bungalow in town. Another top hotel in Manteo is the **Tranquil House Inn** (405 Queen Elizabeth Ave., 800/458-7069, www.tranquilhouseinn.com, from $109 off-season, from $219 summer). It's in a beautiful location, and downstairs is 1587 one of the best restaurants on the Outer Banks. **Burrus House Inn** (509 Hwy. 64-264, 252/475-1636, www.burrushouse.com, $175-250) has direct waterfront access, which, surprisingly, makes it a rare find in Outer Banks B&Bs; the waterfront suites feature double showers and soaking tubs as well as private decks.

The **Cameron House Inn** (300 Budleigh St., Manteo, 800/279-8178, http://cameronhouseinn.com, from $225/night) is a cozy 1919 arts and crafts-style bungalow. All of the indoor guest rooms are furnished in a lovely and understated craftsman style, but the nicest guest room in the house is the porch, which has an outdoor fireplace, fans, and flowery trellises.

The **Wanchese Inn** (85 Jovers Lane, Wanchese, 252/475-1166, www.wancheseinn. com, from $89 off-season, from $139 summer) is a simple and inexpensive bed-and-breakfast in a nice Victorian house with modern guest rooms. There's a boat slip and on-site parking for a boat and trailer. The **Island House** (104 Old Wharf Rd., 888/255-7561 or 252/473-5619, www.islandhouse-bb.com, $140-1785) was built in the early 1900s for a local coast guardsman with wood cut from the property and nails forged on site. It's very comfortable and quiet, and a big country breakfast is served every day.

GETTING THERE AND AROUND

Coming from the mainland, you first reach the town of Mann's Harbor on the inland side of the Croatan Sound; from there you have two choices to cross to Roanoke Island. If you take U.S. 64/264 to the north (left), you'll cross the sound to the north, arriving in Manteo. If you drive straight ahead at Mann's Harbor, you'll be on the U.S. 64/264 Bypass, which crosses to the middle of the island, south of Manteo. Proceed until you get to the main intersection with Highway 345, where you can turn left onto U.S. 64/264 to go to Manteo, or right onto Highway 345 to Wanchese.

To reach Roanoke Island from the Outer Banks, take U.S. 158 or Highway 12 to Whalebone Junction, south of Nags Head, and cross Roanoke Sound on the U.S. 64/264 bridge.

Cape Hatteras National Seashore

Cape Hatteras stretches farther south and east than any other part of the United States, jutting out into the Atlantic and brushing the warm waters of the Gulf Stream. Hatteras draws surfers, anglers, divers, and beach-loving vacationers by the thousands. It's also a haven to migratory birds, home to important inshore and offshore fisheries, making it popular for bird-watching. In Hatteras Village, Waves, Salvo, and Avon, museums and historic sites tell the history of the Outer Banks as well as the story of the birth of the Coast Guard. In these towns, there are also galleries packed with the work of local artists and fish markets with trays and coolers full of today's catch.

Due to Hatteras' position so close to the strong currents of the Gulf Stream, a shifting set of sandbars called Diamond Shoals extends from the cape's pristine beaches far out into the Atlantic. While the lighthouses at Cape Hatteras and Bodie Island provide guidance for ships, in years past, many ran afoul of the shoals, sinking outright or beaching on the sandbars. These ships are part of what's called the Graveyard of the Atlantic, an incredible number of shipwrecks that line the coast of North Carolina but congregate here. Ships range from colonial sailboats to Civil War blockade runners to German U-Boats sent to harass supply and troop ships in World War II. Hundreds of species of fish are drawn to the wrecks, as are divers and anglers.

BODIE ISLAND

Bodie Island hasn't been a true island in decades, but the name stuck around. Today Bodie Island sits at the southern tip of the thin peninsula, which constitutes the most recognizable (and populous) portion of the Outer Banks, just north of Oregon Inlet and Hatteras Island. It is the northern end of the Cape Hatteras National Seashore, which runs the length of the islands from Whalebone Junction, where U.S. 64/264 joins N.C. 12, to Hatteras Inlet and separates Hatteras and Ocracoke Islands.

You'll spot the horizontal black-and-white stripes of the 170-foot **Bodie Island Lighthouse** (6 miles south of Whalebone Junction, 252/473-2111, www.nps.gov/caha, visitors center 9am-5pm daily, $8 adults, $4 seniors and age 11 and under) from several miles away. The Bodie Light's huge Fresnel lens first beamed in 1872, but this is the third lighthouse on this location. The first iteration of the Bodie Light (pronounced "body") was built in the 1830s, but due to engineering errors and shifting sand it leaned like the Tower of Pisa and didn't last too long. The next one stood straight but proved such a tempting target for the Yankee Navy during the Civil War that the Confederates blew it up themselves. The third light still stands, although a flock of geese nearly put it out of commission soon after its first lighting when they collided with and damaged the lens.

The Bodie Island Lighthouse opened to the public for climbs in 2013 and remains popular. Self-guided tours (daily late Apr.-early Oct.) take you on a strenuous climb up the lighthouse, but it is worth it for the view. Solid shoes are required to climb the lighthouse, so no heels, flip-flops, or bare feet.

The nearby Lighthouse Keeper's Cottage serves as a visitors center, and it is also the trailhead for self-guided nature trails to Roanoke Sound. These trails wind through beautiful marsh on the sound side of Bodie Island.

The **Oregon Inlet Campground** (12001 N.C. 12, reservations 877/444-6777, campground information 252/441-6246, open late April through Columbus Day, www.recreation.gov, $28), operated by the National Park Service, offers tent and RV camping behind the sand dunes, with cold-water showers, potable water, and restrooms.

Historic Lighthouses

Centuries of mariners have plied the waters off North Carolina's coast, harvesting its aquatic beasts, protecting or prowling the shore, and skirting or foundering on its dangerous shoals. As beautiful as North Carolina's lighthouses are, they were built to perform a service of life-and-death importance. Today, the historic lights—some still in operation—are popular destinations for visitors. Most are open for climbing and offer fantastic views. The following are some of North Carolina's favorites.

Cape Hatteras Lighthouse

- Visitors willing to climb the 214 spiral steps to the top of **Currituck Beach Lighthouse** are treated to a dazzling view of Currituck Sound.

- Climb to the top of **Bodie Island Lighthouse,** which overlooks Lighthouse Bay and the Atlantic Ocean. This striking structure has been sending its signal out to sea since 1872 but was closed to the public until 2013.

- **Cape Hatteras Lighthouse,** the tallest brick lighthouse in the United States, has a black-and-white spiral exterior that makes it visible from miles away. Pay a small admission price to climb all the way to the top.

- Whale oil originally powered the beam of **Ocracoke Lighthouse,** the second-oldest working lighthouse in the United States. Because it's still on duty, visitors can't go inside, but there are lovely places to walk on the grounds.

- The black-and-white diamond-spangled **Cape Lookout Lighthouse,** one of the most iconic symbols of North Carolina, has stood watch since 1859. The nearby keeper's quarters give an intriguing glimpse into the isolated and meditative life of the light keeper. While you're there, explore Cape Lookout's 56 miles of unspoiled beach, where you may have a close encounter with one of the Outer Banks' famous wild horses.

- Commissioned by Thomas Jefferson and built in 1817, **Old Baldy Lighthouse** is North Carolina's oldest lighthouse. From its strategic point on the southern coast of Bald Head Island, Old Baldy has seen has seen nearly two centuries of commerce, war, and peace.

Getting There

To get to the Bodie Island Lighthouse from the northern Outer Banks towns of Corolla, Duck, Kitty Hawk, Kill Devil Hills, and Nags Head, go south along U.S. 158 or N.C. 12; it's a trip of 70 minutes from Corolla or 20 minutes from Nags Head without traffic, or considerably longer with traffic. From any of the Hatteras Island towns south of Bodie Island, head north along N.C. 12; it's a 25-minute drive from Rodanthe, the northernmost Hatteras Island town.

HATTERAS ISLAND

As Cape Hatteras arches dramatically along the North Carolina coast, it shelters Pamlico Sound from the ocean like a giant cradling arm. The cape itself is the point of the elbow, an exposed and vulnerable spit of land that's nearly irresistible to passing hurricanes. Most of the island is included in Cape Hatteras National Seashore, the first of its kind in the country, although a handful of small towns—Rodanthe, Waves, Salvo, Avon, Buxton, Frisco, and the village of Hatteras—dot the coastline. For the most part Hatteras Island isn't much wider than the dune line and Highway 12, which makes for a great deal of dramatic scenery on all sides.

One of the first things you'll notice about Hatteras Island is its wildness. Since most of the island is part of the Cape Hatteras National Seashore, there's little permanent human habitation here, save the seven communities of Rodanthe, Waves, Salvo, Avon, Buxton, Frisco, and Hatteras Village. This makes it a favorite spot for those seeking a little solitude, especially surfers and kiteboarders hoping to take advantage of wind and wave without worrying about knocking into beachgoers, beachcombers, nature lovers, and anglers.

Rodanthe, a town made notable by North Carolina author Nicholas Sparks' novel *Nights in Rodanthe* and the Richard Gere film of the same name (based on the book) is the first community on Hatteras Island as you travel south on N.C. 12 from Nags Head. It's a small, attractive beach town, home to the Chicamacomico Life-Saving Station (the first such established along the North Carolina coast) and a lovely stretch of beach where fans of the namesake novel and film still come to visit.

Waves and **Salvo** are similarly small, though Salvo has an interesting story behind its name. It's said that during the Civil War, a Union Ship spied the town (then known as Clarksville or Clarks, depending on the map), couldn't identify it on his map, ordered his gunners to "Give it a salvo anyway," then jotted "Salvo" on his map and the name just stuck. Life in Salvo is geared a little more toward crabbing and fishing, and this is the spot where many tourists will pull off the road to take a few pictures of colorful crab pots stacked and piled on docks just a few feet from the road.

Avon, about halfway down Hatteras Island, is known for being a surf fishing destination. The beaches are stunning here, and in the sound on the west side of town you'll see kiteboarders galore.

Buxton is home to the famous Cape Hatteras Lighthouse and an immensely popular surf fishing spot called Cape Point. Hatteras Island begins to make a turn to the west and south here, growing a little fatter and sporting a bit of maritime forest. Frisco, just south of Buxton on the edge of Buxton Woods, is a quiet little town with two identities: seaside retreat and maritime forest escape.

Hatteras Village, on the southernmost tip of the island, is a little bigger than the other towns, but not by much. Here you'll find the Ocracoke Ferry and a decent sized charter fishing fleet. There are a few showy rental homes in the Village, but more often than not, visitors stay in condos or motels when they come here.

Chicamacomico Life-Saving Station

Life-saving operations are an important part of North Carolina's maritime heritage. Corps of brave men occupied remote stations along the coast, ready at a moment's notice to risk their lives to save foundering sailors in the relentlessly dangerous waters off the Outer Banks. In Rodanthe, the **Chicamacomico Life-Saving Station** (Milepost 39.5, N.C. 12, Rodanthe, 252/987-1552, www.chicamacomico.org, 10am-5pm Mon.-Fri. and 11am-4pm Sat. Apr.-Nov., $8 adults, $7 ages 65 and up and students, $6 ages 4-17, free 3 and under) preserves the original station, a handsome gray-shingled 1874 building, the 1911 building that replaced it and now houses a museum of fascinating artifacts from maritime rescue operations, and a complex of other buildings and exhibits depicting the lives of lifesavers and their families. The antique lifesaving drill demonstrations (2pm Thurs., Memorial Day-Labor Day) are fascinating to see; try to stop by and check it out.

★ Cape Hatteras Lighthouse

At 208 feet tall, **Cape Hatteras Lighthouse** (near Buxton, 252/473-2111, www.nps.gov/caha, 9am-5pm daily, $8, $4 children and seniors, children under 42 inches tall not permitted) is the tallest brick lighthouse in the United States, and its distinctive black-and-white spiral paint job makes it easy to see from miles away on land or sea. Built in 1870, it is open for climbing today during the warm months. If you have a healthy heart, lungs, and knees and are not claustrophobic, get your ticket and start climbing. Tickets are sold on the premises beginning at 9am, and climbing tours run every 10 minutes starting at 9am. Winds at the top can be ferocious, at times strong enough to delay or cancel climbs, so hold onto your hats, cameras, phones, and anything else you don't want to fly away.

Sports and Recreation

Pea Island National Wildlife Refuge (N.C. 12, 10 miles south of Nags Head, 252/987-2394, www.fws.gov) occupies the northern reach of Hatteras Island. Much of the island is covered by ponds, making this an exceptional place for watching migratory waterfowl. Two nature trails link some of the best bird-watching spots, including the 0.5-mile, fully wheelchair-accessible North Pond Wildlife Trail. Viewing and photography blinds are scattered along the trails for extended observation. Throughout the year, guided bird walks, canoe trips, and walking lectures on the wildlife of Pea Island take place.

The Outer Banks owe their existence to the volatile action of the tides, and the same forces that created this habitable sandbar also make it an incredible place for water sports. **Canadian Hole,** a spot in the sound between Avon and Buxton, is one of the most famous windsurfing and kiteboarding places in the world (and, of course, it's perfect for flying kites). The island is extraordinarily narrow at Canadian Hole, so it's easy to tote your board from the sound side over to the ocean for a change of scene.

Hatteras Island is a major East Coast destination for kiteboarders and surfers, and at **REAL Watersports** (25706 N.C. 12, Waves, 866/732-5548, www.realwatersports.com), the largest kite-surfing school in the world, they offer lessons (from $350), camps (from $1,495); you can also rent kiteboarding gear (from $150/day for a full kit). If kiteboarding isn't your thing, the watermen (and waterwomen) at REAL also offer surfing lessons (from $350), and rentals (from $25/half day). They also offer stand-up paddleboarding camps, lessons, and rentals ($20/half day, $50/day, $125/week).

Among the ways to tour Hatteras, **Equine Adventures** (52173 Piney Ridge Rd., Frisco, 252/995-4897, www.equineadventures.com) leads two-hour horseback tours through the maritime forests and along the beaches of Cape Hatteras (rides $100 Sept. 10-May 21, $125 May 21-Sept. 19). With **Hatteras Parasail** (Oden's Dock, 57878 N.C. 12, Hatteras, 252/986-2627, www.hatterasparasail.com, $70 parasail ride, $90 WaveRunner rental, boat rental from $300/day) you can ride 400 feet in the air over the coast.

Hatteras Watersports (Milepost 42.5, 27130 N.C. 12, Salvo, 252/987-2306, www.hatteraswatersports.com, 10am-5pm Mon.-Fri., 10am-2pm Sat., closed Sun.) offers sailboat ($75/two hours), Jet Ski ($89), stand-up paddleboards (from $25/hour or $55/day), and kayak rentals (from $15/hour or $35/day) as well as guided and self-guided kayak tours (prices vary). Their location on shallow Pamlico Sound is a perfect spot to head out in any of their watercraft, even for novices.

Shopping

In a place this beautiful and inspiring, it's no surprise that you'll find a number of galleries and boutiques showcasing the works of local and regional artists. The **Pea Island Art Gallery** (27766 N.C. 12, Salvo, 252/987-2879, www.peaislandartgallery.com, 10am-5pm Mon.-Sat.) has works from more than 100 artists in a range of media in

a gallery that's a replica of a 19th-century Life-Saving Station. **SeaWorthy Gallery** (58401 N.C. 12, Hatteras, 252/986-6510, www.seaworthygallery.com, 10am-5pm Tues.-Sat.) carries pieces ranging from fun, cartoonish folk art representations of area wildlife to painstaking paintings of area landmarks, seascapes, and landscapes. **Blue Pelican Gallery** (57762 N.C. 12, Hatteras, 252/986-2244, www.bluepelicangallery.com, 10am-5pm Mon.-Sat.) carries jewelry from local glassblowers, lockets filled with objects found on and inspired by the shore, jewelry, and a beautiful selection of yarn and supplies for knitting and other needle arts. **Someday, by the sea** (24267 N.C. 12, Rodanthe, 252/305-2352, 10am-5pm Mon.-Fri., 9am-2pm Sun.) carries art and gifts from Outer Banks artists; plus plenty of jewelry, beach glass ornaments and home goods.

The indie **Buxton Village Books** (47918 N.C. 12, Buxton, 252/995-4240, www.buxtonvillagebooks.com, 10am-6pm daily) carries a large selection of books about the Outer Banks and by regional authors, along with the latest in contemporary and Southern fiction. The staff is knowledgeable and can point you to beach reads or something deeper.

Food

Dining options are limited on Hatteras Island, but there are plenty of places to eat. **Café Pamlico at the Inn on Pamlico Sound** (49684 N.C. 12, Buxton, 866/726-5426, www.innonpamlicosound.com, 5pm-9pm daily, $23-33) caters to guests of the inn, but if you call in advance, you may be able to get a reservation for dinner, even if you're staying elsewhere. The chef likes to use fresh-caught seafood, sometimes brought in by the guests themselves earlier in the day. Vegetarian fare and other special requests are available.

For breakfast, try the **Gingerbread House** (52715 N.C. 12, Frisco, 252/995-5204,

http://gbhbakery.com, breakfast 7am-11:30am, dinner 4:30pm-9pm Mon.-Sat. Mar.-late Nov., breakfast $1.50-9, dinner $13-24), which serves great baked goods made on the premises. In the evenings, try pan and hand-tossed pizza made using fresh dough; in addition to the usual toppings, they offer a whole-wheat crust and a number of specialty pies topped with local shrimp, clams, crab, or barbecued chicken. You should also try the apple uglies—monstrous apple fritters—from **Orange Blossom Bakery** (47206 N.C. 12, www.orangeblossombakery.com, 6:30am-11am daily), they'll set your day off to a great start.

Watermen's Bar & Grill (25706 N.C. 12, Waves, 252/987-2000, www.watermensbarandgrill.com, 9am-9pm daily, breakfast $7, lunch $9-21, dinner $15-26) offers smoothies in the morning, sandwiches and wraps for lunch (try the grilled mahi mahi wrap or the blackened tuna sandwich, both with fish caught locally), and a short list of tasty dinner entrées. They run specials every night of the week; BBQ Rib Thursday is especially popular.

If you're in the mood to cook your own dinner, try stopping by **Harbor House Seafood Market** (58129 N.C. 12, Hatteras, 252/986-2039, www.harborhouseseafoodmarket.com, 10am-7pm daily, $4-27) in Hatteras Village. This is a killer seafood market, and the owners and employees know their fish. They also know the fishing boats, some excellent fishing spots, and more ways than you or I will ever know for preparing what you catch or buy. Best of all, if you just don't have the energy to cook a full meal after a day in the sun, they have several oven-ready appetizers, salads, and entrées that you just buy, heat as instructed, and feast.

Accommodations

Among the lodging choices on Hatteras Island is the very fine ★ **Inn on Pamlico Sound** (49684 N.C 12, Buxton, 866/726-5426, www.innonpamlicosound.com, $85-350). The inn is right on the sound, with a private dock and

---

1: the Bodie Island Lighthouse; 2: Cape Hatteras Lighthouse stairs; 3: the entrance to Cape Hatteras Lighthouse; 4: great egret on a wetland beach in Pea Island National Wildlife Refuge

easy waterfront access. The dozen suites are sumptuous and relaxing, many with their own decks or private porches. Small gardens throughout the property provide ingredients to the Inn's kitchen, where you can—actually, should—dine as it's exceptional.

Another good choice is the **Cape Hatteras Bed and Breakfast** (49643 Old Lighthouse Rd., Buxton, 252/995-6004, www.capehatterasbandb.com, Apr.-late Nov., $189-210), which is only a few hundred feet from the ocean. Rooms are simple but lovely, and guests rave about the breakfast.

For a more luxurious stay, consider **Watermen's Retreat** (25682 N.C. 12, Waves, 252/987-6060, www.watermensretreat.com, $250-450, three-night minimum in season) is a 14-room condo and single cottage in Waves. Accommodations are quite nice, especially if you plan to partake in any lessons or excursions offered by REAL Watersports, right next door.

Breakwater Inn (57896 N.C. 12, Hatteras, 252/986-2565, www.unwind.breakwaterhatteras.com, $104-189) is in the heart of Hatteras, next to the marina. It's convenient, spacious and affordable, and anglers or surfers headed to the area should definitely take note: it's close to some great breaks and fishing holes. On site there's also **Breakwater Restaurant** (252/986-2733, www.breakwaterhatteras.com, 5pm-9pm daily, $18-30), where the seafood is outstanding and dishes like the potato-crusted crab cakes are a crowd pleaser.

Simpler motel accommodations include the clean, comfortable, and pet-friendly **Cape Pines Motel** (47497 N.C. 12, Buxton, 252/995-5666, www.capepinesmotel.com, $135-150).

Koru Village Resort and Spa (40920 N.C. 12, Avon, 252/995-3125, www.koruvillage.com, $175-240/night, three-night minimum in summer) is an oceanfront resort focused on health and wellness, and as such, they have a yoga studio, a killer fitness center, and a series of programs (think everything from beachfront yoga to fire dancing) to keep you fit and feeling fine. Their 15-acre campus includes the **Avon Fishing Pier** (252/995-5480, www.avonfishingpier.com, 6am-midnight Summer, 6am-10pm Spring and Fall, closed Winter), a 665-foot pier that's the only one remaining in operation along the Cape Hatteras National Seashore; a **Spa** (252/995-3125, treatments $55-155); and **Pangea Tavern** (252-995-3800, www.pangeatavern.com, 11:30am-9pm Tues.-Sat., $8-14 lunch, $17-24 dinner), where the menu is seafood-centric and dishes like the fish tacos, seafood and chips (a mix of fish and shrimp), and sesame-seared tuna stand out as favorites.

CAMPING

Rodanthe Watersports and Campground (24170 N.C. 12, 252/987-1431, www.rodanthewatersports.com, $26 for 2 people, $7/additional adult or dog, $5 for children, add $5-7 for electrical hookup) has a campground on the sound for tents and RVs under 25 feet, with water and electrical hookups and hot showers.

The National Park Service operates two campgrounds in this stretch of the National Seashore: **Frisco Campground** (53415 Billy Mitchell Rd., Frisco, reservations 877/444-6777, campground information 252/995-5101, late Apr.-mid-Oct., $28), where you actually camp in the dunes, and **Cape Point Campground** (46700 Lighthouse Rd., Buxton, reservations 877/444-6777, campground information 252/465-9602, late-May-Aug., $20), with level campsites located behind the dunes. Both have cold showers, restrooms, and potable water. **Frisco Woods Campground** (53124 N.C. 12, Frisco, 252/995-5208, www.thefriscowoodscampground.com, $32-71) has a full spectrum of camping options, including no-utilities tent sites, RV sites with partial or full hookups, and one- and two-bedroom cabins ($55-95). The campground has wireless internet access, hot showers, and a coin laundry.

Cape Hatteras KOA (2509 N.C. 12, Rodanthe, 252/987-2307 or 800/562-5268, www.koa.com, from $85) offers campsites,

RV sites, and small cabins along with a pool, a play area for kids, a small commissary, and direct beach access.

VACATION RENTAL HOMES

Surf or Sound Realty (40974 N.C. 12, Avon, 252/995-5801 or 800/237-1138, www. surforsound.com) has been renting homes to families, anglers, surfers, weddings, and groups of all sorts since 1978, and their portfolio of homes ranges from the simple to the elegant. Looking for pet friendly? Pool? Hot tub? Elevator? Check, check, check, and check. And if you're looking to have your wedding on Hatteras Island, they have an event coordinator who can help direct you to the perfect home (or homes) for a beach wedding.

Getting There

Hatteras Island can be reached by car, following N.C. 12 17 miles south from Nags Head, but it's another 50 miles to get to Hatteras Village at the south end of the island. Along Highway 12 you'll go through the towns of Rodanthe, Waves, Salvo, and Avon and then around the tip of the cape to Buxton, Frisco, and Hatteras, where the highway ends. From here, you have two choices: backtrack or take a ferry to Ocracoke (free, 60 minutes), which runs hourly from 5am-midnight in the off season and three times hourly during peak season.

★ OCRACOKE ISLAND

Ocracoke Island, one of the most geographically isolated places in the state, is the southernmost part of the Cape Hatteras National Seashore. Accessible only by water and air, this 16-mile-long island seems charmingly anchored in the past. Regular ferry service didn't start until 1960, as most residents were content to stay on their island, separate from the rest of the state, and they didn't have a paved highway until 1963. The natural beauty of the island is mostly intact, and some areas look much like they did in 1585 when the first English colonists ran

aground. It may have been during their time on Ocracoke (called Wococon at the time) that the ancestors of today's wild ponies first set hoof on the Outer Banks. Theirs was not the last shipwreck at Ocracoke, nor was it the first; Spanish explorers reportedly ran aground here, too, and it's possible the now-feral Banker ponies came from their ships. As on the northern stretches of the Outer Banks, Ocracokers subsisted partially on the flotsam and goods that would wash up after shipwrecks, so wherever the wild horses came from, like other gifts from the sea, they have become part of the island's history and lifestyle.

In some ways, Ocracoke is a little creepy. Its isolation has something to do with that, but so do its legends and ghosts. During the early 18th century, Ocracoke was a favorite haunt of the pirate Edward Teach, better known as Blackbeard. He lived here from time to time, married his 14th wife here, and died here. He met his fate in Teach's Hole, a spot just off the island, when a band of privateers (pirate hunters) hired by Virginia's Governor Spottsswood finally cornered and killed him. According to legend, he didn't go down without a fight; it took five musket shots, more than 20 stab wounds, and a near beheading before his fight was over. Afterward, Spottswood's privateers took Blackbeard's head as a trophy and dumped his body overboard where, legend says, it swam around the ship seven times before going under.

All of **Ocracoke Village** (www. visitocracoke.com), near the southern end of the island, is on the National Register of Historic Places. While the historical sites of the island are highly distinctive, the most unique thing about the island and its people is the culture that has developed over the centuries. Ocracokers have a "brogue" or dialect of their own, similar to those of other Outer Banks communities but distinctive and unique to the island.

Ocracoke Lighthouse

A lighthouse has stood on Ocracoke since at

Ocracoke Island

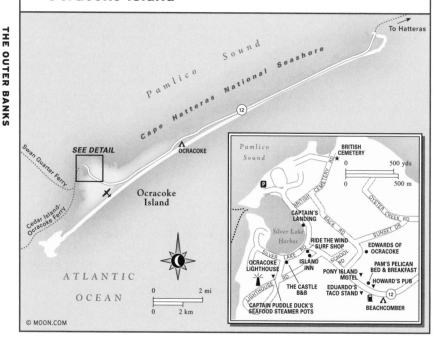

least 1798, but due to the constantly shifting sands, the inlet that it protected kept sneaking away. Barely 20 years after that first tower was built, it was almost a mile from the water. The current **Ocracoke Lighthouse** (Lighthouse Road, Ocracoke) was built in 1823 and originally burned whale oil to power the beam. It is still in operation, the oldest continuously operating light in North Carolina and the second-oldest in the nation. Because it's on active duty, it is not publicly accessible, but a boardwalk nearby gives nice views.

British Cemetery

The **British Cemetery** (243 British Cemetery Rd.) is not a colonial graveyard but rather a vestige of World War II, when the Carolina coast was lousy with German U-boats. Defending the Outer Banks became a pressing concern, and on May 11, 1942, the HMS *Bedfordshire,* a British trawler sent to aid the U.S. Navy, was torpedoed by the German

U-558. The *Bedfordshire* sank, killing all 37 men on board. Over the course of the next week, four bodies washed up on Ocracoke. An island family donated a burial plot, where the four men lie today.

Sports and Recreation

Ride the Wind Surf Shop (486 Irvin Garrish Hwy., 252/928-6311, www.surfocracoke.com, 10am-7pm Mon.-Sat., 10am-6pm Sun.) gives individual and group surfing lessons for adults and children ($95/hour one person, $165/hour two people), covering ocean safety and surfing etiquette in addition to board handling. Ride the Wind also leads sunrise, sunset, and full-moon kayak tours ($39-45, $18 kids age 12 and under) around the marshes of Ocracoke. Kayak, stand-up paddleboard, surfboard, and boogie-board rentals ($12-59/day, $28-150/week) are available.

The *Windfall II* (departs from Community Store Dock, Ocracoke, 252/928-7245, www.

schoonerwindfall.com, from $40/person), a beautiful 32-foot lazy jack schooner, sails out into the Pamlico Sound to visit Teach's Hole, where Blackbeard was brought to justice, and conducts daily sunset cruises.

Tradewinds Tackle Shop (1094 Irvin Garrish Hwy., 252/928-5491, www. fishtradewinds.com, 7am-7pm daily) offers fishing tips and sells all the gear you'll need, including licenses, to land a big one. The Ocracoke Island fishing experts at Tradewinds can tell you where to catch what and how, or they can simply send you to a good fishing guide.

Food

Ocracoke's isolation and size have kept it a small, close-knit community; its dining scene is likewise small. Restaurants tend to be old-guard seafood but new places break through and become island go-tos. One is ★ **Eduardo's Taco Stand** (252/588-0202, 8am-3pm daily, open for dinner 5pm-9pm Mon.-Sat., breakfast $3-10, lunch and dinner $7-12), a place that's not much to look at due to the fact that it's somewhere between a food truck and a semi-permanent trailer restaurant. Order up a crab taco—or stick with some asada or pollo, up to you—and when your name's called, dine at the picnic tables or just a few blocks away at the water's edge. Either way, you'll come back every day you're here.

Howard's Pub & Raw Bar Restaurant (1175 Irvin Garrish Hwy., 252/928-4441, www.howardspub.com, 11am-10pm daily, entrées $15-26) is a cross between a divey beach bar/restaurant and a sports bar; it's fun-loving and relaxing, but not fine dining. They serve steaks, burgers, salads, sandwiches, and a wide assortment of tasty seaside bites, of which you should try the hush puppies and the conch fritters.

There's plenty of excellent seafood as well as pizzas and steak at **Dajio** (305 Irvin Garrish Hwy., 252/928-7119, www.dajiorestaurant. com, 4pm-9pm daily for dinner, 10am-3pm daily for lunch and brunch, lunch $8-25, dinner $16-35). They're all about local seafood (in

a fishing village you kind of have to be) and they treat it right. Their "seachuterie" boards (think charcuterie but with seafood); pizzas topped with clams or shrimp or mussels; and all the fried, broiled, grilled, blackened and otherwise prepared fish prove that they really know how to cook.

Accommodations

The **Captain's Landing** (324 N.C. 12, 252/928-1999, www.thecaptainslanding.com, from $220 summer, from $110 off-season), with a perch right on the harbor (called Silver Lake) looking toward the lighthouse, is a modern hotel owned by a descendant of Ocracoke's oldest families. Suites have 1.5 baths, full kitchens, comfortable sleeper sofas for extra guests, and decks with beautiful views. Also available is a bright, airy penthouse ($2,300/week) with two bedrooms, an office, a gourmet kitchen, and even a laundry room. The Captain's Cottage ($2,200/week) is a private two-bedroom house, also right on the water, with great decks and its own courtyard.

Edwards of Ocracoke (216 Old Beach Rd., 252/928-4801 or 800/254-1359, www. edwardsofocracoke.com, from $70 spring and fall, from $115 summer, weekly rentals $460-875) has several cozy bungalows typical of coastal Carolina, referred to here as "vintage accommodations." The mid-20th-century vacation ambiance is pleasant, the cabins are clean and well-kept, and the rates are great. Private cottages are available, as are two homes perfect for larger groups traveling together.

Pam's Pelican Bed & Breakfast (1021 Irvin Garrish Hwy., 252/928-1661, www. pamspelican.com, $159-199) is a dog-friendly spot not far from the marina. They offer free pick-up service from both the marina and airport, so getting here is easy if you've come over car-free. Pam's Pelican is laid back, and they have bikes, coolers, and grills for guests to use, making for some communal evenings.

The Castle B&B (155 Silver Lake Rd., 252/928-3505, www.thecastlebb.com, $160-260) is a beautiful home with well-appointed guest rooms, spectacular views, a pool, and, of course, breakfast. Get to breakfast early, when the biscuits are hot; they're legendary around these parts.

CAMPING

At **Ocracoke Campground** (4352 Irvin Garrish Hwy., Ocracoke, 252/928-6671, www. recreation.gov, $28), campsites are right by the beach and behind the dunes. Remember to bring extra-long stakes or sand anchors for your tent.

Beachcomber Campground (990 Irvin Garrish Hwy., www.ocracokecamping.com, tents from $41, RVs from $51) is open year-round and is conveniently located near both the Cape Hatteras National Seashore and Ocracoke Island's only gas station, perfect for those late-night munchies. Throughout the season they feature live music. There isn't

a lot of shade, so it is more pleasant during the shoulder seasons, when the weather is milder.

Getting There

Ocracoke can only be reached by ferry. The **Hatteras-Ocracoke Ferry** (800/368-8949, www.ncdot.gov/ferry, 1 hour, free) is the shortest route to Ocracoke. On some maps, Highway 12 is shown crossing from Ocracoke to Cedar Island, as if there were an impossibly long bridge over Pamlico Sound. In fact, that stretch is a ferry route, too. The **Cedar Island-Ocracoke Ferry** (800/293-3779, www.ncdot.gov/ferry), a 2.25-hour ride, costs $15 one-way for a regular-size vehicle. There's also an **Ocracoke-Swan Quarter Ferry** (800/293-3779, 2.5 hours, $15 regular-size vehicle one-way).

Across the Sounds

Traditionally called the Albemarle, although today sometimes called the Inner Banks, the mainland portion of northeastern North Carolina is the heart and hearth of the state's colonial history, the site of its first colonial towns and earliest plantations, and the seat of power for the largely maritime economy.

Inland, early European Carolinians and Virginians named a region they thought of as a diseased and haunted wasteland "the Great Dismal Swamp." They planned to drain it and create more hospitable places to settle, and to a point they succeeded in doing so. But enough of the swamp remains today that it is recognized it as one of the state's prettiest places, valued by human visitors almost as much as by the bears and wolves that live there.

Early cities like Edenton and Bath were influential centers of commerce and government, and today they preserve some of the finest examples of colonial and early Federal architecture in the Southeast. Inland, along the Roanoke River, the small town of

Halifax played a key role in American history; in a tavern in Halifax, representatives from North Carolina wrote and ratified the Halifax Accords, the first documents to denounce British rule over the colonies and to declare American independence. The Halifax Accords were read at the Continental Congress in Philadelphia, which led to the Declaration of Independence and the Revolutionary War.

The vast networks of rivers and creeks feeding the Roanoke River and other major waterways include some of the state's best places for inland canoeing and kayaking. Along the Albemarle Regional Canoe-Kayak Trail, a number of camping platforms allow paddlers to spend an unforgettable night listening to owls hoot and otters splash. The abundant water also irrigates the vast farms in this corner of the state, and if a small town has a restaurant, it'll be either a country kitchen or a fish shack. Either way, you'll get to sample the region's inland seafood traditions.

THE GREAT DISMAL SWAMP

Thought of for centuries as an impediment to progress, the Great Dismal Swamp is now recognized for the national treasure that it is, and tens of thousands of its acres are protected. There are several points to access the interior of the Dismal Swamp. On U.S. 17, a few miles south of the Virginia-North Carolina border, is the **Dismal Swamp Welcome Center** at **Dismal Swamp State Park** (2294 U.S. 17 N., South Mills, 252/771-6593, www.ncparks.gov, 8am-6pm daily Mar.-Oct., 8am-5pm daily Nov.-Feb., closed Dec. 25, visitors center 9am-4:30pm Mon.-Fri., 9:30am-4:30pm Sat.-Sun., bike, canoe, and kayak rentals $5/hour) as well as the **Dismal Swamp Visitors Center** (2356 U.S. 17 N., South Mills, 877/771-8333, www.dismalswampwelcomecenter.com, 9am-5pm daily). Arriving by water, you'll find the Welcome Center at mile 28 on the Intracoastal Waterway. You can tie up to the dock and spend the night, or wait for one of the four daily lock openings (8:30am, 11am, 1:30pm, and 3:30pm) to proceed. There are also picnic tables, grills, and restrooms open 24 hours.

Another area of the swamp to explore is the **Great Dismal Swamp National Wildlife Refuge** (3100 Desert Rd., Suffolk, VA, 757/986-3705, www.fws.gov, trails dawn-dusk daily, auto tour 7:30am-3pm Mon.-Sat.), which straddles the state line. Two main entrances are outside of Suffolk, Virginia, off White Marsh Road (Hwy. 642). These entrances, Washington Ditch and Jericho Lane, are open 6:30am-8pm daily April 1-September 30 and 6:30am-5pm daily October 1-March 31. In the middle of the refuge is Lake Drummond, an eerie 3,100-acre natural lake that's a wonderful place for canoeing. Contact refuge headquarters for directions on navigating the feeder ditch into Lake Drummond. You may see all sorts of wildlife in the swamp, including poisonous snakes like cottonmouths, canebrake rattlers, and copperheads; and possibly even black bears. Controlled hunting is permitted on certain days in October-December, so if you visit in the fall, wear bright-colored clothing and contact refuge staff before your visit to find out about closures.

GATESVILLE

Near the town of Gatesville, west of South Mills on U.S. 158, is another gorgeous natural swamp area, **Merchant's Millpond State Park** (176 Millpond Rd., Gatesville, 252/357-1191, http://ncparks.gov, visitors center 8am-6pm Mon.-Fri. Mar.-Oct. and 8am-5pm Nov.-Feb., park 8am-6pm daily Nov.-Feb., 8am-8pm daily Mar.-May and Sept.-Oct., 8am-9pm daily June-Aug.). There is an amazing variety of wildlife, particularly reptiles, with many species of snakes (most are harmless), turtles (harmless, except for the snappers), and, despite the relatively northerly clime, alligators (most emphatically not harmless). Other denizens include salamanders, mink, and nutrias.

This is a great spot for canoeing or kayaking, with miles of beautiful blackwater backwaters. For those unfamiliar with blackwater, it looks like it sounds: black water. Tannins from decaying vegetation leech into the water, turning it a dark tea or coffee color and creating a beautiful, but eerie, effect. The park has canoe rentals ($5). There are nine miles of hiking trails, all classified as easy, but rangers strongly caution hikers to avoid ticks. Wear bug spray, tuck your pant legs into your socks, wear light-colored clothing to see the ticks better, and when you return, do a tick check by running your fingers over every inch of your body.

Merchant's Millpond has several campsites ($10-23). The family campground, near the park office, is easily accessible, accommodates tents and RVs, and has a washhouse with restrooms, showers, and drinking water. Off the park's Lassiter trail are five backpack campsites, where all supplies, including water, must be packed in; there is a pit toilet nearby. There are also two canoe camping areas accessed by canoe trails, with pit toilets; campers must bring water and other supplies.

ELIZABETH CITY

The free **Museum of the Albemarle** (501 S. Water St., 252/335-1453, www.museumofthealbemarle.com, 9am-5pm Mon.-Sat.) covers the four centuries since the first English settlers arrived at Roanoke. Come to learn about the Lost Colonists, the pirates who swarmed the region, and the folkways of the sound country.

To stay in Elizabeth City and get a feel for the charm here, opt for a bed-and-breakfast. **Foreman House Bed & Breakfast** (311 W. Church St., 252/562-6539, www.foremanhousebb.com, $115-135) was built in 1899. Each of its four rooms is perfectly lovely, but what makes this place is the openness of the innkeepers; their friendly nature, ease around guests, and devotion to ensuring an exceptional stay make this B&B quite the experience. **Grice-Fearing House Bed and Breakfast** (200 S. Road St., 252/333-1792, www.gricefearinghouse.com, $100-135) is the oldest home in the city, dating back to around 1798; the house was expanded in 1840 and again in 1885, then updated in 2004 when the current owners turned it into a bed-and-breakfast. There are only two suites at Grice-Fearing, but that only adds to the homey feel. Weather permitting, breakfast is served on the brick patio, a lovely place to start the day.

Two newer homes are also B&Bs of note in Elizabeth City. The **Pond House Inn** (915 Rivershore Rd., 252/335-9834, www.thepondhouseinn.com, $130-180) is on the banks of the Pasquotank River and has boat access, an unusual amenity for a B&B. Each of the large guest rooms in this 1941 home has its own fireplace, but as charming as that is, sharing a bottle of wine by the river is the real treat. Built in the 1930s, the **Culpepper Inn** (609 W. Main St., 252/335-9235, www.culpepperinn.com, $115-160), just a few blocks from Albemarle Sound, has several comfortable guest rooms in the main house as well as cozy accommodations in a carriage house and a cottage.

You'll find vintage and antique items, fine art and crafts, and plenty of decorative items at **Tina Clancy's Art and Antique Collection** (116 N. Poindexter St., 252/339-3868, 10am-7pm Tues.-Sat.). With plenty of beautiful untouched antiques and upcycled pieces, the selection is always fun to explore.

Cypress Creek Grill (113 Water St., 252/334-9915, www.cypresscreekgrill.com, 11am-9pm Mon.-Thurs., 11am-10pm Fri., 5pm-10pm Sat., entrées $11-27) is close to downtown and serves gulf-style seafood, Tex-Mex cuisine, and a few creole dishes. The owners are from Texas, and they've blended their native flavors with the local ingredients of eastern North Carolina to make for some tasty dining.

At **Montero's Restaurant & Bar** (414 N. McArthur St., 252/331-1067, www.monterosrestaurant.com, 4:30pm-9pm Tues.-Thurs., 4:30pm-10pm Fri.-Sat., 10:30am-8pm Sun., brunch $6-20, dinner $10-27) they dish up pasta, ribs, steak, and a selection of seafood dishes. The food's quite good, which is one reason every hotel staffer and B&B host will recommend this spot. Most entrées have two size options available, so you can have a tasty meal without busting your dietary budget.

EDENTON

Incorporated in 1722, Edenton is North Carolina's second-oldest town even though it was the state's first permanent settlement. For 50 years prior to incorporation, colonists called the lovely waterside town home. Edenton, as one of the largest ports in the colony, served as the first colonial capital until 1743. It's home to a beautiful collection of historic homes and sites along the Maritime Underground Railroad; in the historic district, more than 250 years of architectural styles are on display, including the state's oldest courthouse. The Chowan County Courthouse, built in 1767, is still in use today.

The folks around here are proud of their town and are ready to give you a recommendation on what to see and where to eat. While you could ask just about anyone on the street, the best place for questions is the **Penelope Barker House** (505 S. Broad St.,

252/482-7800, http://ehcnc.org, 10am-5pm daily), part of the town's Historic Site and the home of the Edenton Welcome Center. You can also contact the **Chowan County Tourism Development Authority** (800/775-0111, www.visitedenton.com, 9am-5pm Mon.-Fri.) with travel inquiries.

Historic District

All of Edenton is lined with historic buildings, and several especially important sites are clustered within a few blocks of the waterfront. The easiest starting point for a walking tour is the headquarters of the **Edenton State Historic Site** (108 N. Broad St., 252/482-2637, www.nchistoricsites.org, 9am-5pm Tues.-Sat., guided tours $2.50-5). From here, it's a short walk to any of a number of historic sites, including the **1886 Roanoke River Lighthouse** (open daily 10am-4pm, $2.50 ages 13 and up, $1.50 ages 3-12, free 2 and under), an exquisitely restored original river lighthouse. The 1758 **Cupola House** (408 S. Broad St., tickets and information at Edenton Visitors Center, 108 N. Broad St., 252/482-2637, www.cupolahouse.org, 9am-4:30pm daily) is a home of great architectural significance and a National Historic Landmark. Although much of the original interior woodwork was removed in 1918 and sold to the Brooklyn Museum in New York, where it remains, Cupola House has been meticulously restored inside and out and its colonial gardens recreated. Also a designated National Historic Landmark is the **Chowan County Courthouse** (117 E. King St., 252/482-2637, www.nchistoricsites.org, hours vary, $2.50), a superb 1767 brick building in the Georgian style. It's the best-preserved colonial courthouse in the United States and the oldest in-use courthouse in the nation.

Downtown you'll find yourself surrounded by beautiful examples of Jacobean, Georgian, Federal, and Victorian homes as well as a number of other important historical sites, including **St. Paul's Episcopal Church** (W. Church St. and N. Broad St., 252/482-3522, http://stpauls-edenton.org), the second-oldest church structure in the state, and **Colonial Waterfront Park** (Edenton waterfront, parking on W. Water St. and S. Broad St.), a stop on the **Maritime Underground Railroad** (www.harrietjacobs.org). African American workers would find sailors sympathetic to the cause of freeing slaves and arrange their passage on ships to a free state. Harriet Jacobs' description of her 1842 escape by sea from Edenton is one of the few existing written accounts. Learn more about her story at http://harrietjacobs.org or on a guided or self-guided walking tour that highlights her years in Edenton.

Leisurely guided **trolley tours** depart from the Penelope Barker House Welcome Center at 10:30am, 11:30am, 1:30pm, and 2:30pm Mon. and Wed.-Sat., and at 10:30am, 11:30am, and 12:30pm on Sundays. Tickets are $12.50 for adults and $2.25 for children ages 6-12; kids 5 and under ride free.

Sports and Recreation

Right on the water, Edenton is surrounded by miles of paddling trails (www.visitedenton.com), but there is only one kayak and canoe rental outfit, the **Edenton Town Harbor Dock Master** (Edenton Harbor, 252/482-2832, www.visitedenton.com, kayaks from $5/hour, canoes $10/hour, $20/overnight). You can take a cruise around Edenton Bay in an all-electric boat, the *Liber-Tea* (800/367-5786, www.edontonbaycruises.com, $18 adults, $12 age 13 and under, discount with trolley receipt). The *Liber-Tea* departs from Edenton Harbor at the end of S. Broad Street, and cruises, which are seasonal, depart at 10:30am, 11:30am, 12:30pm, 1:30pm, and 2:30pm Thursday-Monday, weather permitting. The views from the water are incredible, and the stories you'll hear from Captain Thesier are enlightening to say the least.

Food and Accommodations

★ **The Inner Banks Inn & Restaurant** (103 E. Albemarle St., 252/482-3641, www.innerbanksinn.com, $139-349), formerly known as The Pack House Inn, occupies

1

2

3

4

three exceptional historic buildings: the 1900 grand Victorian mansion known as The Lords Proprietor's; the 1915 Pack House, which started its life as a tobacco packing house on a nearby plantation; and the 1879 Tillie Bond House cottage. Each is artfully restored with soft and restful furnishings. A three-course breakfast, which features gluten-free and vegetarian selections if arranged in advance, is served every morning in the Tillie Bond Dining Rooms. Lunch and dinner are also available at **The Table Restaurant** (www.thetablenc.com, 4:30pm-9pm Sun.-Thurs. and 4:30pm-10pm Fri.-Sat for dinner, 11am-3pm Sun. for brunch, brunch $9-16, dinner $22-32), where the chef serves a farm-to-table menu that's among the best in town.

WINDSOR

A small historic town on the Cashie (cuh-SHY) River, Windsor is the seat of Bertie (ber-TEE) County. Historic architecture, good food, and wetlands exploration are equally compelling reasons to visit this lesser-known treasure of the Albemarle region.

Sights

Hope Plantation (132 Hope House Rd., 252/794-3140, www.hopeplantation.org, visitors center 9am-4pm Mon.-Fri., museum and tours 10am-5pm daily, last tour out at 3:15pm, $12 adults, $11 seniors, $8 students and children) was built in 1803 for David Stone. Stone did not live to see his 50th birthday, but by the time of his death he had been governor of North Carolina, a U.S. senator and representative, a state senator, and a Superior Court judge and had been elected seven times to the State House. He graduated from Princeton and passed the bar when he was 20, fathered 11 children, and was one of the founders of the University of North Carolina. As busy as he was, he also managed to oversee the construction of this impressive house. Characterized by a mixture of Georgian and Federal styles

with significant twists of regional and individual aesthetics, Hope House is on the National Register of Historic Places. Also on the register, and now on the grounds of the plantation, is the brick-end, gambrel roof **King-Bazemore House**, built in 1763 and also a significant example of its type.

The **Roanoke-Cashie River Center** (112 W. Water St., Windsor, 252/794-2001, 10am-4pm Mon.-Sat., $2, $1 children) has interpretive exhibits about this region's history and ecology. There is a canoe ramp outside where you can access the Cashie River, and canoe rentals ($10/hour, $25/half-day, $35/full day) are available.

Southeast of Windsor on the Cashie River, the **Sans Souci Ferry** (Woodard Rd. and Sans Souci Rd., 252/794-4277, 6:30am-6pm Mar. 16-Sept. 16, 6:45am-5pm Sept. 17-Mar. 15) operates, as it has for generations, by a cable and a honk of the horn. To cross the river, pull up to the bank and look for the ferry. If it's across the river, honk your horn and wait. The ferry operator will cross to you and pull you to the opposite bank. There's only room for two cars at a time, but it's a charming way to cut 20 miles off your journey.

Recreation

The headquarters of the **Roanoke River National Wildlife Refuge** (114 W. Water St., 252/794-3808, www.fws.gov) is located in Windsor. The refuge stretches over nearly 21,000 acres in Bertie County, through the hardwood bottomlands and cypress-tupelo wetlands of the Roanoke River Valley, an environment that the Nature Conservancy calls "one of the last great places." The refuge is an exceptional place for bird-watching, with the largest inland heron rookery in North Carolina, a large population of bald eagles, and many wintering waterfowl and neotropical migratory species.

Food

Bunn's Bar-B-Q (127 N. King St., 252/794-2274, 9am-5pm Mon.-Tues. and Thurs.-Fri., 9am-2pm Wed. and Sat., from $5) is a

1: the 1886 Roanoke River Lighthouse; 2: the Great Dismal Swamp; 3: the 1758 Cupola House; 4: cannons outside of the Penelope Barker House

barbecue joint of renown, an early gas station converted in 1938 to its present use. Service here is blazing fast, primarily because there are just a few choices on the menu. Super-finely chopped barbecue is the specialty, and you get it on a plate or a sandwich, with tart or creamy coleslaw and cornbread. It comes lightly sauced, the way the locals like it, but if you want more, or hotter, sauce, you'll find a bottle close at hand.

SCOTLAND NECK

In the little Halifax County community of Scotland Neck, west of Windsor, is the **Sylvan Heights Bird Park** (500 Sylvan Heights Park Way, off Lees Meadow Rd., 252/826-3186, www.shwpark.com, 9am-5pm Tues.-Sun., $11 adults, $10 over age 62, $8 ages 2-12, free under age 2), a center for the conservation of rare species of birds and home to the world's largest collection of waterfowl, comprising more than 1,000 birds of 170 different species. You'll see birds native to every continent except Antarctica; it gets a little hot here for penguins. A visit to Sylvan Heights is an unbeatable opportunity to get up close to birds you won't encounter elsewhere and a great spot for wildlife photography—you won't even need your zoom lens.

HISTORIC HALIFAX AND ROANOKE RAPIDS

Sometimes the biggest things come from the smallest places. Fewer than 300 people call the tiny hamlet of Halifax home, but it is the birthplace of a nation, where the first official documents calling for independence from British rule were written. Once an important town due to its proximity to the river and trade routes, Halifax dwindled as nearby Roanoke Rapids rose in significance. Today, Halifax is not much more than a state historic site, with the vast majority of local shopping, dining, and infrastructure located in Roanoke Rapids.

In its heyday Roanoke Rapids was home to several textile mills. But, as in so many other Southern towns, the mill jobs left, and the town suffered. Once part of a complex series of locks allowing river traffic to bypass the falls on the Roanoke River, the Roanoke Canal Museum and Trail has become a historical sight and a well-used walking and cycling path.

Sights

The main attraction is **Historic Halifax** (25 St. David St., Halifax, 252/583-7191, www.nchistoricsites.org, 9am-5pm Tues.-Sat., free). Several colonial-era buildings still stand, including a prominent merchant's home and the Tap Room tavern, both from 1760, and the 1790 Eagle Tavern; there are also several early-19th-century buildings, including a home, an attorney's office, the clerk's office, and the jail. Five tours run throughout the day and take anywhere from 30 minutes to 1 hour. On April 12, the Halifax Day celebration commemorates the date of the 1776 Halifax Resolves, which are believed to have been signed in the Eagle Tavern. Events, speakers, tours, and usually costumed Colonial-era reenactors fill the day with the sights, sounds, smells, and activities that would have given the community so much energy so long ago.

In Roanoke Rapids, the **Roanoke Canal Museum and Trail** (15 Jackson St. Ext., 252/537-2769, www.roanokecanal.com, museum 10am-4pm Tues.-Sat., trail dawn-dusk daily, museum $4, trail free) is more than a museum, it includes a 7.5-mile nature trail. At the trailhead, a museum tells the story of this 200-year-old canal, originally opened to allow river traffic to bypass the falls, and all its subsequent incarnations. In 1882 investors developed it into an early hydroelectric power source, and by 1900, two powerhouses were in full operation. The investors couldn't maintain it, and it was sold to a power company that operated it for several decades; in 1976 what remained of the canal was placed on the National Register of Historic Places. Learn about this in greater detail in the museum, which also provides an overall feel for the history of the Roanoke River Valley.

Sports and Recreation

The **Roanoke Canal Trail** (15 Jackson St. Ext, trailheads at Roanoke Rapids Lake, near Oakwood Ave., Roanoke Rapids; and Rockfish Dr., near U.S. 158/301, Weldon, dawn-dusk daily) runs for 7.5 miles along the tow path beside the 19th-century canal. Expect river views and secluded woodsy sections along the path; bring water and bug spray.

Every spring, anglers from around the country come to nearby Weldon to catch striped bass, known here as rockfish; as they travel up the river to spawn, the fishing is excellent. The Roanoke River's other fish species include shad, largemouth bass, and catfish. Outfitters can provide gear as well as the requisite fishing license. A comprehensive list of outfitters and guides is maintained by the **Halifax County Convention and Visitors Bureau** (www.visithalifax.com).

If kayaking is more your speed, **Roanoke River Partners** (www.roanokeriverpartners. org) maintains an index of outfitters and guides happy to help you with a solo or guided exploration of the river.

Shopping

At the western end of the Roanoke Canal Trail is **Riverside Mill** (200 Mill St., Weldon, 252/536-3100, www.riversidemill. net, 10am-6pm daily), an antiques mall and artisans gallery in a historic cotton mill. It's a fun place to explore because of the eclectic mix of local pottery, paintings, crafts, and antiques.

An odd and strangely fun thing to do is hook up with the **U.S. 301 Endless Yard Sale** (www.301endlessyardsale.com), a 100-mile yard sale stretching across five counties and lining the roads, parks, parking lots, fields, and any available space along U.S. 301 from Halifax to Johnston County with stuff. It's a two-day affair occurring in June, and it's your chance to find some unusual—read: treasure, trash, junk, oddities, and everything in between—items to take home. At the very least, it's quality people-watching.

Food and Accommodations

David's Restaurant (1011 Roanoke Ave., Roanoke Rapids, 252/537-3262, 4:30pm-10pm Tues.-Sat., 11am-3pm Sun., $13-39) is one of a handful of non-chain dining options, but fortunately it's pretty good. The menu ranges from steaks to seafood to pasta, so most folks will be able to find something for dinner here. **The Hen & The Hog** (16 S. King St., Halifax, 252/583-1017, www.thehenthehog.com, 11am-3pm Tues.-Fri., 5pm-10pm Thurs.-Sat., lunch $6-12, dinner $16-36) uses local farms and ranches to supply the ingredients for tremendous Southern dishes that stay focused on regional cuisine, but strays to include other southern specialties. The pork chop with seasonal veggies and the shrimp and grits are dinner favorites, and the shrimp po' boy is a lunchtime crowd pleaser.

Accommodations in the area consist mostly of chain hotels and a few mom and pop motels that open and close periodically. A reliable option is the **Hilton Garden Inn Roanoke Rapids** (111 Carolina Cross Road Pkwy., 252/519-2333, www.hiltongardeninn3. com, from $120).

Nearby Enfield, just a few miles south of Roanoke Rapids, is home to one B&B. **Bellamy Manor and Gardens Bed and Breakfast** (613 Glenview Rd., Enfield, 252/445-2234, www.manorbnb.com, $175) has four charming guest rooms in a beautiful home. Extensive gardens provide a place to walk and unwind, and if you're the sporting type, request a skeet-shooting outing when you make your reservation.

Getting There and Around

From the Outer Banks, Halifax is a 2.5-hour drive west. Follow U.S. 64 across Roanoke Island and onto the mainland, then continue along this route for approximately 53 miles. Turn right on N.C. 45 North, and follow this road for 13 miles until it meets U.S. 17. Turn left onto U.S. 17 and then take the U.S. 17 Bypass to N.C. 308, approximately 11 miles. Follow N.C. 308 for 28 miles until you reach U.S. 258/N.C. 561, where you'll turn left. After

7 miles, turn right onto N.C. 561 and take it the rest of the way into Halifax.

Weldon is approximately 10 minutes north along U.S. 301, and Roanoke Rapids is 10 minutes west of Weldon via U.S. 158.

WILLIAMSTON AND VICINITY

Williamston is at the junction of U.S. 17 and U.S. 64. If you're passing through town, Williamston is a great place to stop for barbecue or a fresh seafood meal at one of the few remaining traditional seafood houses.

Sights

One of the oddest sights in eastern North Carolina may be **Deadwood** (2302 Ed's Grocery Rd., 252/792-8938, www.deadwood. live, 5pm-9pm Thurs., 5pm-10pm Fri., noon-11pm Sat, noon-9pm Sun.), a tiny amusement park with an Old West flair. The owner calls this 10-acre park "a weird, out-of-hand backyard project" inspired by Dolly Parton's Dollywood in Tennessee. Amusements here include miniature golf, a miniature train ride, a kid-friendly roller coaster, and a murder-mystery dinner show (first Sat. of the month, $30, $15 kids 12 and under), complete with pratfalls, a gunfight, and a hearty dinner. It's well worth the stop, even if all you do is play a round of mini golf and eat ice cream.

Food

The ★ **Sunny Side Oyster Bar** (1102 Washington St., 252/792-3416, 5:30pm-8:30pm Mon.-Wed and Thurs., 5:30pm-10pm Fri.-Sat., 5:30pm-8pm Sun., $7-25), a seasonal oyster joint open during the months which have names that contain the letter *R*—that is, oyster season—draws diners from hundreds of miles away. It has been in business since 1935 and is a historic and gastronomic landmark. Oysters are steamed behind the restaurant and then hauled inside and shucked at the bar. Visit the restaurant's website to meet the shuckers. In eastern North Carolina, a good oyster shucker is as highly regarded as a good artist or athlete, and rightly so.

The Smokehouse Grill (252/792-8516, www.deadwoodnc.com, 5pm-9pm Thurs., 5pm-10pm Fri., noon-11pm Sat, noon-9pm Sun., $9-23), in the Deadwood amusement park, serves steaks, ribs, chicken, shrimp, and Tex-Mex specialties in a kitschy but charming Old West venue.

EAST ON U.S. 64

The eastern stretch of U.S. 64 runs along the Albemarle Sound between Williamston and the Outer Banks, passing through the towns of Plymouth, Creswell, and Columbia before it crosses to Roanoke Island. Here you'll encounter evidence of North Carolina's ancient past in old-growth forests, its recent past in the form of a plantation with a long and complex history of slavery, and its present in art galleries and abundant wildlife-watching and recreational opportunities.

Plymouth

Plymouth is an attractive little town on the Roanoke River with a rich maritime and military history. Most notably it was the site of the 1864 Battle of Plymouth, the second-largest Civil War battle in North Carolina, fought by more than 20,000 soldiers. At the **Roanoke River Lighthouse and Maritime Museum** (W. Water St., 252/217-2204, www. roanokeriverlighthouse.org, 11am-3pm Tues.-Sat. and by appointment, $3 adults, $2 students), visitors can explore a pretty replica of Plymouth's 1866 screw-pile lighthouse; across the street in an old car dealership, the maritime museum, featuring artifacts and photographs from the region's water-faring heritage. On East Water Street is the **Port O'Plymouth Museum** (302 E. Water St., 252/793-1377, www.portoplymouthmuseum.org, 9am-4pm Tues.-Sat., $3.50 adults, $2.50 ages 12-17, $1.50 ages 8-12, free under 8, guided tour $5 adults, $3 ages 12-17). This tiny museum is packed with Civil War artifacts, including a collection of beautiful pistols, telling the story of the Battle of Plymouth, the last major Confederate victory of the Civil War and the third largest battle in North Carolina. Surprisingly, some

5,000 North Carolinians from around here joined the Union navy. On site there's a fully-functioning, scale replica of the Ironclad *CSS Albemarle*; see it and more at a living history event held the last weekend in April.

★ Somerset Place Historic Site

Somerset Place Historic Site (2572 Lake Shore Rd., Creswell, 252/797-4560, www.nchistoricsites.org, 9am-5pm Tues.-Sat., free) was one of North Carolina's largest and most profitable plantations for the 80 years leading up to the Civil War. In the late 18th and early 19th centuries, 80 African-born men, women, and children were purchased as slaves and brought to Somerset to labor in the fields. The grief and disorientation they experienced and the subsequent trials of the slaves, whose numbers grew to include more than 300 people, are told by the historian Dorothy Spruill Redford in the book *Somerset Homecoming*. Somerset is a significant historical place for many reasons, but the story of its African Americans makes it one of this state's most important historic sites. Visitors can walk around the estate at their leisure. A small bookshop on the grounds is a good source for books about North Carolina history in general and African American history in particular.

★ Pettigrew State Park

Pettigrew State Park (2252 Lakeshore Rd., Creswell, 252/797-4475, http://ncparks.gov, 8am-6pm Nov.-Feb., 8am-8pm Mar.-May and Sept.-Oct., 8am-9pm June-Aug., closed Dec. 25, park office 8:30am-6pm Mon.-Fri.), on the banks of **Lake Phelps,** preserves an unusual ancient waterscape that's unlike anything else in the state. Archaeology reveals that there was a human presence here at least 10,000 years ago. The lake, which is five miles across and never more than nine feet deep, is only fed by rainfall and has yielded more than 30 ancient dugout canoes, some as old as 4,400 years and measuring more than 30 feet. The natural surroundings are ancient, too, encompassing some of eastern North Carolina's only remaining old-growth forests. **Pungo Lake,** a smaller body of water within the park, is visited by 50,000 migrating snow geese over the course of the year, an unforgettable sight for wildlife watchers. Visitors can camp at the family campground ($23), which has drive-in sites and access to restrooms and hot showers, or at primitive group campsites (from $15).

Sports and Recreation

Palmetto-Peartree Preserve (entrance on Pot Licker Rd./Loop Rd./State Rd. 1220, east of Columbia, 252/796-0723 or 919/967-2223, www.conservationfund.org) is a 10,000-acre natural area, wrapped in 14 miles of shoreline along Albemarle Sound and Little Alligator Creek. Originally established as a sanctuary for the red cockaded woodpecker, this is a great location for bird-watching and spotting other wildlife, including alligators, wolves, bears, and bobcats, as well as hiking, cycling, and horseback riding along the old logging trails through the forest or canoeing and kayaking. The preserve's excellent paddle trail passes by Hidden Lake, a secluded cypress-swamp blackwater lake. There is an overnight camping platform at the lake, which can be used in the daytime without a permit for bird-watching and picnicking. To stay overnight, arrange for a permit through **Roanoke River Partners** (252/792-3790, www.roanokeriverpartners.org, $25).

Once the southern edge of the Great Dismal Swamp, **Pocosin Lakes National Wildlife Refuge** (205 S. Ludington Dr., 6 miles south of Columbia, 252/796-3004, www.fws.gov) is an important haven for many species of animals, including migratory waterfowl and reintroduced red wolves. Five important bodies of water lie within the refuge: Pungo Lake, New Lake, the 16,600-acre Lake Phelps, and stretches of the Scuppernong and Alligator Rivers. All of these areas are good spots for observing migratory waterfowl, but Pungo Lake is special in the fall and winter, when snow geese and tundra swans visit in massive numbers—approaching 100,000—on their arctic journeys.

Also east of Columbia on U.S. 64 is the **Alligator River National Wildlife Refuge** (between Columbia and Roanoke Island, 252/473-1131, www.fws.gov). The large refuge covers most of the peninsula bounded by the Alligator River to the west, Albemarle Sound to the north, Croatan Sound to the east, and Pamlico Sound to the southeast. This large swath of woods and pocosin represents one of the most important wildlife habitats in the state, home to more than 200 species of birds as well as alligators, red wolves, and more black bears than anywhere in the coastal Mid-Atlantic. In the 1980s, red wolves were introduced into the Alligator River Refuge as they became extinct in the wild elsewhere in their original range. The Columbia-based **Red Wolf Coalition** (252/796-5600, http://redwolves.com) works to educate the public about the wolves in the hope of helping to establish free-ranging, self-sustaining red wolf populations at a number of sites.

There are many other ways to enjoy the Alligator River National Wildlife Refuge, including hiking, kayaking, and bird-watching. The refuge does not have a physical headquarters or traditional visitors center, but detailed directions and visitor information are available on the website.

Art Galleries

Eastern North Carolina has always had a folk-art tradition. **Pocosin Arts** (Main St. and Water St., Columbia, 252/796-2787, www.pocosinarts.org, 9am-5pm Mon.-Fri.) has helped keep the tradition of arts and crafts alive, teaching community classes in ceramics, fiber arts, sculpture, jewelry making, metalwork, and other media. The sales gallery has beautiful handmade items, and the main gallery displays many examples of folk art from eastern North Carolina.

WASHINGTON, BATH, AND BELHAVEN

North of the Pamlico River, as you head toward the Mattamuskeet National Wildlife Refuge and the Outer Banks, the towns of Washington, Bath, and Belhaven offer brief but beautiful diversions into the nature and history of the region.

North Carolina Estuarium

The **North Carolina Estuarium** (223 E. Water St., Washington, 252/948-0000, 10am-4pm Tues.-Sat., $5, $3 children, free 4 and under) is a museum dedicated to both the natural and cultural history of the Tar-Pamlico River basin. In addition to the exhibits, which include live native animals, historic artifacts, a 0.75-mile boardwalk along the Pamlico River, and hands-on displays, the Estuarium operates pontoon boat tours (10:30am Wed.-Sat., 1:30pm Wed.-Fri., reservations required, free).

Moss House

Located in the historic district a block from the river, **The Pamlico House B&B** (400 E. Main St., 252/946-5001, www.pamlicohousebb.com, $138-175) has five luxury rooms in the heart of the historic district. Breakfast gets rave reviews, but the real star is the comfortable feel and beauty of the place. An easy walk from the Moss House is **Bill's Hot Dogs** (109 Gladden St., 252/946-3343, www.billshotdogsnc.com, 8:30am-5pm daily, $1.50-2.25), a longtime local favorite for a quick snack. It's been around since 1928, so they've got their process down—you can only order when they ask for your order—and they know how to produce the dogs on the double.

Goose Creek State Park

Goose Creek State Park (2190 Camp Leach Rd., 252/923-2191, http://ncparks.gov, 8am-6pm daily Nov.-Feb., 8am-8pm daily Mar.-May and Sept.-Oct., 8am-9pm daily June-Aug., closed Dec. 25, park office 8am-5pm daily) is on the banks of the Pamlico River where Goose Creek joins it. It's an exotic environment of brackish marshes, freshwater swamps, and tall pine forests that are home to a variety of wildlife, including bears, a multitude of bird species, and lots of snakes. Eight miles of hiking trails as well as boardwalks and paddle trails traverse the hardwood swamp environment, and miles of shoreline and creek await exploration from a kayak or canoe (bring your own). Twelve primitive campsites (year-round, $10) are available, with access to toilets and water, including one campsite that is wheelchair-accessible.

Historic Bath

North Carolina's oldest town, Bath was chartered in 1705. The town has changed so little that even today it is mostly contained within the original boundaries laid out by the explorer John Lawson. For its first 70 years Bath enjoyed the spotlight as one of North Carolina's most important centers of trade and politics, home to governors, a refuge from the Indian wars, and frequently host to and victim of the pirate Blackbeard. Bath faded into obscurity as the town of Washington grew in the years after the Revolution, and today almost all of Bath is designated as **Historic Bath** (252/923-3971, www.nchistoricsites.org, visitors center and tours 9am-5pm Tues.-Sat., admission charged for both the Palmer-Marsh and Bonner Houses, $2 adults, $1 students). Important sites on the tour of the village are the 1734 St. Thomas Church, the 1751 Palmer-Marsh House, the 1790 Van Der Veer House, and the 1830 Bonner House, which overlooks a plot of land where Blackbeard once had a house. Bath has its fair share of legends, including a set of indelible hoof prints said to have been made by the devil's horse and "Teach's light"—supposedly ghostly remnants of the pirate Blackbeard.

If you decide to stay the night, try the **Inn on Bath Creek** (116 S. Main St., 252/923-9571, www.innonbathcreek.com, two-night minimum Fri.-Sat. Apr.-Nov., $140). This bed-and-breakfast, built on the site of the former Buzzard Hotel, fits in nicely with the old architecture of the historic town, but because it was built in 1999, it has modern conveniences to make your stay comfortable. Breakfast is big—think scratch-made blueberry pancakes, scrambled-egg wraps, and quiche along with the usual fruit, coffee, and pastries—and vegetarian options are available.

Belhaven

Belying its innocuous name, **Belhaven Memorial Museum** (210 E. Main St., 919/943-6817, www.beaufort-county.com, 1pm-5pm Thurs.-Tues., free) is actually a very strange little institution that houses the collection of Miss Eva Blount Way, who died in 1962 at the age of 92, a collector of oddities. She was described in a 1951 newspaper article as "housewife, snake killer, curator, trapper, dramatic actress, philosopher, and preserver of all the riches of mankind." Among her earthly treasures is a collection of pickled tumors (one weighs 10 pounds), a pickled one-eyed pig, a pickled two-headed kitten, cataracts (pickled), and three human infants (also pickled). It is without a doubt one of the weirdest museums you'll find.

Belhaven has an especially nice inn, the **Belhaven Water Street Bed and Breakfast** (567 E. Water St., 866/338-2825, www.belhavenwaterstreetbandb.com, $95-125). The guest rooms in this 100-year-old house face Pantego Creek and have their own fireplaces and private baths as well as wireless internet access.

One place you must stop to dine is ★ **Spoon River Artworks & Market** (263 Pamlico St., 252/945-3899, www.spoonrivernc.com, lunch 11:30am-2:30pm Fri.-Sat., dinner 5:30pm-9:30pm Mon. and Wed.-Sat., brunch 10:30am-2:30pm., brunch $8-18, dinner $18-30). Known for their artful plating of delicious farm-to-fork food, Spoon River is a great find in this corner of the state, where an excellent meal is hard to find. Seafood, oysters and shrimp, in particular, are excellent, but you'll see almost as many steaks coming out of the kitchen.

★ MATTAMUSKEET NATIONAL WILDLIFE REFUGE

Near the tiny town of Swan Quarter, **Mattamuskeet National Wildlife Refuge** (856 Mattamuskeet Rd., off Hwy. 94, between Swan Quarter and Englehard, 252/926-4021, www.fws.gov) preserves one of North

Carolina's most remarkable natural features as well as one of its most famous buildings. Lake Mattamuskeet, 18 miles long by 6 miles wide, is the state's largest natural lake, and at an average of 1.5 feet deep—5 feet at its deepest point—it is a most unusual environment. The hundreds of thousands of waterfowl who rest here on their seasonal rounds make this a world-famous location for bird-watching and wildlife photography.

Hiking and biking trails thread through the refuge, but camping is not permitted. In hunting season, which runs during spring and autumn months, beware of hunters (wearing a bright color like safety orange isn't a bad idea), and keep an eye out for copperheads, cottonmouths, two kinds of rattlesnakes, and alligators. Bears and red wolves abound here as well.

Within the administration of the Mattamuskeet Refuge is the **Swanquarter National Wildlife Refuge** (252/926-4021, www.fws.gov), located along the north shore of the Pamlico Sound, and accessible only by water. It is a gorgeous waterscape full of wildlife and worth exploring if you have the time and the means to get here. In spring, songbirds like robins, warblers, and red-winged blackbirds return by the thousands to nest and breed, and summer brings fledgling and juvenile birds like great blue herons, green herons, and great and snowy egrets. During fall, the Refuge is thick with ducks and geese, and it stays that way for much of winter. In colder weather, and for the annual waterfowl hunts in December and January, you'll spot green-winged teal, northern pintail, American coots, gadwalls, and ring-necked ducks among others.

GREENVILLE

Thirty minutes west of Washington is Greenville, a college town that's home of East Carolina University and one of eastern North Carolina's legendary barbecue joints, B's Barbecue. This city of 90,000 is the largest in this part of the state, and the energetic, relatively young populace takes a great deal of pride in their home, building an eclectic art and cultural scene. The **Greenville-Pitt County Convention & Visitors Bureau** (www.visitgreenvillenc.com) operates a **Visitors Center** (417 Cotanche Street, Ste. 100, 252/329-4200, Mon.-Fri. 8am-5pm) in Uptown Greenville to help point visitors, and the families of prospective college students, to some of the best things the city has to offer.

Sights

Uptown Greenville is a lively spot; here you'll find many shops, galleries, and eateries. Among the best galleries are the Greenville Museum of Art and Emerge Gallery and Art Center. **Greenville Museum of Art** (802 S. Evans St., 252/758-1946, www.goma.org, 10am-4:30pm Tues.-Fri., 1pm-4pm Sat.-Sun., free), though on the small side, is a fine art museum. Exhibits in the permanent collection include 19th- and 20th-century works by American artists, along with galleries dedicated to showing works and artists of particular local and regional interest. The Pitt County Arts Council operates **Emerge Gallery and Art Center** (404 S. Evans St., 252/551-6947, www.pittcountyarts.org, 10am-9pm Tues.-Fri., 10am-4pm Sat., 1pm-4pm Sun., free), a combo workshop and gallery space. The two galleries here show rotating exhibits and pieces for sale, often featuring local works or works created on site. The public can take a number of art classes, including a few one-day studio classes.

Trollingwood Taproom & Brewery (707 Dickinson Ave., 252/210-6295, www.trollingwoodbrewery.com, 4pm-10pm Tues., 4pm-midnight Wed., 1pm-midnight Thurs.-Sat., 1pm-6pm Sun.) has a cozy taproom with an outdoor area where you can enjoy their growing list of brews. Currently they make a dozen beers in rotation, but kegs of their Barrel Tipper rye ale and their Whistler dry stout seem to kick frequently.

At **Uptown Brewing Company** (418 Evans St., 252/689-6487, www.uptownbrewingcompany.com, 2pm-10pm Tues.-Wed., 2pm-midnight Thurs.-Fri., noon-midnight Sat., 1pm-7pm Sun.) you'll find a big taproom where they play good music, host frequent events and musical guests, and serve some excellent beer. They may have a wide range of styles, from the expected IPAs and wheat ales, to porters, lagers, and even barleywines and sours. Their gose is excellent, as is their Cerveza, a Mexican-style lager that's perfect for the long summers here.

Sports and Recreation

The Tar River flows by the city and some of the best recreational opportunities are tied to the water. **Knee Deep Adventures** (2800 E. 10th St, 252/714-5836, www.kneedeepadventures.com, noon-6pm Thurs.-Mon.) rents kayaks and paddleboards (from $35/hour), allowing you to explore the Tar River on your own, and provides guide service ($95). **River Park North** (1000 Mumford Rd., 252/329-4562, www.greenvillenc.gov, 6am-8pm daily May-Aug., 7am-7pm daily Sept.-Oct. and Mar.-Apr., 8am-5pm daily Nov.-Feb., free) has 1.2 miles of Tar River frontage, five ponds for fishing and pedal boating ($4/half hour), a handful of campsites ($10/night), hiking trails, and plenty of space for picnicking; you can also rent a Jon boat ($7/half-day) or kayak (from $9/3 hours) if you want to get out on the river. There's also a small nature center here; the **Walter L. Stasavich Science & Nature Center** (252/329-4560, 9:30am-5pm Tues.-Sat., 1pm-5pm Sun, $3 ages 13 and up, $1.50 ages 12 and under) has a 10,000-gallon freshwater aquarium, live animals of the kind you'd find around Greenville, and displays on the fauna and flora of the area.

A favorite way for locals to enjoy the Tar River is by taking a stroll, jog, or bike ride along the **South Tar River Greenway** (www.greenvillenc.gov). Part of Greenville's larger greenway system, the South Tar River Greenway links the Town Common to the Tar River on a wide, well-maintained, and well-used path. If you are looking for a longer walk, the Green Mill Run Greenway goes from the river to College Hill on the ECU campus.

There are plans in the works for expanding the city's greenway systems significantly.

Food

You can't come to Eastern North Carolina and not try some barbecue, and you can't come to Greenville without trying B's, a giant in the world of Eastern N.C. 'cue. **B's Barbecue** (751 B's Barbecue Rd., 252/758-7126, 10am-2pm Tues.-Sat., under $10) does it right: whole hog, pepper-laced vinegar sauce, sides like what you'd eat at home. From the outside B's could use a coat of paint and some TLC, but they focus all of their efforts on the plate, and that's why they sell out of barbecue every day they're open. B's claims to be open until 2pm, but I've never known them to last much longer than 12:30, so if you have a hankering for barbecue, fried chicken, and country sides, get in line early, it'll be out the door any day they're open.

One of the most lauded barbecue joints in North Carolina is Skylight Inn, between Greenville and Kinston, but the son of the famous Jones barbecue family has opened his own spot in Winterville. ★ **Sam Jones BBQ** (715 W. Fire Tower Rd., Winterville, 252/689-6449, www.samjonesbbq.com, 11am-9pm Mon.-Sat., 11am-8:30pm Sun., $8-19) serves chopped whole-hog 'cue in trays, plates and sandwiches, but he pushes out into other barbecue territory, too. Smoked chicken and turkey, ribs (which, surprising to many, aren't a part of North Carolinas' barbecue tradition), wings, catfish, and burgers. A barbecue sandwich is a must, but don't miss the fried pork skins and pimento cheese.

Sup Dogs (213 E. 5th St., 252/752-7682, www.supdogs.com, 11am-2:30am Sun.-Wed., 11am-3am Thurs.-Sat., under $10) is a fun hot dog joint that's open late every night, cheap, and tasty, so it's just right for the college crowd. They have an impressive array of specialty dogs and burgers and a range of beer and boozy drinks that are college-town perfect.

Accommodations

The 5th Street Manor (1105 E. 5th St.,

252/335-0699, www.the5thstreetmanor. com, $99-129) is the only bed-and-breakfast in town, but fortunately it's a lovely one. Located in the College View Historic District, the white three-story home cuts a fine figure on its lot across the street from ECU. Elegant and well-appointed without feeling like one of those antique-filled, not-sure-if-I-can-touch-anything B&Bs, 5th Street Manor ticks all the boxes when it comes to a comfortable, welcoming stay.

There are several choices when it comes to chain hotels in Greenville, but the best of them are the **Hilton Greenville** (207 SW Greenville Blvd., 252/355-5000, www3.hilton.com, from $180) and the **Residence Inn by Marriott** (1820 W. 5th St., 252/364-8999, www.marriott.com, from $130).

GETTING THERE AND AROUND

This remote corner of North Carolina is crossed by two major north-south routes, U.S. 17 and U.S. 168, both from Chesapeake, Virginia. U.S. 168 passes to the east through Currituck, and U.S. 17 is the westerly route, closest to the Dismal Swamp and Elizabeth City, passing through Edenton, Windsor, and Williamston. At Williamston, U.S. 17 meets U.S. 64, a major east-west route that leads to Plymouth, Creswell, and Columbia to the east.

If you continue south on U.S. 17 from Williamston, the next major town is Washington, where you can turn east on U.S. 264 to reach Bath and Belhaven. Alternately, you can reach U.S. 264 from the other direction, taking Highway 94 at Columbia and crossing Lake Mattamuskeet. West of Washington along U.S. 264 is the town of Greenville; from Greenville you have easy access to I-95 by following U.S. 264 west.

There is one state ferry route in this region, at the far northwest corner between Currituck and Knotts Island (877/287-7488, 45 minutes, six trips daily, free).

Beaufort and the Crystal Coast

Long before you smell the ocean salt on the air,

you can feel the ocean drawing near. The sky seems wider, and it takes on a deeper shade of blue.

Hardwoods and hills give way to towering pines and flat fields, and then more and more water—creeks, wetlands, and widening rivers. Somewhere between Kinston and New Bern, still an hour's drive from the beaches and sounds of Carteret County, you can sense the Atlantic.

Along the Crystal Coast, as North Carolina's central coast is known in these parts, you'll find New Bern and Beaufort, two old North Carolina towns that were centers of colonial commerce and provided access to the Atlantic. Beautifully preserved, these two towns have great examples of historic commercial and residential architecture

Highlights

Look for ★ to find recommended sights, activities, dining, and lodging.

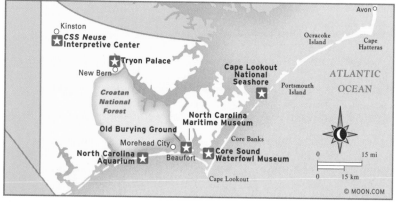

© MOON.COM

★ **Tryon Palace:** The splendid, and in its day controversial, seat of colonial government is worthy of a day's leisurely exploration (page 83).

★ **CSS *Neuse* Interpretive Center:** Far up the Neuse River, a Confederate ironclad was built, scuttled, and burned to prevent its capture. It stayed in the river for nearly a century before being salvaged for historic preservation. This museum tells its story, complete with the recovered hull (page 93).

★ **North Carolina Maritime Museum:** The state's seafaring heritage, ranging from pirate history to its current maritime culture, is represented by fascinating exhibits and activities (page 98).

★ **Old Burying Ground:** One of the prettiest and most storied cemeteries in the South, this Beaufort churchyard is home to the "Little Girl

Buried in a Barrel of Rum" and other fascinating residents (page 98).

★ **Core Sound Waterfowl Museum:** Actually a museum about people rather than ducks, the Waterfowl Museum eloquently tells of the everyday lives of past generations of Down Easterners while bringing their descendants together to reforge community bonds (page 106).

★ **Cape Lookout National Seashore:** The more than 50 miles of coastline along Core and Shackleford Banks, now home only to wild horses and turtle nests, were once also the home of Bankers who made their livings in the fishing, whaling, and shipping trades (page 108).

★ **North Carolina Aquarium:** Sharks, jellies, otters, and their aquatic kin show their true beauty in underwater habitats at the aquarium (page 112).

dating as far back as three centuries, including one home that belonged to the dreaded pirate Blackbeard.

The Neuse River winds through pine forests, passing Kinston—a town with an unusual Civil War past and a food scene that's worth the visit—and widening as it enters the coastal plain, feeding the primeval forest, creeks, hidden lakes, and tiny towns in the Croatan National Forest. To the northeast, the Cedar Island National Wildlife Refuge is a vast swath of marshes, gradually easing into the Pamlico Sound, where Cape Lookout National Seashore shelters the mainland from storms. Along the seashore are miles of beach where the only occupants are wild horses, the Banker ponies, and the beautiful diamond-patterned Cape Lookout Lighthouse. You won't find homes here. Portsmouth Village, a once-thriving whaling port washed away by a series of storms, is a ghost town and part of the National Park Service.

Sometimes people in North Carolina refer to any part of the coast, from Wilmington to Nags Head, as "Down East." In the truest sense of the term, Down East refers to northeast Carteret County, the area north of Beaufort. Here the islands, marshes, and towns bordering Core Sound are undergoing colossal cultural shifts as people from "Up North" (meaning "anywhere but here") move into the area and local youth leave generations of family life for greener economic pastures. Changes in global trade and in the environment have made traditional maritime occupations like fishing and shrimping untenable. Nonetheless, Down Easterners work to preserve the treasure of their home, the Core Sound, with conservation and historic preservation as well as folkways education. Witness the Core Sound Waterfowl Museum on Harkers Island, where community members have assembled an interesting collection of family photos, quilts, baseball uniforms,

oyster knives, net hooks, and other treasures to tell their story.

PLANNING YOUR TIME

Beach-season rules apply along the coastal areas and river towns, meaning that prices and crowds increase dramatically between Memorial Day in May and Labor Day in early September; conversely, they drop to rock bottom during the off-season. Visiting during shoulder seasons can mean warm water, empty beaches, and no waiting for restaurant tables, but your accommodations and dining choices can be limited, particularly in smaller towns.

When you visit, try the fresh, local seafood. To ensure you're getting the best local catch, **Carteret Catch** (www.carteretcatch.org) provides downloadable cards and information on the seasonally fresh seafood caught in the area.

Across the Southeast, late summer and early autumn are hurricane season. The paths of hurricanes can be quite unpredictable. Even if reports say a storm will dissipate over Cuba, that doesn't mean it won't turn into a hurricane and head for the Carolina coast. Chances are that you'll have sufficient warning before any major storm, but it's advisable to keep an eye on the weather forecast. A storm that stays offshore, even at some distance, can cause foul beach conditions; surfers love the big waves that precede a storm, but they know the danger of powerful tides, strong undertow, rip currents, and the general unpredictability that storms bring. Not unique to this region, the risk is the same anywhere on the North Carolina coast.

Barring storms, fall is a fabulous time to visit. Days and nights are still warm, the ocean is swimmable, and the crowds are smaller. Mild weather often holds through the end of October into November, but the water becomes chilly for swimming then, although

BEAUFORT AND THE CRYSTAL COAST

Beaufort and the Crystal Coast

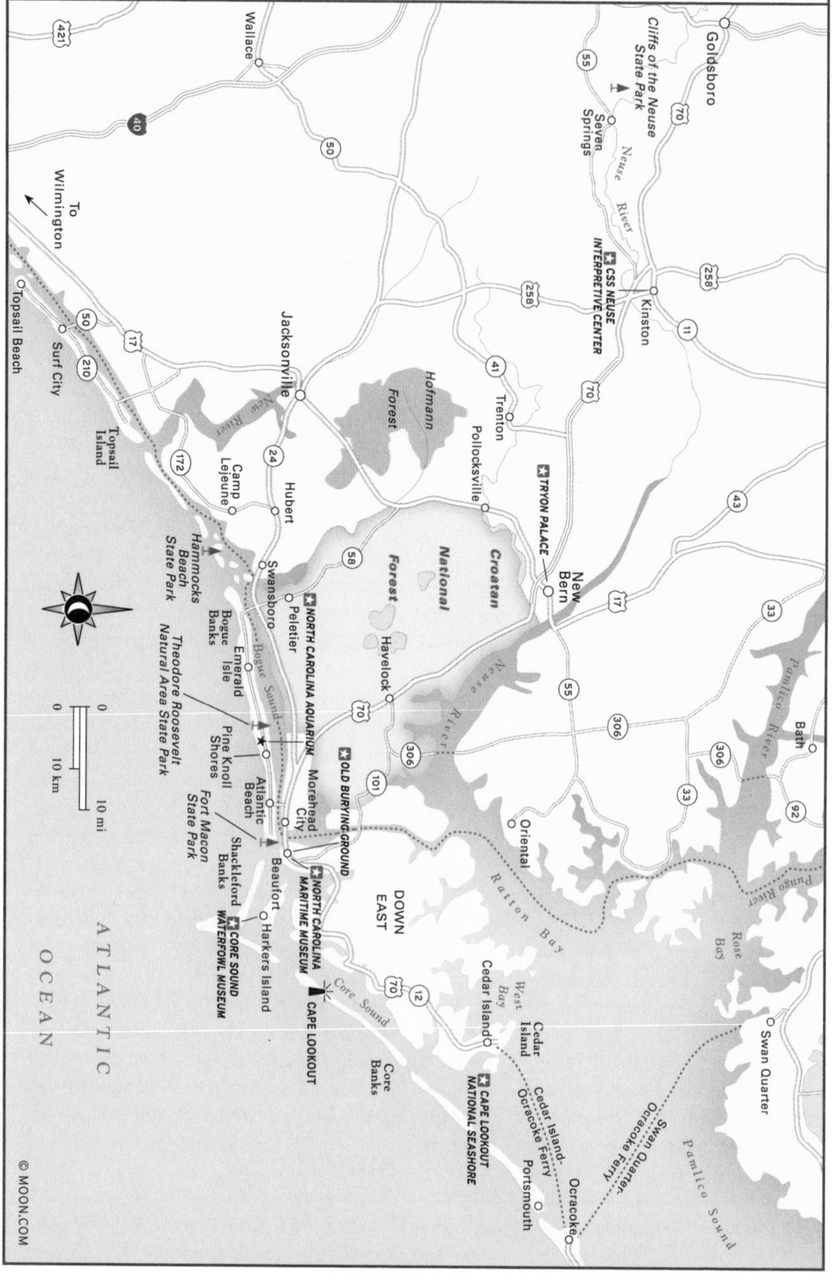

air temperatures are still nice for strolling on the sand.

INFORMATION AND SERVICES

Hospitals in the area include **Carteret General Hospital** (3500 Arendell St., 252/499-6000, www.carterethealth.org) in Morehead City, **Carolina East Medical Center** (2000 Neuse Blvd., 252/633-8111, www.carolinaeasthealth.com) in New Bern,

Vidant Duplin Hospital (401 N. Main St., 910/296-0941, www.vidanthealth.com) in Kenansville, **Lenoir UNC Health Care** (100 Airport Rd., 252/522-7000, www.unclenoir. org) in Kinston, and **Wayne UNC Health Care** (2700 Wayne Memorial Dr., 919/736-1110, www.waynehealth.org) in Goldsboro.

Extensive travel information is available from the **Crystal Coast Tourism Authority** (3409 Arendell St., 252/726-8148, www. crystalcoastnc.org) in Morehead City.

New Bern

New Bern's history attracts visitors, but the natural beauty of this artistic community keeps many of them returning year after year. Situated at the confluence of the Trent and Neuse Rivers, it's a prime spot for sightseeing and retirement living. Despite the attention it gets and the consequent traffic, New Bern has retained its charm and is still a small and enormously pleasant town. An important note: It's pronounced "NYEW-bern" or "NOO-bern," sometimes even like "neighbor," but never "new-BERN."

At the junction of two major highways, New Bern is easily reached by car. U.S. 17 passes through New Bern north-south, and U.S. 70 crosses east-west, with Beaufort and Morehead City an hour to the southeast and Kinston 45 minutes to the west; Wilmington is 2.5 hours to the southwest via Highway 17, and Raleigh 2.5 hours west-northwest.

HISTORY

New Bern's early days were marked by tragedy. It was settled in 1710 by a community of Swiss and German colonists under the leadership of English surveyor John Lawson (author of the 1709 *A New Voyage to Carolina,* available today in reprint) and Swiss entrepreneur Christoph von Graffenried (from Bern, Switzerland). More than half of the settlers died en route to the New World, and those who made it alive suffered tremendous hardship in the first years. Lawson and Graffenried were both detained in 1711 by the indigenous Tuscarora people, whom the colonists had evicted from their land without compensation. Graffenried was released, according to some accounts because he wore such fancy clothes that the Tuscarora feared executing such a high-ranking official. Lawson was tried and burned at the stake, and the conflict escalated into the Tuscarora War.

Despite early disasters, New Bern was on its feet again by the mid-18th century, when it was home to the colony's first newspaper and its first chartered academy. It also became North Carolina's capital, an era symbolized by the splendor of Tryon Palace, one of the most recognizable architectural landmarks in the state.

During the Civil War, New Bern was captured early on by Ambrose Burnside's forces. Despite multiple Confederate attempts to retake the city, it remained a Union stronghold for the balance of the war. It became a center for African American resistance and political organization through the Reconstruction years, a story grippingly told in historian David Cecelski's book *The Waterman's Song.*

SIGHTS
★ Tryon Palace

Tryon Palace (529 S. Front St., 800/767-1560, www.tryonpalace.org, 9am-5pm Tues.-Sat.,

New Bern

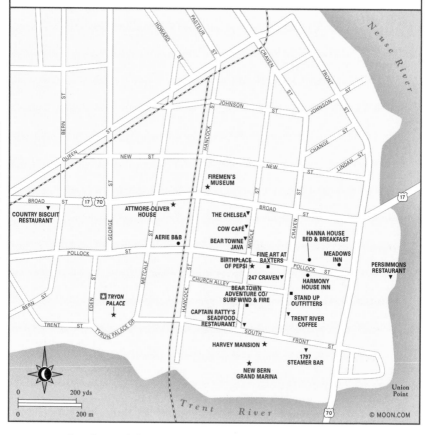

noon-5pm Sun., last guided tour 4pm, gardens 9am-6pm Tues.-Sat. and noon-6pm Sun. Mar.-Nov., 9am-5pm Tues.-Sat. and noon-5pm Sun. Nov.-Mar., museum shop 9am-5pm Tues.-Sat., 1-5pm Sun., full admission $20 adults, $10 schoolchildren, galleries and gardens only $12 adults, $6 children, gardens only $6 adults, $3 children) is a remarkable feat of historic re-creation, a reconstruction of the 1770 colonial capitol and governor's mansion done from the ground up. It was a magnificent project the first time around, too, when Governor William Tryon bucked the preferences of Piedmont Carolinians and had the colonial government's new home built

here on the coastal plain. He hired English architect John Hawks to design the complex, a Georgian house on an estate laid out in the Palladian style. The palace's first incarnation was short-lived, standing for a scant 25 years before burning down in 1798. As the new state had relocated its governmental operations to Raleigh, there was no need to rebuild the New Bern estate, but it was not forgotten. In the early 20th century a movement arose to rebuild Tryon Palace. By the 1950s both the funds and, incredibly, Hawks's original drawings and plans had been secured, and the palace was rebuilt over a period of seven years using the drawings as well the stables, the only original building not destroyed in the fire, as a model. Today, it is once again one of the most striking and recognizable buildings in the state.

Tryon Palace is open for tours year-round, and it hosts various lectures and living-history events throughout the year. One of the best times to visit is during the December holiday season, when the estate is decorated beautifully and a recreated **Jonkonnu,** a colonial African American celebration once seen throughout the Caribbean and Southeast, is celebrated. Also known by the name Junkanoo, John Canoe, and several other variations, it was a Mardi Gras-like festival with deep African roots, involving a parade through plantations with music and outlandish costumes, some representing folk characters associated with the celebration. Like Mardi Gras, it was a sort of upside-down day, when the social order was temporarily inverted and enslaved people could boldly walk right onto the master's porch and demand gifts or money. Some slave owners got into the spirit of the celebration and played along with the remarkable pantomime. It was a tradition fraught with both joy and sorrow. Tryon Palace puts on a lively and enlightening re-creation.

Tryon's living-history interpreters do a wonderful job of enlightening visitors to certain aspects of colonial life, on a guided tour of the palace and on a walk through the nearby kitchen. In the kitchen, costumed interpreters show what was involved in running an 18th-century household, utilizing the nearby kitchen garden for most of what they cook with during the demonstrations. Lately the cooking demonstrations have expanded, pairing the beauty of the palace with the talents of a local chef to put on dinner events, including the on-site Savoring Spring event that makes use of the bounty of the kitchen garden.

At the Tryon Palace ticket office is the **North Carolina History Center,** a collection of galleries and exhibits that illustrate the history of the region and New Bern in particular. The **Pepsi Family Center** is a hit with kids as interactive displays transport you back to 1835, when the region was busy producing valuable things like turpentine for the nation's young navy. Visitors interested in Jonkonnu will find enlightening exhibits on the festival, and art lovers will appreciate the best of the region in the **Duffy Exhibit Gallery.** Admission to the Pepsi Family Center, Duffy Exhibit Gallery, and Regional History Museum are included in the admission cost for Tryon Palace.

Visiting Tryon Palace and its gardens along with the North Carolina History Center can fill an afternoon or even a full day. When you're done exploring, the surrounding neighborhood contains some wonderful old homes.

New Bern Firemen's Museum

The **New Bern Firemen's Museum** (420 Broad St., 252/636-4087, www.newbernfiremuseum.com, 10am-4pm Mon.-Sat., $5 adults, $2.50 children, free under age 7) is a fun museum for gearheads that has an antiquarian bent. The museum—in an old fire station—houses a collection of 19th- and early-20th-century fire wagons and trucks and chronicles the lively and contentious history of firefighting in New Bern. The city was the first in North Carolina and one of the first in the country to charter a fire department. After the Civil War, three fire companies operated in New Bern; one was founded before the war, one was founded after, and the third was a boys' bucket brigade, a training program for junior firefighters. They competed, even fought, to put out fires. Learn their stories and the tale of the disastrous fire of 1922 which left more than 1,800 residents homeless.

Attmore-Oliver House

The beautiful 1790 **Attmore-Oliver House** (511 Broad St., 252/638-8558, www.newbernhistorical.org, 10am-4:30pm Mon.-Fri., guided tours by appointment, free) is a historic house museum with exhibits about New Bern's Civil War history. It's also the headquarters of the New Bern Historical Society.

Birthplace of Pepsi

We often think of Coca-Cola as the quintessential Southern drink, but it was here in New Bern that Caleb Bradham, a drugstore owner, put together what he called Brad's Drink—later Pepsi-Cola. The Pepsi-Cola Bottling Company operates a soda fountain and gift shop at the location of Bradham's pharmacy, called the **Birthplace of Pepsi** (256 Middle St., 252/636-5898, www.pepsistore.com). A few Pepsi antiques sit in display cases, and there's a mural showing the original recipe, but aside from some T-shirts and souvenirs, there's little else here.

SPORTS AND RECREATION

Given the town's location right on the river and near miles of tributaries to explore by boat, it's no surprise that watersports dominate New Bern's outdoor offerings. **Dragonfly Boat Tours** (departing from New Bern Grand Marina Dock E at 101 Craven St., 252/675-0657, www.dragonflyboattours.com, $30) offers a combined nature and history tour of the Trent River in an electric boat; tours are 90 minutes long and run at 10am and 2pm Fri.-Sat. at 2pm and 4pm Sun. **Cruise the Neuse Boat Tours** (departing from New Bern Grand Marina Dock D at 101 Craven St., 252/876-7232, www.cruisetheneuse.com) offers a daytime and sunset cruise. Daytime cruises ($30) run at 10am, noon and 2pm, and sunset cruises ($35) at 7pm (varies seasonally, call for times).

For a self-propelled kayak or stand-up paddleboard tour of New Bern's waterfront, see **Stand Up Outfitters** (1305 Country Club Rd., 252/638-3000, www.standupoutfitters.com, lessons from $450, rentals from $75 per day); they'll set you up with everything you need for a day of SUPing. If you're feeling limber and balanced, check out their SUP yoga classes ($30, days and times vary).

Bear Town Adventure Company (230 Middle St., 252/288-5823, www.beartownadventure.com, kayak and SUP from $40/three hours, tours $50, bike rentals $8/hour or $28/day, bike tours $20-30) can equip you with the boards, bikes, and vessels you need to go exploring on your own, or you can join them on a tour of the town. Bear Town is located inside **Surf, Wind and Fire** (10am-6pm Mon.-Thurs. and Sat., 10am-8pm Fri., noon-4pm Sun.), an outdoor lifestyle shop carrying clothing and gear from Patagonia, The North Face, and other brands.

Golfers visiting New Bern will want to check out **Harbour Pointe Golf Club** (1105 Barkentine Dr., 252/638-5338, www.harbourpointegolfclub.com, 18 holes, par 72, greens fees $42 for 18 holes, $30 for 9 holes, $25 twilight, $30 military, fees include cart). The course presents challenges but gives you plenty of opportunities to take strokes back. And the must-see hole is number 14, where the green's sweeping view of Broad Creek and the Neuse River can even take the sting out of a double bogey. The **Emerald Golf Club** (5000 Clubhouse Dr., 252/633-4440, www.emeraldgc.com, 18 holes, par 72, greens fees $56 for 18 holes, $34 for 9 holes, $45 after 11am, rates include cart) is a pretty course with wide fairways flanked by trees, bunkers, and water.

ENTERTAINMENT AND EVENTS

New Bern's historic Harvey Mansion has a cozy, old-fashioned pub in its cellar and an Italian restaurant upstairs, the **Circa 1810 Harvey Mansion Restaurant & Bar** (221 S. Front St., 252/635-3232, www.circa1810.com, restaurant 4pm-10pm Tues.-Thurs. and Sun., 4pm-11pm Fri.-Sat., bar 4pm-2am daily). The Italian dishes are quite good, especially the pork *osso bucco* and the shrimp Fra Diavolo. In the bar, get pizza by the slice, calzones, wings and fried snacks. This basement bar is rare; originally the house's kitchen, it's a perfect hangout.

Captain Ratty's Seafood Restaurant (202-206 Middle St., 252/633-2088 or

---

1: New Bern Firemen's Museum; **2:** gardens at Tryon Palace

800/633-5292, www.captainrattys.com, 11:30am-9:30pm Mon.-Fri., 8am-9:30pm Sat.) has a rooftop bar that's a popular gathering spot for locals and travelers alike, and the impressive wine list, combined with a few choice appetizers, make this a great place to watch the sun go down.

SHOPPING

Given its age, the fact that New Bern is a great place for antiques shopping comes as no surprise. Check out **New Berne Antiques and Collectibles** (1000 Greenleaf Cemetery Rd., 252/637-0206, www.new-bern-antiques-and-collectibles.com, 9:30am-5:30pm Mon.-Sat., 1pm-5pm Sun.), where they've got 12,500 square feet of space that's "packed to the rafters" with antiques, stuff, and junk. **JL Kirkman's Antique Mall** (1198 Hwy. 17 N., Bridgeton, 252/634-2745, www.jlkirkmans.com, 9am-6pm Mon.-Fri., 10am-6pm Sat.), five minutes north of New Bern, has a varied selection with more than a few surprises.

Tryon Palace is a fun shopping spot for history buffs and home-and-garden fanciers. The historical site's **Museum Shop** (Jones House, Eden St., and Pollock St., 252/639-3532, 9am-5pm Tues.-Sat., 1pm-5pm Sun.) has a nice variety of books about history and architecture as well as handicrafts and children's toys and games.

Strolling the streets of New Bern, you'll notice a number of art galleries, including the **Craven Arts Council & Gallery's Bank of the Arts** (317 Middle St., 252/638-2577, www.cravenarts.org, 11am-5pm Tues.-Sat., free), a onetime bank that's now a great exhibition space. **Fine Art at Baxters** (323 Pollock St., 252/634-9002, www.fineartatbaxters.com, 10am-6pm Mon.-Fri., 10am-5pm Sun.), a well-curated gallery and working studio with architecture almost as beautiful as the artwork, is in a former jewelry store and has the original antique cases and even the safe. Both of these are great stops for art and architecture buffs. **Carolina Creations Fine Art and Contemporary Craft Gallery** (317-A Pollock St., 252/633-4369, www.

carolinacreationsnewbern.com, 10am-6pm Mon.-Thurs., 10am-8pm Fri., 10am-6pm Sat., 11am-4pm Sun. spring-summer, 10am-6pm Mon.-Sat., 11am-3pm Sun. winter) has a mix of fine arts and functional craft items. You'll find everything from turned wooden bowls to oil paintings and hand-forged menorahs.

FOOD

One of the top restaurants in New Bern also happens to have the best view. At **Persimmons Restaurant** (100 Pollock St., 252/514-0033, www.persimmonsrestaurant.net, 11am-3pm Tues.-Sun., 5pm-9pm Tues.-Sat., 4pm-8pm Sun., $13-30) you can take in the water views from a seat in the comfortable dining room or outside on the dockside deck. There's an excellent chef at Persimmons, and the dishes are seafood-centric and executed at a much higher level than at other restaurants in town.

Moore's Olde Tyme Barbeque (3621 Doctor M.L.K. Jr. Blvd., 252/638-3937, www.mooresbarbeque.com, 10am-9:30pm Sun.-Thurs., 10am-10pm Fri.-Sat., $3-9) is a family business in operation since 1945. They roast and smoke their own barbecue in a pit on site, burning the wood that you'll see piled up by the shop. The menu is short and simple—pork barbecue, chicken, shrimp, fish, hush puppies, fries, and slaw—and the prices are lower than many fast-food joints. In addition to making some good 'cue, Moore's is a Guinness World Record holder for making the world's largest open barbecue sandwich with slaw, on July 4, 2010. Weighing in at more than half a ton, it was one big sandwich.

There are lots of good snack stops in New Bern to grab a bite or a cup of coffee before a day of touring on foot or on the water. The **Trent River Coffee Company** (208 Craven St., 252/514-2030, 8am-5pm Mon.-Sat., 10am-5pm Sun.) is a casual coffee shop serving a good cup in a cool downtown storefront. It's sometimes patronized by well-behaved local

1: Fine Art at Baxters, one of New Bern's best galleries; **2:** luxe accommodations at the Aerie Bed and Breakfast in New Bern

dogs that lie patiently under the tables while their owners read the newspaper. This is a nice meeting place and a shaded oasis in the summer heat.

For a down-home breakfast, the **Country Biscuit Restaurant** (809 Broad St., 252/638-5151, http://thecountrybiscuit.com, 5am-2:30pm Mon. and Tues., 5am-9pm Wed.-Fri., 5am-2:30pm Sat., breakfast $2-9, lunch and dinner $5-9), is popular, not surprisingly, for its biscuits. They say they serve "real food for real folks," and indeed, the food is simple, homey, and filling.

Christoph's on The Water (100 Middle St. in the Doubletree by Hilton, 252/638-0305, www.christophsnewbern.com, breakfast 6am-10:30am Mon.-Fri. and 7am-11am Sat.-Sun., dinner 5pm-10pm nightly, lounge 4pm-late Mon.-Thurs. and noon-late Fri.-Sun., The Deck 4pm-9pm Fri.-Sun., breakfast $4.50-15, dinner $6.50-28, The Deck $5-13) serves breakfast (omelets and pancakes and a breakfast buffet) and dinner (fish and chips, pork chops, steaks and fish). At The Deck, find sliders, flatbreads, and finger foods of the pub variety.

The **Cow Café** (319 Middle St., 252/672-9269, www.cowcafenewbern.com, 10am-7pm Mon.-Thurs., 10am-9pm Fri.-Sat., 11:30am-5pm Sun., $2-10) is a pleasant downtown creamery and restaurant with some unusual and classic homemade ice cream flavors you can't find anywhere else in town. Expect cones and cups, banana splits and shakes on the sweet side, barbecue, turkey and chicken sandwiches for something heartier. The fun logo and Holstein cow decor make it hard to miss.

One restaurant on many visitors' must-eat list is **The Chelsea** (335 Middle St., 252/637-5469, www.thechelsea.com, 11am-9pm Mon.-Thurs., 11am-10pm Fri.-Sat., closed Sun., lunch $7-19, dinner $9-28). The menu runs the gamut from crab cakes and shrimp and grits to New Orleans-style pasta, and everything is tasty. Don't miss the crab soup, the seared tuna appetizer, or the duck spring rolls.

Sea Glass Café and Bakery (1803 S. Glenburnie Rd., 252/634-2327, www.theseaglasscafe.com, 6am-2pm Mon.-Fri., 7:30am-2pm Sat.-Sun., around $8) is a local favorite for their pecan cranberry toast made with bread baked on site and their scones. Open for breakfast and lunch, they put out food ranging from scrambled eggs to chicken salad on pecan cranberry bread or seared ahi tuna over salad. The place is small, but the food is worth the wait if there are no tables free when you arrive.

ACCOMMODATIONS

Pollock Street is lined with charming 19th-century houses decorated in classic bed-and-breakfast style. The ★ **Benjamin Ellis House Bed & Breakfast** (215 Pollock St., 252/636-3810, www.benjaminellishouse.com, $109-189) has seven well-appointed guest rooms and three suites. Two of the suites feature king beds and two-person jetted tubs, while the third offers a queen bed and a separate living room with queen sleeper sofa. Breakfast is exceptional as the owners draw on their love of Southern food and culinary influences from their world travels and put out a spread that includes eggs Florentine with Mornay sauce, grits soufflé, and muesli.

The **Aerie Bed and Breakfast** (509 Pollock St., 252/636-5553, www.aerienc.com, $129-199) is the current incarnation of the 1880s Street-Ward residence. All of its seven luxurious guest rooms are decorated with Victorian furniture reflecting the house's earliest era. There is a lovely courtyard for guests to enjoy, and the inn is only one block from Tryon Palace.

At the **Hanna House Bed and Breakfast** (218 Pollock St., 252/635-3209 or 866/830-4371, http://hannahousenc.net, no children under age 6, $99-150), expect one of the best breakfasts you can get at a B&B. The owners take pride in their morning spread and offer a selection of dishes ranging from eggs *en croûte* to a variety of frittatas and my favorite, stuffed French toast. Hanna House isn't all breakfast; each of the five guest rooms is comfortable and spacious for both single travelers and couples.

Several hotels can be found around New Bern as well, including **Hampton Inn** (200 Hotel Dr., 252/637-2111, www.hamptoninn.com, from $129), **SpringHill Suites** (300 Hotel Dr., 252/637-0017, www.marriott.com, from $130), and **Bridge Pointe Hotel & Marina** (101 Howell Rd., 877/283-7713, www.bridgepointe.com, from $108), which has 115 guest rooms and great water views.

Camping

New Bern's **KOA Campground** (1565 B St., reservations 800/562-3341, information 252/638-2556, www.koacamping.com, tent sites from $31, RV sites from $40, cabins from $73) is on the other side of the Neuse River from town, right on the riverbank. Choices include 20-, 30-, and 40-amp RV sites; "Kamping Kabins and Lodges"; and tent sites.

Pets are allowed, and there is a dog park on site. The campground has free wireless internet access. Stop by the New Bern Convention Center's visitor information center before checking in and pick up a KOA brochure for some valuable coupons.

GETTING THERE AND AROUND

New Bern is located on the Neuse River, at the point where the river opens wide and prepares to meet the Pamlico Sound. A pair of recognizable roads run through town, including U.S. 70 from the east and Highway 17 from the south. N.C. 70 continues through New Bern down to Morehead City on the coast, an hour-long drive through the Croatan National Forest. New Bern is 2 hours north of Wilmington (via Hwy. 17), and 2.25 hours southeast of Raleigh (via U.S. 70). Nags Head and the Outer Banks are 2.75 hours from New Bern (via Hwy. 17 and U.S. 64).

Croatan National Forest and Vicinity

A huge swath of swampy wilderness, the Croatan National Forest is all the land bounded by the Neuse, Trent, and White Oak Rivers and Bogue Sound, from New Bern to Morehead City and almost all the way to Jacksonville. Despite its size, Croatan is one of the lesser-known and least developed federal preserves in the state. All three nearby towns in Jones County (population just over 10,000) enjoy a similar atmosphere of sequestration, where barely traveled roads lead to dark expanses of forest and swamp as well as narrow, old village streets.

CROATAN NATIONAL FOREST

Headquartered just off U.S. 70 south of New Bern, the **Croatan National Forest** (141 E. Fisher Ave., New Bern, 252/638-5628, www.fs.usda.gov) has few amenities for visitors but plenty of land and water trails to explore.

Hiking and Biking

The main hiking route is the **Neusiok Trail,** which begins at the Newport River Parking area and ends at the Pinecliff Recreation Area on the Neuse River. It traverses 20 miles of beach, salt marsh, swamp, pocosin, and pine woods. Part of North Carolina's Mountains to Sea Trail (a 900-mile route from Jockey's Ridge on the Outer Banks to Great Smoky Mountains National Park in the west), Neusiok is blazed with white circles and is quite an old trail, used by everyone from Native Americans to hunters, woodsmen, and even moonshiners. Dogs are permitted so long as they're leashed. This long trail is a popular hike for backpackers; you can camp anywhere, but a trio of shelters offers a dry spot to sleep in this otherwise wet forest. The 1.3-mile **Cedar Point Tideland National Recreation Trail** covers estuary marshes and woods, starting at the Cedar Point boat ramp near Cape Carteret. The 0.5-mile **Island Creek Forest Walk** passes through virgin hardwood forests and includes interpretative signage installed as part of an Eagle Scout project. If you want to bike, the best place is at the Neuse River Campground, where there are two miles of bike trails.

Boating

The spectacular **Saltwater Adventure Trail** is a water route nearly 100 miles in length that starts at Brice's Creek, south of New Bern, and winds north to the Neuse River, following the Neuse River to the Harlowe Canal. The route then leads down to Beaufort and Bogue Sound, turning back inland on the White Oak River and ending at Haywood Landing north of Swansboro. If you're up for the challenge, it's an incredible trip.

There are eight popular boat launches in Croatan National Forest: Brices Creek, Catfish Lake, Great Lake, Siddie Fields, Cahooque Lake, Cedar Point, Haywood Landing, and Oyster Point. You can launch a shallow-drafting motor boat from any of these as well as use them as launch points for kayaks, canoes, and stand-up paddleboards.

For boat rentals, not many outfitters serve the national forest. **White Oak River Outfitters** (7660 New Bern Hwy., Maysville, 910/743-2744, www. whiteoakrivercampground.com, single kayaks $40/half-day, $50/full day, double kayaks and canoes $50/half-day, $60/full day, reservations required) rents out canoes and kayaks, has a shuttle service that makes trips a lot easier, and offers guided tours on the White Oak River and other waters in the area. They also have camping available, with tent ($15) and RV ($20) sites to rent (910/595-4163).

Great Lake is a popular spot to explore via canoe, kayak, or small flat-bottomed boat. Surrounded by centuries-old cypress trees, it's easy to feel like you're in another world or another time. A handful of campsites lets you extend your stay or just enjoy the day paddling

around or fishing for crappie, perch, and bullhead, all easy catches.

The **Oyster Point Campground,** which is also the trailhead for the Neusiok Trail, offers a boat launch suitable for both motorized and paddle watercraft. It's easy to explore the marshy fringes of the forest from here or head into one of the tributaries or winding marsh creeks nearby.

Camping

There are four developed campsites in the Croatan Forest (877/444-6777, www. recreation.gov). **Neuse River** (also called Flanners Beach Campground, $12-24) has 41 sites with showers and flush toilets. **Cedar Point** (single sites $20, double sites $40, electric hookup additional $7-14) has 40 campsites with electricity, showers, and flush toilets. Oyster Point Campground ($8) is small, with only eight sites, but **Fisher's Landing** (free) is smaller with only nine sites and no facilities other than vault toilets. Primitive camping areas are at Great Lake, Catfish Lake, and Long Point.

OHV Area

OHV, or Off Highway Vehicle, Trails are growing more popular in forests and recreation areas across the United States. Here in Croatan National Forest, the designated, and only permitted, OHV riding area is the **Black Swamp OHV Trail** ($5/day, purchased at the Croatan District Office in New Bern), and it's a hot one. The easy-to-intermediate trails are suited for ATVs, trail bikes, and SUVs with a small wheel base (50 inches or less). At Black Swamp, there are several miles of trails completed with many more in the planning and developmental stages.

GETTING THERE AND AROUND

The main highway running through Croatan National Forest is U.S. 70. It runs south and east through the forest, connecting New Bern (to the north) with Morehead

City (to the south). Highway 17 forms the western boundary of the National Forest, and inside the forest proper, there are dozens of state routes and roads crisscrossing the land. Detailed maps are available from the Croatan National Forest Office or online.

KINSTON

In years past you wouldn't find Kinston on many must-see lists, but this formerly prosperous tobacco town two hours northwest of Wilmington has made quite a turnaround in recent years. A couple of locals have spearheaded renewal, opening a renowned restaurant and a brewery with a growing reputation for great craft beer and changing the face of downtown. Add to that a top-of-the-line museum dedicated to the town's Civil War history and a community that's passionate about preserving its past.

Sights

Like many towns that were once prosperous and suddenly experienced a downturn, Kinston is an architectural time capsule. Driving, or better, walking the several downtown blocks of **Queen Street,** the town's main artery, is an education in early-20th-century commercial architecture. The Hotel Kinston is the town's tallest building, an 11-story structure with a ground level that's a crazy blend of art deco and Moorish motifs. The 1914 post office is a big, heavy beaux arts beauty, and the Queen Street Methodist Church is turreted to within an inch of its life. The People's Bank building testifies to the heyday of early-20th-century African American commerce. With its many strange and daring experiments in building styles, Queen Street is a crazy quilt, but the buildings are beautifully complementary in their diversity. In the Herritage Street neighborhood, near the bend of the river, block after block of grand old houses stand in threadbare glory. On the other side of town are shotgun houses, the icon of Southern folk housing, lining the alleys of the old working-class neighborhood.

★ CSS *NEUSE* INTERPRETIVE CENTER

The remains of the Confederate ironclad gunboat CSS *Neuse* are on display in Kinston in a museum located near the spot where she was scuttled in 1865 to keep her out of the hands of the advancing Union Army. All that remains is the core of the 158- by 34-foot hull, but even in such deteriorated condition the *Neuse* is a striking feat of boatbuilding. At the **CSS *Neuse* Interpretive Center** (100 N. Queen St., 252/522-2107, 9am-5pm Tues.-Sat., $5 adults, $4 seniors and military, $3 ages 3-12, free under 3) you can see what remains of the hull, which sat in the river for more than 100 years before it was salvaged. If you're lucky, one of the volunteers will be a Kinston old-timer who can tell you stories about using the *Neuse* as a diving board for summer swims. On display are artifacts including the ironclad's bell, cannonballs and shells, coal rakes, and other small items. The centerpiece is the overhead view of the ironclad's hull. Now outfitted with a ghostly shape showing the original form of the ship, it's an impressive sight. For a full-scale look at the CSS *Neuse,* check out the **CSS *Neuse* II** (Herritage St. and Gordon St., 252/560-2150, www.cssneuseii. org, 10am-4pm Sat. or by appointment, free), a 158-foot facsimile of the gunboat. Climb aboard to feel how tight the quarters were, peer out the gun ports, and imagine sleeping, eating, and fighting on board.

MOTHER EARTH BREWING

Mother Earth Brewing (311 N. Herritage St., 252/208-2437, www.motherearthbrewing. com, brewery tours on the hour 10am-5pm Tues.-Fri. and 1pm-8pm Sat., free, tap room 4pm-10pm Tues.-Thurs., 1pm-10pm Fri.-Sat., 1pm-7pm Sun., trading post 10am-6pm Tues.-Thurs., 10am-8pm Fri., 1pm-9pm Sat.) has been making craft beer in Kinston since 2008 and racking up awards ever since. In 2013, they became the first brewery to attain LEED Gold Certification, and their tap room and distillery are solar powered. Brewery tours are free, but as it is a working brewery, some days the tours may be crowded, limited to certain areas, or canceled altogether. Tours start and end in the **Mother Earth Brewing Tap Room,** solar-powered and serving up the best Mother Earth brews. A mix of original art, exposed brick walls, sleek modern lines, and contemporary lighting make this room one of a kind. Cozy up to the bar or grab a pint to take to a nearby table or to the patio out back. I'm fond of the Dark Cloud Dunkel and Old Neighborhood Oatmeal Porter, but the *kölsch, witbier,* and IPA are also popular.

Mother Earth also operates **Mother Earth Spirits** (same location, call for tour information), where they make gin, rum, and whiskey. As North Carolina laws change regarding distilled spirits, you may be able to purchase on site, but until then, you can find Mother Earth Spirits in ABC Stores across the state; locally you'll find their spirits in cocktails at The Boiler Room, Chef & the Farmer and The Red Room.

Sports and Recreation

Oddly, there's a water park in Kinston. **Lions Water Adventure** (2602 W. Vernon Ave., 252/939-1330, www.lionswateradventure.com, 11:30am-5:30pm Mon.-Sat., 12:30pm-5:30pm Sun., $11, $60 for 6), has three three-story high slides—the zebra slide, a twisty tube ride; the lion slide, a straightforward waterslide with a decent drop at the end; and the low-splash slide. There's a 5,000-square-foot kiddie lagoon, a lazy river longer than a football field, a lap pool, and a heated therapeutic pool. They serve food, mainly kid-friendly bites and snacks, but the water park is close enough to town that you can head out for a real meal with little effort.

In Kinston you can enjoy disc golf or a traditional round. At the **Barnet Disc Golf Course** (100 Sand Clay Rd., 252/939-3332, http://kinstondiscgolf.com, dawn-dusk daily, 18 holes, par 67, free), you'll need to bring your own discs, but this fun course layout rewards aggressive but accurate players. For a day on a regular, albeit short, golf course, at Bill Fay Park there's a **Par 3 Course** (1007 Phillips Rd., 252/939-3356, www.kinstonrec.com, 18 holes, par 54, $6) where you can work on your short game.

Entertainment and Events

Kinston is fortunate to have a great local arts engine, the **Kinston Community Council for the Arts** (KCCA, 400 N. Queen St., 252/527-2517, www.kinstoncca.com, 10am-6pm Tues.-Fri., 10am-2pm Sat.), which has the kind of energy and artistic vision one would expect to find in a much larger city. It occupies an old storefront on Queen Street, remodeled into a gorgeous gallery and studio space. In addition to the many community events hosted here, KCCA has consistently hosted innovative exhibits in the main gallery, including avant-garde photography and collage art, and a recent exhibition of dozens of custom motorcycles.

Every spring, typically the last weekend in April, barbecue enthusiasts flock to Kinston for the **BBQ Festival on the *Neuse*** (www.bbqfestivalontheneuse.com). This four-day festival features competitions pitting barbecue teams against one another in categories such as showmanship, quality, and sauce. During the festival, downtown is crowded with food, smoke from a dozen barbecue cookers, carnival rides, concerts, a wine garden, and beer from Mother Earth Brewing. Many artists come for the opening day's Plein Air Paint Out, a competitive painting event, which awards the winner with an image of their painting for the next upcoming year's festival poster. The Art Fest event invites everyone to create art inspired by the festival; it's a hit with kids as well as adults who shake off their artistic inhibitions. With concerts, fireworks, and heaping plates of 'cue, there's plenty to do, see, and eat.

The Red Room (220 N. Herritage St., 252/520-2000, www.thered-room.com, 8pm-2am Thurs.-Sat.) is a small bar and music

---

1: the Croatan National Forest; **2:** Mother Earth Brewing; **3:** young ospreys in the nest; **4:** Kinston's kitschy-cool Mother Earth Motor Lodge

hall in downtown Kinston, just a couple of blocks from Mother Earth, The Boiler Room, and Chef & the Farmer. They serve Mother Earth's beers and spirits as well as a slate of other North Carolina spirits and a decent selection of wine by the glass and bottle. Check their schedule to see what musical acts will be performing here during your visit.

Food

Kinston's reputation as a food town has been on the rise lately, thanks in large part to a trio of locals—chef Vivian Howard Knight and brewery owners Stephen Hill and Trent Mooring. They collectively opened a renowned restaurant, a top-notch brewery and taproom, and an oyster bar. Though these may be the best known, they're not the only food options in town.

You might know ★ **Chef & the Farmer** (120 W. Gordon St., 252/208-2433, www. chefandthefarmer.com, 5pm-9pm Mon.-Thurs., 5pm-10:30pm Fri.-Sat., $12-30) from the PBS show *A Chef's Life*. Here, chef-owner Vivian Howard Knight elevates the simple Southern food she grew up eating on a farm not far from here into true fine-dining dishes that have been recognized by the James Beard Foundation. The menu changes with the local crops and catch, but a few staples remain, including the wood-fired-oven pizzas, massive burgers, and Pimp My Grits menu (where you can get your grits topped with a variety of interesting cheeses, meats, and veggies). Whether you're there for a multicourse affair (the desserts are fantastic) or just the best grits of your life at the kitchen counter, you'll leave full and happy. And if you're looking for something lighter or you just want to zip in and out, look in the back, where they have a great selection of wine and beer along with an abbreviated food menu.

Queen Street Deli (117 S. Queen St., 252/527-1900, www.queenstreetdeli.com, 9am-7pm Mon.-Fri., breakfast from $2, lunch and dinner from $8) bakes vegan and non-vegan cookies and makes great sandwiches for breakfast and lunch. For breakfast, try the Million Dollar Pound Cake French Toast; at lunch, go for the filling Queen's Chicken Salad, which comes with toasted pecans and cranberries. Their take on the BLT, called Prides Pimento, is another good option made with pimento cheese, sliced tomatoes, and bacon.

The entrepreneurial owners of Mother Earth Brewing and Chef & the Farmer also have opened **The Boiler Room** (108 W. North St., 252/208-2433, www.boilerroomoysterbar. com, 4:30pm-10pm Mon.-Tues., 11am-10pm Wed.-Thurs., 11am-11pm Fri.-Sat.; 11am-8pm Sun., $8-26), an oyster bar, raw bar, and gourmet burger joint so named because of the massive boiler standing in the dining room. One of my favorite restaurants along the coast, the dive-y atmosphere and simple, smartly-done food are a great match for the space, and everything I've eaten—burgers, oysters in any preparation, beef fat fries, a Cheerwine Float—has been good enough to make me mark my calendar for a return trip.

Lovick's Cafe (320 N. Herritage St., 151/523-6854, www.lovickscafe.com, 6am-2pm Mon.-Fri., 6am-11am Sat., closed Sun., breakfast $3-9, lunch $5-12) has been a Kinston fixture since 1941, when Milton and Eva Lovick borrowed $180 and opened Lovick's Quick Lunch. Since then, not much has changed except the prices. Bacon and eggs, pancakes, biscuits, and breakfast sandwiches are served until 1:30 on weekdays; lunch consists of pork chops, hamburger steak, barbecue and barbecue chicken, and their "Dough Burger." The Dough Burger—a flour- and spice-laced hamburger—was on the original menu as a way to make meat, a precious commodity during WWII, go a little further. Strange as it sounds to us today, it's pretty tasty.

The North Carolina Barbecue Trail's eastern terminus is in Ayden, just a short drive from Kinston. Here the world-famous ★ **Skylight Inn** (4618 S. Lee St., Ayden, 252/746-4113, www.skylightinnbbq.com, 10am-7pm Mon.-Sat., under $10) serves eastern North Carolina-style barbecue done up in the traditional manner: chopped and served with a vinegary sauce that brings out the flavor in the pork like no other sauce can. When you pull in to the gravel parking lot, you'll notice a mountain of wood waiting to become the coals in the huge smokehouse just a few steps away. The Jones family has been cooking 'cue since 1830, so they know their way around a hog; their current location dates to 1947 and son Sam Jones has opened his own restaurant a few miles north of here, just outside Greenville.

Accommodations

The O'Neil (200 N. Queen St., 252/208-1130, www.the-oneil.com, from $189), a boutique hotel in the former Farmers & Merchants Bank, stands in the heart of downtown. Construction on this building ran from 1919 to 1924, and it's got that powerful, early-20th-century look about it. The hotel was the vision of Mother Earth's Stephen Hill, and the renovation kept much of the building's character by preserving elements like the main vault and teller windows. There are only a few rooms, but it's an absolutely lovely place.

Another of Hill's visions was the retro-sexy ★ **Mother Earth Motor Lodge** (501 N. Herritage St., 252/520-2000, www.motherearthmotorlodge.com, from $109). This massive remodel converted a derelict motel into a beautiful homage to motels from the '50s through the '70s. Bold colors, a kidney-shaped pool, and modern furniture in each room highlight this cozy lodge, and Mother Earth Brewery, Chef & the Farmer, and everything else in Kinston are within easy walking distance.

There's only one bed-and-breakfast in town. **The Bentley** (117 W. Capitola Ave., 252/523-2337, $169-184) has four beautiful guest rooms and 13 acres of gardens, lawns, and woods. The house and grounds are large enough to host lavish events like weddings and receptions but have a luxe, homey feel you don't find in many places. As for hotels, the **Hampton Inn** (1382 U.S. 258 S., 252/523-1400, www.hamptoninn.com, around $110) is convenient and comfortable, and the staff are especially nice.

CLIFFS OF THE NEUSE STATE PARK

In Seven Springs, a historic little town about 30 minutes' drive southwest of Kinston, is **Cliffs of the Neuse State Park** (240 Park Entrance Rd., 919/778-6234, http://ncparks.gov, visitors center 9am-5pm daily, 7am-6pm Dec.-Feb., 7am-8pm March-April, 7am-9pm May-Sept., 7am-8pm Oct.-Nov.), a highly unusual blend of environments, including high red bluffs overlooking the Neuse River, hardwood and pine forests, and cypress swamps. Hiking trails follow the cliff line through Spanish moss-draped forests. Boating and swimming (11am-6:45pm daily late May-early Sept.) are permitted at the park's artificial lake during the summer; swimming is allowed only when a lifeguard is on duty. Boats must be rented ($5/hour)—no private watercraft are permitted.

Family camping ($20/night) is available year-round. There is a washhouse with hot showers and electricity, and several water stations are located in the campsite. Note that unless you have a medical emergency, when you're camping you must stay inside the park from the time the gates close until 8am the next morning—so no slipping out for a late supper.

GETTING THERE AND AROUND

Kinston sits at the junction of U.S. 70, U.S. 258, and N.C. 58. Raleigh is 80 minutes west along U.S. 70; New Bern is 36 miles east on U.S. 70, and Greenville is 30 minutes north on N.C. 11. You can be in Atlantic Beach in 80 minutes by following U.S. 70 east.

Beaufort and Vicinity

The small waterside town of Beaufort has unusual problems stemming from its geography—there's also a Beaufort in South Carolina—and the idiosyncrasies of regional Southern dialects. This Beaufort is pronounced in the French way, "BO-fert," while the name of town in South Carolina is pronounced "BYEW-fert." Pronunciation notwithstanding, Beaufort is a beautiful little town. The third-oldest colonial settlement in North Carolina, it matches its elders, Bath and New Bern, in the charm department. Once North Carolina's window to the world, Beaufort was a surprisingly cosmopolitan place that would often receive news from London or Barbados sooner than from other colonies. Today, you'll find the streets crowded with old homes, many built in that double-porch, steep-sided roof style that shows off the early cultural ties to the Caribbean.

It was long rumored that the pirate Blackbeard ran his ship aground in the inlet here, which is plausible because he did frequent Beaufort, and his pirate base at Ocracoke Island isn't far away. In the late 1990s the rumor was proved to be true: In Beaufort Inlet the *Queen Anne's Revenge,* the French slave ship that Blackbeard captured in 1717 and made into the flagship of his dreaded fleet, was found mired in nearly three centuries of silt. Blackbeard had increased his ship's arsenal to 40 cannons, a fact that helped confirm the identity of the wreck. A few months after he ran his flagship aground, Blackbeard himself was killed at Ocracoke after putting up a tremendous fight with privateers (pirate hunters) sent from Virginia. In the intervening time between the shipwreck and its discovery, incredible artifacts from the *Queen Anne's Revenge* washed up on the shores here, a number of which are on display at the North Carolina Maritime Museum.

From the Maritime Museum, a short walk leads to Beaufort's cafés, boutiques, antiques shops, restaurants, and dock. Across the waterway you can see Carrot Island, home to a herd of wild horses, one of the few remaining in eastern North Carolina. You can also catch a ride on a ferry or tour boat to Cape Lookout National Seashore, where the stunning Cape Lookout Lighthouse has guarded the coast for more than 150 years. Or simply tour the marshes for a close-up glimpse of the area's wildlife.

SIGHTS

★ North Carolina Maritime Museum

The **North Carolina Maritime Museum at Beaufort** (315 Front St., 252/540-7740, www.ncmaritimemuseums.com, 9am-5pm Mon.-Fri., 10am-5pm Sat., 1pm-5pm Sun., free) is among the best museums in the state and one of three state maritime museums; the others are in Southport and on Roanoke Island. Even if you don't think you're interested in boat-building or maritime history, you'll get caught up in the exhibits here. Historic watercraft, reconstructions, and models of boats are on display, well presented in rich historical and cultural context. The display of artifacts and weapons recovered from Blackbeard's *Queen Anne's Revenge* wows visitors. There's also a lot about the state's fishing history, including related occupations, such as the highly complex skill of net-hanging. Far from being limited to the few species caught by today's fisheries, early North Carolinians did big business hunting sea turtles, porpoises, and whales.

★ Old Burying Ground

One of the most beautiful places in North Carolina is Beaufort's **Old Burying Ground** (Anne St., www.beauforthistoricsite.org, dawn-dusk daily, tours through Beaufort Historic Site 2:30pm Tues.-Thurs. June-Sept.,

Beaufort and Vicinity

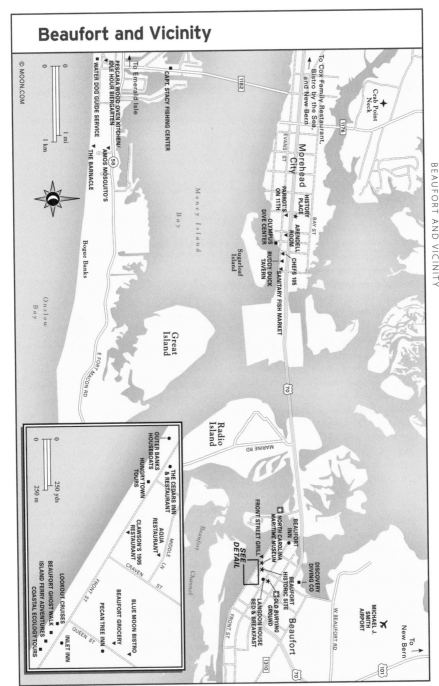

© MOON.COM

0   1 mi

0   1 km

Crab Point Neck

To Cox Family Restaurant, Bistro by the Sea, and New Bern

To New Bern

To Emerald Isle

Morehead City

EVANS ST

BAY ST

1182

1176

CAPT. STACY FISHING CENTER

PESCARA WOOD OVEN KITCHEN/ IDLE HOUR BIERGARTEN

WATER DOG GUIDE SERVICE

AMOS MOSQUITO'S

THE BARNACLE

58

M o n e y B a y

Bogue Banks

O n s l o w B a y

E FORT MACON RD

Great Island

Sugarloaf Island

PARROT'S ON 11TH

OLYMPUS DIVE CENTER

HISTORY PLACE

ARENDELL ROOM

CHEFS 105

RUDDY DUCK TAVERN

SANITARY FISH MARKET

70

Radio Island

MARINE RD

Beaufort Channel

70

1310

70

101

MICHAEL J. SMITH AIRPORT

W BEAUFORT RD

Beaufort

DISCOVERY DIVING CO

NORTH CAROLINA MARITIME MUSEUM

BEAUFORT INN

BEAUFORT HISTORIC SITE

OLD BURYING GROUND

LANGDON HOUSE BED & BREAKFAST

FRONT STREET GRILL

SEE DETAIL

0   250 yds

0   250 m

OUTER BANKS HOUSEBOATS

THE CEDARS INN & RESTAURANT

HUNGRY TOWN TOURS

AQUA RESTAURANT

CLAWSON'S 1905 RESTAURANT

MIDDLE LN

CRAVEN ST

FRONT ST

QUEEN ST

BLUE MOON BISTRO

BEAUFORT GROCERY

PECAN TREE INN

LOOKOUT CRUISES

BEAUFORT GHOST WALK

ISLAND FERRY ADVENTURES

COASTAL ECOLOGY TOURS

INLET INN

$10 adults, $5 children), a picturesque cemetery that's quite small by the standards of some old Carolina towns and crowded with 18th- and 19th-century headstones. Huge old live oaks, Spanish moss, wisteria, and resurrection ferns, which unfurl and turn green after a rainstorm, give the Burying Ground an irresistibly Gothic feel. Many of the headstones reflect the maritime heritage of the town, including a sea captain whose epitaph reads:

> The form that fills this silent grave
> Once tossed on ocean's rolling wave
> But in a port securely fast
> He's dropped his anchor here at last.

Captain Otway Burns, an early privateer who spent much time in Beaufort, is buried here; his grave is easy to spot, as it is topped by a cannon from his ship, the *Snap Dragon*. Nearby is another of the graveyard's famous burials, the "Little Girl Buried in a Barrel of Rum." This unfortunate child died at sea and was placed in a cask of rum to preserve her body for burial on land. Visitors often bring toys and trinkets to leave on her grave, which is marked by a simple wooden plank. Though hers is the most gaudily festooned, you'll see evidence of this old tradition of funerary gifts on other graves here as well, most often coins and shells. This is a tradition found throughout the coastal South and the Caribbean, with roots tracing back to Africa. Feel free to add to her haul of goodies, but beliefs hold that it's not karmically advisable to tamper with those already here.

Beaufort Historic Site

The **Beaufort Historic Site** (100 Block Turner St., 252/728-5225, www.beauforthistoricsite.org, 9:30am-5pm Mon.-Sat.) recreates life in late-18th- and early-19th-century Beaufort in several restored historic buildings. The 1770s "jump and a half" (1.5-story) Leffers Cottage reflects middle-class life in its day; a merchant, whaler, or, as in this case, a schoolmaster would have lived in such a home. The Josiah Bell and John Manson Houses, both from the 1820s, reflect the Caribbean-influenced architecture prevalent in the early days of the coastal South. A restored apothecary shop, a 1790s wooden courthouse, and a haunted 1820s jail that was used into the 1950s are among the other important structures. There are tours led by costumed interpreters (10am and 2:30pm, Mon.-Sat., $12 adults, $6 kids) as well as driving tours of the old town on a double-decker bus (11am and 1:30pm Mon., Wed., Fri., and Sat., and 1:30pm Tues. and Thurs. April-Oct., $12 adults, $6 children), and tours of the Old Burying Ground (2:30pm Tues.-Thurs. June-Sept., $10 adults, $5 children).

SPORTS AND RECREATION
Diving

North Carolina's coast is a surprisingly good place for scuba diving. The **Discovery Diving Company** (414 Orange St., 252/728-2265, www.discoverydiving.com, $70-115 per excursion) leads half-day and full-day scuba trips to explore the reefs and dozens of fascinating shipwrecks nearby. The water here is often exceptional—hence the name Crystal Coast—and warm, both of which make for a great day underwater.

Cruises and Tours

Hungry Town Tours (400 Front St., 252/648-1011, www.hungrytowntours.com) offers bicycle and walking tours of Beaufort on a number of themes. Culinary bike tours ($59-75) take you through town for a mini-history tour and stops at several restaurants. Sightseeing bike tours ($20) get you out and about to see some of the town's prettiest spots, including locations from and inspired by Beaufort author Nicholas Sparks. Walking tours ($20-69) range from sightseeing and history tours to culinary-themed walks. Combined with the bus tour from the Historic Site, you'll have a

---

1: Boaters love Beaufort and Morehead City for the convenient docks. **2:** Take a ride out to Cape Lookout on this catamaran. **3:** Beaufort Historic Site; **4:** Beaufort's Old Burying Ground

good sense of the town's past and present by the time you're through.

Coastal Ecology Tours (252/241-6866, www.goodfortunesails.com) runs tours of the Cape Lookout National Seashore and other island locations in the area on the *Good Fortune*, a 41-foot ketch (that's a sailboat), as well as a variety of half-day, full-day, overnight, and short trips to snorkel, shell, kayak, and bird-watch. There are also cruises to Morehead City restaurants and other educational and fun trips. Prices range from $120/ person for a 2.5-hour dolphin-watching tour to $600 plus meals for an off-season overnight boat rental.

Island Ferry Adventures (610 Front St., 252/728-4129, www.islandferryadventures. com, $10-30 adults, $5-10 children, ferry $15-30 adults, $10-20 children) runs dolphin-watching tours, trips to collect shells at Cape Lookout, and trips to see the wild ponies of Shackleford Banks. Lookout Cruises (600 Front St., 252/504-7245, www.lookoutcruises. com, $35-80 adults, $15-70 under age 13) carries sightseers on lovely catamaran rides in the Beaufort and Core Sound region, out to Cape Lookout, and on morning dolphin-watching trips.

Port City Tour Company leads a Beaufort Ghost Walk (108 Middle Ln., 252/772-9925, http://pctourco.com, $16) through town. Highlights include supposedly haunted homes, tales of Blackbeard and other ghost pirates, ghost ships, mysterious murders, and more. Many people report taking photos in the cemetery and seeing ghostly figures, orbs, and other unexplained phenomena in the resulting images. If you'd like something a little less scary, opt for the Pirate Walk ($16), where you'll hear tales of Blackbeard, Calico Jack, Anne Bonny, and Stede Bonnet.

There's also a pair of escape rooms ($25) run by Port City Tour Company. Race the clock to "escape" (or solve the mystery or save the world) by solving puzzles and using the clues found in the room to lead you to your end goal. Puzzle themes vary, but there's always a pirate-themed room here.

Take a Shackleford Wild Horse and Shelling Safari (252/838-1167, www.shacklefordwildhorseandshellingsafari.com, $33 adults, $32 Seniors and Military, $ 23 kids ages 3-11, free age 2 and under), departing from Grayden Paul Park at 702 Front St., to catch sight of the Banker ponies on the small islands here. Your tour starts with a talk about the history of the Banker ponies and of the area, then you'll search the dunes and woods and shoreline for the horses, after, you'll spend time shelling, searching for conchs, whelks, and more.

FOOD

For generations, local families have plied the waters off Beaufort to earn a living and catch fish for their families. To ensure residents and visitors dine at eateries utilizing locally caught seafood when possible, Carteret Catch (http://carteretcatch.org) provides a list of such restaurants. Not only does this help the local fishing industry, it allows chefs to provide the best and freshest seafood possible, meaning your dinner tastes even better.

★ Beaufort Grocery (117 Queen St., 252/728-3899, www.beaufortgrocery.com, 11:30am-2:30pm and 5:30pm-late Mon. and Wed.-Sat., 11am-2pm Sun., $23-42), despite its humble name, is a sophisticated little eatery. Lunch features salads and crusty sandwiches along with Damn Good Gumbo and specialty soups. In the evening the café atmosphere gives way to that of a more formal gourmet dining room. For starters, the ahi tuna napoleon is both beautiful and delicious, and Aunt Marion's Apple and Onion Salad makes an interesting plate to share. Some of the best entrées include Thai chicken curry; duck two ways (seared and leg confit); a whole rack of lamb, served with a chèvre and mint *gremolata*, and a New York strip done in the Korean barbecue *bulgogi* style. Try the cheesecake for dessert.

Weather permitting, you must dine on the patio at City Kitchen (232 W. Beaufort Rd., Unit A, 252/648-8141, 5:30pm-8:30pm Tues.-Thurs., 5:30pm-9pm Fri.-Sat., $15-26) because the sunsets are good enough to make you almost forget to order dessert. The rib eye is a star dish here, as is the Duck Bolognese, though it seems that every table in the restaurant orders the sticky toffee pudding for dessert.

★ **Aqua Restaurant** (114 Middle Lane, 252/728-7777, www.aquaexperience.com, 5:30pm-9pm Tues.-Thurs., 5:30pm-10pm Fri.-Sat., small plates $8-14, big plates $23-28) uses local seafood in a number of their dishes, including a fresh catch tostada, shrimp and grits, and bouillabaisse. Along with local seafood, they use locally and regionally sourced produce and meats. The menu changes frequently, but structurally it's always composed of tapas, small plates, salads, and big plates. With a number of vegetarian and gluten-free items, the menu is amenable to most dietary needs.

Clawson's 1905 Restaurant (425 Front St., 252/728-2133, www.clawsonsrestaurant. com, 11:30am-9pm Mon.-Thurs., 11:30am-9:30pm Fri.-Sat., 11am-3pm Sun., lunch $8-21, dinner $10-30) was a grocery store long before it was a restaurant. Starting in 1905, Clawson's sold canned goods, fresh produce, and freshly baked bread until the Great Depression forced it to close in 1934. Now a restaurant, it serves everything from burgers to ribs, but the specialty is seafood. It's hard to beat their lump crab cakes or fried seafood plate, but one standout dish is the mahi mahi, grilled and served over tortellini with sweet peas and a champagne dill sauce.

The crab cakes from **The Spouter Inn Restaurant and Bakery** (218 Front St., 252/728-5190, www.thespouterinn.com, 11am-9pm daily, lunch and brunch $9-17, dinner $15-36) will keep you coming back, but dishes like the linguine and clams and the seafood mixed grill are dinner staples. At lunch, go for one of their fresh seafood sandwiches or a burger.

If you're traveling with a cooler and want to buy some local seafood to take home, try the **Fishtowne Seafood Center** (100 Wellons Dr., 252/728-6644, www.fishtowneseafood.

com, 9am-6pm Mon.-Sat.). Fresh fish selections include flounder, grouper, speckled trout, red snapper, trigger fish, redfish (or drum), spots, tuna, and black bass. Include in that mix the fresh shrimp, clams, oysters (in season), and crabs and you have a great mix of seafood. The website lists what is seasonally available.

ACCOMMODATIONS

Catty-corner to the Old Burying Grounds is the ★ **Langdon House Bed and Breakfast** (135 Craven St., 252/728-5499, www.langdonhouse.com, $137-238). One of the oldest buildings in town, this gorgeous house was built in the 1730s on a foundation of English ballast stones. Unlike most other B&Bs, Langdon House allows guests to customize their breakfast (and overall room rate) by selecting from options that range from coffee and tea only to the two-course Hallmark Breakfast, which includes fresh fruit, waffles, French toast, omelets, and more; it's quite a production.

The **Beaufort Inn** (101 Ann St., 252/728-2600, www.beaufort-inn.com, $104-254) is a large hotel on Gallants Channel, along one side of the colonial district. It's an easy walk to the main downtown attractions, and the hotel's outdoor hot tub and balconies have great views. The **Pecan Tree Inn** (116 Queen St., 800/728-7871, www.pecantree.com, $145-195) is such a grand establishment that the town threw a parade in honor of the laying of its cornerstone in 1866. The house is still splendid, as are the 5,000-square-foot gardens. The **Inlet Inn** (601 Front St., 800/554-5466, www.inlet-inn.com, $85-185) has one of the best locations in town, right on the water near where many of the ferry and tour boats land. If you're planning to go dolphin-watching or hop the ferry to Cape Lookout, you can get ready at a leisurely pace and just step outside to the docks. Even in high season, prices are quite reasonable.

Beaufort Harbour Suites (313 Cedar St., 252/728-3483, www.beaufortharboursuites. com, from $125 in summer, from $90 in winter; pet-friendly rooms from $155 summer, from $120 winter) has 16 suites with full kitchens, and pet-friendly rooms.

MOREHEAD CITY

Giovanni da Verrazzano may have been the first European to set foot in present-day Morehead City when he sailed into Bogue Inlet. It wasn't until the mid-19th century that the town came into being, built as the terminus of the North Carolina Railroad to connect the state's overland commerce to the sea. Despite its late start, Morehead City has been a busy place. During the Civil War it was the site of major encampments by both armies. A series of horrible hurricanes in the 1890s, culminating in 1899's San Ciriaco Hurricane, brought hundreds of refugees from the towns along what is now the Cape Lookout National Seashore. They settled in a neighborhood that they called Promise Land, and many of their descendants are still here. The Atlantic and North Carolina Railroad operated a large hotel here in the 1880s, ushering in Morehead's role as a tourism spot, and the bridge to the Bogue Banks a few decades later increased holiday traffic considerably.

Morehead is also an official state port, one of the best deepwater harbors on the Atlantic Coast. This mixture of tourism and gritty commerce gives Morehead City a likeable, real-life feel missing in many coastal towns today.

Sights

Morehead City's history is on display at the **History Museum of Carteret County** (1008 Arendell St., 252/247-7533, www. carterethistory.org, 10am-4pm Tues.-Fri., and 10am-4pm first Sat. each month). There are many interesting and eye-catching historical artifacts on display, but the most striking exhibit is that of a carriage, clothes, and other items pertaining to Morehead City's Emeline Piggott, considered a heroine by the Confederacy. She was a busy woman all through the Civil War, working as a nurse, a spy, and a smuggler. The day she was

captured, they found 30 pounds of contraband hidden in her skirts, including Union troop movement plans, a collection of gloves, several dozen skeins of silk, needles, toothbrushes, a pair of boots, and five pounds of candy.

Sports and Recreation

Many of this region's most important historic and natural sites are underwater. From Morehead City's **Olympus Dive Center** (713 Shepard St., 252/726-9432, www. olympusdiving.com, 6am-8pm daily, intro lessons from $340, advanced lessons from $90, half-day charters from $70, full day from $130), scuba divers of all levels of experience can take charter trips to dozens of natural and artificial reefs that teem with fish, including the ferocious-looking but not terribly dangerous eight-foot-long sand tiger shark. This is the Graveyard of the Atlantic, so there are many shipwrecks to choose from, including an 18th-century schooner, a luxury liner, a German U-boat, and many Allied commercial and military ships that fell victim to the U-boats that infested this coast during World War II.

Inshore fishing has its own fans, and **Water Dog Guide Service** (252/728-7907 or 919/423-6310, www.waterdogguideservice. com, tours from $325) knows where to find the fish, including speckled trout, flounder, and red drum, in the sounds, marshes, and creeks. They also fish at near-shore wrecks and reefs for bluefish, mahi mahi, and Spanish mackerel. Check their website to see what's biting, and plan a trip around the red drum spawn, when red drum invade the marsh in huge numbers. Or try fly fishing for false albacore.

Crystal Coast Ecotours (252/808-3354, www.crystalcoastecotours.com, $100 per hour, $325 half-day, $425 full day) is run by a marine biologist with a passion for introducing people to the world of the marshes, creeks, barrier islands, and waterways where she makes her home. Tours lead you to secluded barrier islands, the Cape Lookout National Seashore, and even into near-ocean waters so you can explore the area by birding, dolphin-watching, shelling, snorkeling, and watching wild horses.

Entertainment and Nightlife

Seafood is a serious art in Morehead City. The enormous **North Carolina Seafood Festival** (252/726-6273, www.ncseafoodfestival.org), the state's second-largest fair (behind the State Fair in Raleigh), takes place here the first weekend in October. The city's streets shut down, and some 150,000 visitors descend on the waterfront. Festivities kick off with a blessing of the fleet, followed by music, fireworks, competitions such as the flounder fling (where you compete for distance by flinging a frozen flounder), fishing tourneys, and, of course, loads of food to sample.

Arendell Room (715 Arendell St., 252/240-2753, www.arendellroom.com, 5pm-midnight Mon.-Thurs., 5pm-2am Fri.-Sat.) is an unexpected find here: an upscale cocktail bar. They make drinks both classic and nouveau, and although they open at 5, the bartender is here most of the day, squeezing, juicing, peeling, slicing, dicing, and macerating all of their garnishes, juices, mixes, bitters, and cocktail accouterements. Order off the menu, or do what I do and opt for the Bartender's Choice; after a few questions about what you like in a cocktail, the barkeep will whip up something just for you.

Food

The ★ **Sanitary Fish Market** (501 Evans St., 252/247-3111, www.sanitaryfishmarket.com, 11:30am-9pm daily, $13-31) is not only the most widely known eatery in Morehead City, it's probably its best-known institution. The odd name reflects its 1930s origins as a seafood market that was bound by its lease and its fastidious landlord to be kept as clean as possible. Today, it's a huge family seafood restaurant, and they claim to have served more than 7.6 million pounds of shrimp to 15 million customers. Of particular note are its famous hush puppies, which have a well-deserved reputation as some of the best in the state, and the monstrous Famous Deluxe Shore Dinner—soup, fried fish, shrimp, oysters, scallops, soft-shell crab, fries, and, of course, hush puppies.

El's Drive-In (3706 Arendell St., 252/726-3002, www.elsdrivein.com, 10:30am-10pm Sun.-Thurs., 10:30am-11pm Fri.-Sat., around $7), a tiny place across from Carteret Community College, seems like it has been around almost as long as the town. It's most famous for its shrimp burgers but serves all sorts of fried delights. It's a hit among locals and road-food fans, and most everyone agrees that the shakes are great, as are the onion rings. Be forewarned: It's car-side service, and the place is mobbed with gulls at times; they'll swoop down and snatch a French fry.

The Banks Grill (2900 Arendell St. Suite 3, 252/499-9044, www.thebanksgrill.com, 7am-2pm Mon.- Fri., 7:30am-2pm Sat.-Sun., breakfast $3-9, lunch $8-12) serves breakfast and lunch of the stick-to-your-ribs variety. At breakfast, the XXL Buttermilk Biscuit—served with a pair of fried eggs, cheddar cheese, breakfast meat, and topped with sausage gravy or creamy tomato gravy (optional)—should be on your radar. When it's lunch time, go for the Shack-style Steak and Cheese, their spin on a cheesesteak.

The **Bistro-by-the-Sea** (4031 Arendell St., 252/247-2777, www.bistro-by-the-sea.com, 5pm-9:30pm Tues.-Thurs., 5pm-9:45pm Fri.-Sat., $10-25) participates in Carteret Catch, a program that ensures that fresh, locally caught seafood graces area tables. They serve a number of seafood dishes, but don't just stick to the sea; they also offer steaks, prime rib, and even fresh calf liver. Most interesting, though, are the small plates, with items such as a half-slab of baby back ribs, baked oysters, or a Japanese bento box. Grab a seat at the piano bar on Friday and Saturday nights; it's entertaining.

Ruddy Duck Tavern (509 Evans St., 252/726-7500, www.ruddyducktavern.com, 11am-10pm daily, $9-22) has a fun bar, a few outdoor tables, and a menu that takes a playful international approach to seafood and area delicacies. Pecan crusted flounder has some Caribbean flavors, their jambalaya is spicy and packed with local seafood, and the crispy duckling is a hard dish to pass up.

Cox Family Restaurant (4109 Arendell St., 252/726-6961, 6am-9pm Mon.-Sat., 6am-8pm Sun., breakfast $2-11, lunch and dinner $3-16) also has served down-home cooking for many years and is known for its friendly staff and coterie of local regulars. The food here is anything but fancy; it's simple home cooking, but it's very well done.

Floyd's 1921 Restaurant (400 Bridges St., 252/727-1921, www.floyds1921.com, noon-late Tues.-Sat., noon-4pm Sun., $10-34) serves a blend of southern classics and contemporary southern cuisine. You're just as likely to see meatloaf being delivered to a table as you are fried oysters or shrimp and grits. Their wine and spirits menu is extensive.

HARKERS ISLAND

The Core Sound region stretches east-northeast from Beaufort, many miles up to the Pamlico Sound. Filled with birds, boats, and not much else, it's a hauntingly beautiful landscape. As along much of the North Carolina coast, the marshes and pocosins serve as way stations for countless flocks of migratory birds as they migrate, adding greatly to the year-round bird population. Fishing has always been a way of life here, but so has hunting, particularly hunting waterfowl. In earlier generations, men who earned a living fishing most of the year had sideline businesses hunting birds. They ate the birds they shot, sold the feathers for women's hats, trained bird dogs, and worked as birding outfitters to visiting hunters. Consequentially, many Down Easterners became expert decoy carvers. The beautifully carved decoys started as functional pieces, but today most are produced as art for art's sake; either way, the tradition survives.

Woodworking on a much grander scale has defined the culture of the people of Harkers Island, as it is home to generations of boat builders whose creations are as elegant as they are reliable. Keep an eye out as you drive through; you may see boats under construction in backyards and garages—not canoes or dinghies, but full-size fishing boats.

To get to Harkers Island, follow U.S. 70 east from Beaufort around the dogleg that skirts the North River. East of the town of Otway, you'll see Harkers Island Road; go right and head south toward Straits. Straits Road will take you through the town of Straits and then across a bridge over the straits themselves, finally ending up on Harkers Island.

★ Core Sound Waterfowl Museum

The **Core Sound Waterfowl Museum** (1785 Island Rd., 252/728-1500, www.coresound. com, 10am-5pm Mon.-Sat., 2pm-5pm Sun., $5), which occupies a modern building on Shell Point next to the Cape Lookout National Seashore headquarters, is a community-wide labor of love. The museum is home to exhibits crafted by members of the communities it represents, depicting the Down East maritime life through decoys, nets, and other tools of the trades as well as everyday household objects, beautiful quilts, and other utilitarian folk arts. This is a sophisticated modern institution, but its community roots are evident in touching details like the index-card labels, written in the careful script of elderly women, explaining what certain objects are, what they were used for, and who made them. The museum hosts Core Sound Community Nights on the second Tuesday of every month. These get-togethers are a taste of the old home days when families and long-lost friends reunite over home-cooked food to reminisce about community history and talk about their hopes and concerns for the future.

The museum's gift shop has a nice selection of books and other items related to Down East culture. Be sure to pick up a copy of *Island Born and Bred: A Collection of Harkers Island Food, Fun, Fact and Fiction* by the Harkers Island United Methodist Women. This cookbook has become a regional classic for its wonderful blend of authentic family recipes and community stories. You may also be able to find a Core Sound Christmas Tree, made by Harvey and Sons in nearby Davis. This old family fishery has made a hit in recent years manufacturing small Christmas trees out of recycled crab pots. It's a fun, playful item, but it carries significant messages about the culture of the Core Sound region.

Core Sound Decoy Carvers Guild

Twenty years ago, over a pot of stewed clams, some decoy-carving friends Down East decided to found the **Core Sound Decoy Carvers Guild** (1575 Harkers Island Rd., 252/838-8818, www.decoyguild.com, call for hours). The guild is open to the public and gives demonstrations, competitions, and classes for grown-ups and children; the museum shop is a nice place to browse. It's also a cultural spot akin to the Appalachian craft guilds you find in the mountains: members preserve and celebrate history and a deep-rooted way of life for families around here. Spend a little time talking with decoy artists old and young and see for yourself just how far down the family tree this art goes.

Events

The Core Sound Decoy Carvers Guild also hosts the **Core Sound Decoy Festival,** usually held in the early winter. Several thousand people come to this annual event—more than the number of permanent residents on Harkers Island—to buy, swap, and teach the art of making decoys.

Food

Captain's Choice Restaurant (977 Island Rd., 252/728-7122, 10am-9pm Tues.-Thurs., 7am-9am Fri.-Sun., closed Mon., breakfast $2-10, lunch and dinner $6-25) is a great place to try traditional Down East chowder. Usually made of clams but sometimes with other shellfish or fish, chowder in Carteret County is a point of pride. The point is the flavor of the seafood itself, which must be extremely fresh and not hidden behind lots of milk and spices. Captain's Choice serves chowder in the old-time way—with dumplings. Breakfast is weekend only. If you want a taste of seafood done in the local style, the Down East Seafood Buffet on Friday and Saturday nights brings in old timers who claim it tastes like home used to.

Fish Hook Grill (980 Island Rd., 252/728-1790, 11am-9pm Sat.-Mon., 11am-10pm Fri., 11am-3pm Sun.., $6-26) is a small-town restaurant serving big portions of seafood, burgers, and more. They're known locally for their chowder, crab cakes, potato salad, hush puppies, fried oysters, coleslaw, and, well, just about everything on the menu. Check to see if Miss Faye, the owner and operator, is here when you visit; if she is, stop by and say hello. She's as friendly as the food is good.

VILLAGE OF CEDAR ISLAND

For a beautiful afternoon's drive, head back to the mainland and follow U.S. 70 north. You'll go through some tiny communities—Williston, Davis, Stacy—and if you keep bearing north on Highway 12 when U.S. 70 heads south to the town of Atlantic, you'll eventually reach the tip of the peninsula and the village of Cedar Island. This little fishing town has the amazing ambience of being at the end of the earth. From the peninsula's shore you can barely see land across the sounds. The ferry to Ocracoke departs from Cedar Island, a two-hour-plus ride across Pamlico Sound. The beach here is absolutely gorgeous, and horses roam on it; they're not the famous wild horses of the Outer Banks, but they move around freely as if they were.

A spectacular location for bird-watching is the **Cedar Island National Wildlife Refuge** (U.S. 70, east of Atlantic, 252/926-4021, www.fws.gov). Nearly all of its 14,500 acres are brackish marshland, and it's often visited in season by redhead ducks, buffleheads, surf scoters, and many other species. While there are trails for hiking and cycling, this refuge is primarily intended as a haven for the birds. That said, they do allow hunting here and have a 200-acre area designated for waterfowl hunts. Fishing is allowed here, too, but both activities are closely regulated, so check on rules, seasons, permits, and other information before you head out.

GETTING THERE AND AROUND
Car
One of the state's main east-west routes, U.S. 70 provides easy access to most of the destinations in this chapter. From Raleigh to Beaufort is a little over 150 miles, but keep in mind that long stretches of the highway are in commercial areas with plenty of traffic and red lights. U.S. 70 continues past Beaufort, snaking up along Core Sound through little Down East towns like Otway and Davis and finally ending in the town of Atlantic. At Sea Level, Highway 12 branches to the north, across the Cedar Island Wildlife Refuge and ending at the Cedar Island-Ocracoke Ferry.

Down south, to reach the Bogue Banks (Atlantic Beach, Emerald Isle, and neighboring beaches) by road, bridges cross Bogue Sound on Highway 58 at both Morehead City and Cedar Point (not to be confused with Cedar Island).

Ferry
Inland, a 20-minute free passenger and vehicle ferry (800/339-9156, pets allowed) crosses the Neuse River between Cherry Branch (near Cherry Point) and Minesott Beach in Pamlico County every 30 minutes.

Lower Outer Banks

The southern stretch of the Outer Banks of North Carolina contains some of the region's most diverse destinations. Core and Shackleford Banks lie within Cape Lookout National Seashore, the fifth national seashore established in the country and the second in North Carolina (Cape Hatteras National Seashore to the north was the first in the country). It's a wild place, a maritime environment populated by birds, herds of wild horses, and not a single human. The towns of Bogue Banks—Atlantic Beach, Salter Path, Pine Knoll Shores, Indian Beach, and Emerald Isle—are classic beach towns with clusters of motels and restaurants and even a few towel shops and miniature golf courses. Both areas are great fun; Cape Lookout especially so for ecotours and history, and Bogue Banks for those looking for a day on the beach followed by an evening chowing down on good fried seafood.

TOP EXPERIENCE

★ CAPE LOOKOUT NATIONAL SEASHORE
Cape Lookout National Seashore (visitors center at 1800 Islands Rd., Harkers Island, 252/728-2250, www.nps.gov/calo) is an otherworldly place: 56 miles of beach stretched out across four barrier islands, a long tape of sand seemingly so vulnerable to nature that it's hard to believe there were ever any towns on its banks. There were: Cape Lookout was settled in the early 1700s, and people in the towns of the south Core Banks made their living in fisheries that might seem brutal by today's terms: whaling and catching dolphins and sea turtles, among the more mundane species. Portsmouth was an important port to the early economy of North Carolina. Portsmouth declined slowly, but catastrophe rained down all at once on the people of the southerly Shackleford Banks, who were driven

out of their own long-established communities to start new lives on the mainland when a series of terrible hurricanes decimated the islands in the 1890s.

Among the dunes, patches of maritime forest fight for each drop of fresh water, while ghost forests of trees that were defeated by advancing saltwater look on. Along the endless beach, loggerhead turtles come ashore to lay their eggs, and in the waters just off the strand, three other species of sea turtles are sometimes seen. Wild horses roam the beaches and dunes, and dolphins frequent both the ocean and sound sides of the islands. Other mammals are all of the small and scrappy variety: raccoons, rodents, otters, and rabbits. Like all of coastal North Carolina, it's a great place for bird-watching as it's located in a heavily traveled migratory flyway. Pets are allowed on leash; the wild ponies on Shackleford Banks can pose a threat to dogs that get among them, and the dogs can frighten the horses, so be careful not to let them mingle.

Portsmouth Village

Portsmouth Village, at the northern tip of the Cape Lookout National Seashore, is a peaceful but eerie place. The village looks much as it did 100 years ago, with the handsome houses and churches all tidy and in good repair. But with the exception of caretakers and summer volunteers, no one has lived here since 1970 when the last two residents moved away. What had once been a town of 700 people and one of the most important shipping ports in North Carolina died. Founded before the Revolution, Portsmouth was a lightering station, a port where huge seagoing ships that had traveled across the ocean would stop and have their cargo removed for transport across the shallow sounds in smaller boats. There is a visitors center located at Portsmouth, open varying hours April-October, where you can learn about the village before embarking on a stroll to explore the quiet streets.

In its busy history, Portsmouth was captured by the British during the War of 1812

and by Union troops in the Civil War, underscoring its strategic importance. By the time of the Civil War, though, its utility as a way station was already declining. An 1846 hurricane opened a new inlet at Hatteras, which quickly became a busy shipping channel. After abolition, the town's lightering trade was no longer profitable without enslaved people to perform much of the labor. The fishing and lifesaving businesses kept the town afloat for a few more generations, but Portsmouth was never the same.

Once a year, an unusual thing happens: Boatloads of people arrive on shore, the church bell rings, and the sound of hymns come through the open church doors. At the Portsmouth Homecoming, descendants of the people who lived here come from all over to pay tribute to their ancestral home. They have an old-time dinner on the grounds and then tour the little village together. It's like a family reunion with the town itself as the matriarch. The rest of the year, Portsmouth receives visitors and National Park Service caretakers, but one senses that it's already looking forward to the next spring, when its children will come home again.

Shackleford Banks

The once-busy villages of Diamond City and Shackleford Banks are like Portsmouth in that, although they have not been occupied for many years, its residents' descendants retain a profound attachment to their ancestors' homes. Diamond City and nearby communities met a spectacular end. The hurricane season of 1899 culminated in the San Ciriaco Hurricane, a disastrous storm that destroyed homes and forests, killed livestock, flooded gardens with saltwater, and washed the Shackleford dead out of their graves. The Bankers saw the writing on the wall and moved to the mainland en masse, carrying as much of their property as would fit on boats. Some actually floated their houses across Core Sound. Harkers Island absorbed most of the refugee population, and many went to Morehead City; their traditions are still an important part of Down East culture. Daily and weekly programs held at the Light Station Pavilion and the porch of the Keepers Quarters during the summer months teach visitors about the natural and human history of Cape Lookout, including what day-to-day life was like for the keeper of the lighthouse and the keeper's family.

Descendants of the Bankers feel a spiritual bond to their ancestors' home, and for years they would return, occupying fish camps that they constructed along the beach. When the federal government bought the Banks, it was made known that the fish camps would soon be off-limits to their deedless owners. The outcry and bitterness that ensued reflected the depth of the Core Sounders' love of their ancestral grounds. The National Park Service may have thought that the fish camps were ephemeral and purely recreational structures, but to the campers, the Banks were still home, even if they had been born on the mainland and had never lived here for longer than a fishing season. Retaining their sense of righteous, if not legal, ownership, many burned down their own fish camps rather than let the government take them down.

Cape Lookout Lighthouse

By the time you arrive at the 1859 **Cape Lookout Lighthouse** (252/728-2250, www. nps.gov/calo, visitors center and Keeper's Quarters Museum 9am-5pm daily Apr.-Nov., lighthouse climbs 10am-3:45pm Wed.-Sat. early May-mid-Sept., $8 adults, $4 seniors and under age 12), you will have seen it portrayed on dozens of brochures, menus, signs, and souvenirs. With its striking diamond pattern, it looks like a rattlesnake standing at attention. This 163-foot-tall lighthouse was first lit in 1859. Like the other lighthouses along the coast, it's built of brick. At its base, the walls are nine feet thick, narrowing to two feet at the top. The present lighthouse isn't the first to guard this section of the coast; originally a lighthouse was built only a few yards away, but it was plagued with problems and replaced by the current structure.

Accommodations

There are cabins (877/444-6777, www.nps. gov/calo, reservations www.recreation.gov, Sept.-Nov.) to rent on Cape Lookout, but you must reserve well in advance to obtain one. On **Long Point** ($112-145) **and Great Island** ($54-168), you can rent cabins with hot and cold water, gas stoves, and furniture, but in some cases visitors must bring their own generators for lighting as well as linens and utensils. Before you make a reservation, remember that with no air-conditioning, fall and spring are far more comfortable than summer.

CAMPING

Camping is permitted within Cape Lookout National Seashore. There are no designated campsites or camping amenities, and everything you bring must be carried back out when you leave. Campers can stay for up to 14 days, and large groups (25 or more campers) require special permits. The National Park Service website for Cape Lookout (www.nps. gov/calo) has full details on camping regulations and permits.

Getting There

Except for the visitors center at Harkers Island, Cape Lookout National Seashore can only be reached by ferry. Portsmouth, at the northern end of the park, is a short ferry ride from Ocracoke, but Ocracoke is a very long ferry ride from Cedar Island. The **Cedar Island-Ocracoke Ferry** (800/293-3779) is part of the state ferry system and costs $15 one way for regular-size vehicles (pets allowed). It takes 2.25 hours to cross Pamlico Sound, but the ride is fun, and embarking from Cedar Island feels like sailing off the edge of the earth. The **Ocracoke-Portsmouth Ferry** is a passenger-only commercial route, licensed to Captain Rudy Austin of **Austin Boat Tours** (252/928-4361 or 252/928-5431, $20 pp, 3-person minimum, daily as weather

---

1: the Cape Lookout Lighthouse; **2:** up early for the fresh catch at Atlantic Beach; **3:** The shrimp burger from Big Oak Drive-In and Bar-B-Q is a regional favorite.

permits). Call to ensure a seat. Most ferries operate April-November, with some exceptions.

Commercial ferries cross every day from mainland Carteret County to the southern parts of the national seashore. There is generally a ferry route between Davis and Great Island, but service can be variable; check the Cape Lookout National Seashore website (www.nps.gov/calo) for updates.

From Beaufort, passenger ferries include **Island Ferry Adventures** (610 Front St., 252/728-7555, www.islandferryadventures. com), which has a three-hour tour to Cape Lookout leaving at 9am (reservations required, $30 adults, $15 age 11 and under).

Cape Lookout Cabins and Camps (125 Davis Lane, Davis, 252/729-9751 or 252/729-9752, www.cape-lookout-cabins-camps-ferry-davis-nc.com), 30 minutes east of Beaufort on U.S. 70, midway to Cedar Island, runs regular ferries from Davis to the South Core Banks and Cape Lookout. Trips run from mid-March to the end of the year, and prices range from $16 (adults age 11 and up) to $150 for trucks hauling a trailer. You can also rent a 4x4 vehicle for $150/day.

The **Morehead City Ferry Service** (709 Shepherd St., 252/504-2488, $10-35 adults, $9-25 ages 11 and under) provides tours to several of the smaller islands for shelling, birding, and sightseeing trips, even a guided tour of Ft. Macon State Park.

BOGUE BANKS

Most folks around here call the long island off the coast of Morehead City and Beaufort by the wrong name: Emerald Isle. Emerald Isle is the name of one of the beach towns on the island known officially as Bogue Banks. But if you, and they, get it wrong, no one is going to hold it against anyone. The Bogue Banks are home to several beach towns, the most prominent of which are the aforementioned Emerald Isle and Atlantic Beach. These two towns, and their smaller counterparts, have the typical North Carolina Coast laid-back feel. There's a quieter, slower pace here, as opposed to the fun-fun-fun neon jungles of beaches

elsewhere. The major attractions, Fort Macon State Park and the North Carolina Aquarium at Pine Knoll Shores, are a bit more cerebral than, say, amusement parks and bikini contests. The other major draw is the beach itself, a long, south-facing stretch of sand that's perfect for surfing, fishing, beachcombing, or just relaxing.

★ North Carolina Aquarium

The **North Carolina Aquarium at Pine Knoll Shores** (1 Roosevelt Blvd., Pine Knoll Shores, 252/247-4003, www.ncaquariums. com, 9am-5pm daily, closed Thanksgiving and Dec. 25, $13 adults, $12 seniors and military, $11 ages 3-12, free under age 3) is one of the state's three great coastal aquariums. Here at Pine Knoll Shores, exhibit highlights include a 300,000-gallon aquarium in which sharks and other aquatic beasts go about their business in and around a replica German U-boat (plenty of originals lie right off the coast and form homes for reef creatures); a "jelly gallery" (they really can be beautiful); a tank filled with the beautiful but invasive lionfish; a pair of river otters; and many other wonderful animals and habitats.

Trails from the parking lot lead into the maritime forests of the 273-acre **Theodore Roosevelt Natural Area** (1 Roosevelt Dr., Atlantic Beach, 252/247-4003), where a network of trails takes your through secluded marshes, on a high dune ridge, and under a coastal forest canopy, providing plenty of opportunities for bird-watching and wildlife viewing. The trails close at 4:30pm, so get an early start.

Fort Macon State Park

At the eastern tip of Atlantic Beach is **Fort Macon State Park** (2303 E. Fort Macon Rd., 252/726-3775, http://ncparks.gov, visitors center and bookstore 9am-5pm daily, fort 9am-5:30pm daily, bathhouse area 8am-5:30pm Nov.-Feb., 8am-8pm Mar.-May and Sept.-Oct., swimming area 10am-5:45pm daily May-Sept. as staffing allows, free). The central feature of the park is Fort Macon, an 1820s federal fort that was a Confederate garrison for one year during the Civil War. Guided tours are offered, and there are exhibits inside the casemates. For such a stern and martial building, some of the interior spaces are surprisingly pretty. The park has 1.5 miles of beach, perfect for fishing, swimming, sunbathing, or simply strolling. At different times throughout the year, the park is filled with costumed Civil War reenactors.

Sports and Recreation

The ocean side of Bogue Banks offers plenty of public beach access. In each of the towns—Atlantic Beach, Pine Knoll Shores, Salter Path, Indian Beach, and Emerald Isle—are parking lots, some free and some paid. The beach at **Fort Macon** is bounded by the ocean, Bogue Sound, and Beaufort Inlet. Because there's a Coast Guard station on the Sound side and a jetty along the inlet, swimming is permitted only along one stretch of the ocean beach. A concession stand and bathhouse are located at the swimming beach.

You can get out on the water and try something different with **Carolina Kitesurfing** (142 Fairview Dr., Suite 6M, Emerald Isle, 252/876-2595, www.carolinakitesurfing.com). You harness yourself to a giant kite (it's really more of a parachute), strap your feet to what looks like a wakeboard, and then let the wind pull you around while you turn, carve, spin, and fly through the air on a thrilling ride. Lessons—and you'll need lessons—are $150 for two hours ($50 for each hour after that). If you want a little slower pace, they have that, too, with SUP rentals ($50/half-day, $75/24 hours) and tours ($50) as well as SUP surfing instruction ($150 for two hours).

Atlantic Beach Surf Shop (515 W. Fort Macon Rd., Atlantic Beach, 252/762-9382, www.absurfshop.com, SUP rentals $50/day, surf rentals $25/day) opened in 1964 because the 14-year-old owner loved surfing so much, he had to help others get into the sport. Now they sell and rent surfboards and stand-up paddleboards and carry a big line of surf lifestyle clothing. They work with **Progression**

Surf Lessons (252/342-3020, call for rates and availability) for those interested in learning a new sport.

There's a small store stocked with all the gear you'll need for a day on the water at **Hot Wax Surf Shop** (200 Mallard Dr., Emerald Isle, 252/354-6466, www.hotwaxsurf.com). Here you can arrange for surfing and stand-up paddleboard lessons ($75-125), rent surf ($25/day) and SUP ($65/day) equipment, or take a tour with their guides. They also rent bodyboards and skimboards (from $25/day) as well as fishing kayaks and kayak fishing excursions ($75-160).

Barrier Island Kayaks (160 Cedar Point Rd., Swansboro, 252/393-6457, www.barrierislandkayaks.com) offers custom trips, excursions to Bear Island at the southern edge of this region, eco-adventures focused on wandering marsh creeks and viewing wildlife up close. They also rent out kayaks and stand-up paddleboards (from $30 for two hours, $40 half-day, $55 full day, $35 additional days).

AB Watersports (612 Atlantic Beach Causeway, 252/422-0520, www.abwatersport.com, 8am-6pm Mon.-Sat. and 9am-6pm Sun.) has tours and rentals for just about every watersport you can imagine. Get out on the water via parasailing ($80/single, $150/double), kiteboarding ($350/two hours, $500/half day, $1000/day, small group lessons $400/person), jet skis ($60/half hour, $100/hour, Cape Lookout Tour $195), stand-up paddleboards ($50/half day, $75 full day, $25/additional day), kayaks (single kayaks $40/half day, $60/full day, $25/additional day; double kayaks $50/half day, $70/full day, $35/additional day), or pontoon boat ($300/half day, $425 plus fuel/full day).

Anglers love this part of the coast for its inshore and offshore fishing; find an up-to-date list of Morehead City charter boats at www.downtownmoreheadcity.com. Just over the bridge from Morehead City, **Captain Stacy Fishing Center** (416 Atlantic Beach Causeway, Atlantic Beach, 252/276-4675 or 800/533-9417, www.captstacy.com, from $100 adults, $65 children) has been hauling in big fish off the coast for decades. Charter options include a nighttime shark fishing expedition. Full-day and half-day bottom-fishing excursions take you offshore into deep water, where you can expect to catch black sea bass, spot-tail porgies, triggerfish, red snapper, and other good eating fish. Serious anglers may want to join one of the overnighters April to November; these trips include a two-day bag limit and have a reputation for bringing in loads of fish.

Pelagic Sportfishing (212 Smith St., 252/904-3361, www.pelagicsportfishing.com, fishing $500-1,850, cruising $100/hour) has 31-foot and 61-foot boats at Atlantic Beach for half-day and full-day charters for tuna, mahimahi, and redfish. Sunset cruises and sightseeing tours are also offered.

BEACHES

The 21-mile-long island known as the Bogue Banks on maps, and Emerald Isle by locals, is actually made up of five beach towns and communities. From west to east they are Emerald Isle, Indian Beach, Salter Path, Pine Knoll Shores, and Atlantic Beach. The two most prominent of these communities are Emerald Isle and Atlantic Beach. Atlantic Beach, on the eastern end of the island due south from Morehead City, is the more developed of the communities in terms of commercial spots—shops, restaurants, and outfitters—but it's still a quiet little beach town. At the western end, Emerald Isle is larger, but less commercial; there are many more homes on this end of the island, however. Beaches along the length of the Bogue Banks are south-facing, so waves and winds are slightly different than at other beaches, but unless you surf or sail, the only difference you'll notice is that the sun rises and sets over the Atlantic Ocean. Families flock to the Bogue Banks because it's what the Outer Banks was 25 years ago—beautiful beaches, great houses, no crowds—and the distractions offered by the kayak and bike outfitters, fishing and sightseeing charters, and the mix of seafood and family restaurants that deliver on that ideal beach vacation.

Food

Before dinner, or after, or both, grab a drink at one of the coolest bars in Atlantic Beach, **The Barnacle** (700 E. Ft. Macon Rd., 252/726-0863, www.oceanapier.com, 5pm-9:30pm Thurs.-Fri., noon-9:30pm Sat.-Sun.). The Barnacle is a sort of boozy hut with the sunset view you're looking for. Perched as it is 1,000

Beaches on the Cape Lookout National Seashore are wide open.

feet out into the Atlantic, you can capture the sun, clouds, waves, and shore in one stunning glance. Cocktails are simple but good, and the selection of beer and wine is limited, but out here they all taste great. The sister to The Barnacle is **Oceana Pier House Restaurant** (252/726-0863, www.oceanapier.com, breakfast 6am-11am daily, lunch and dinner 11am-late), where you can grab breakfast ($2-10.50), lunch or dinner ($4.50-23). Breakfast is simple eggs and bacon, but lunch gets into burgers, hot dogs, and chicken sandwiches as well as shrimp burgers and fresh seafood platters.

The beer selection at **Idle Hour Biergarten** (121 Atlantic Blvd., Atlantic Beach, 252/773-0008, www.idlehourbiergarten.com, noon-late Wed.-Sun., $6-14) is a fun one. With several takes on traditional German styles like dunkels, pilsners, weizenbachs, and kölsches, plus some great domestic and craft beer, this place gives you that community feel you want in a Biergarten. The menu consists of small and large plates of pretzels and a tasty schnitzel sandwich, plus seafood bites like fried oysters and a lobster salad sandwich.

The ★ **Big Oak Drive-In and Bar-B-Q** (1167 Salter Path, 252/247-2588, www.bigoakdrivein.com, 11am-3pm Tues.-Thurs. and Sun., 11am-8pm Fri. and Sat., around $6) is a classic beach drive-in: a little red, white, and blue-striped building with a walk-up counter and drive-up spaces. They're best known for their shrimp burgers ($5), a fried affair slathered with Big Oak's signature red sauce, coleslaw, and tartar sauce. Then there are the scallop burgers, oyster burgers, clam burgers, hamburgers, and barbecue, all cheap and made for snacking on the beach.

★ **The Island Grille** (401 Money Island Dr., Atlantic Beach, 252/240-0000, www.igrestaurant.net, 5pm-9pm Mon.-Tues. and Fri.-Sat., 5:30pm-8:30pm Wed., Thurs. and Sun., brunch 11am-2pm Sun., diner $19-36, brunch $8-16) came highly recommended from a friend who grew up nearby, and I'm glad I listened. They bill themselves as "Atlantic Beach's gourmet hole in the wall"

and I can't think of any way to say it better. The food's southern coastal—scallops and shrimp sautéed in butter and served with mushrooms and fresh vegetables, crab cakes, pork chop—and outstanding. Do yourself a favor and make a reservation now, then plan your trip around it.

At ★ **Pescara Wood Oven Kitchen** (208 West Dr., Atlantic Beach, 252/499-9300, www.pescararestaurant.com, 5pm-9pm Wed.-Thurs. and Sun., 5pm-10pm Fri.-Sat., around $24) they serve some fine coastal Italian in a beautifully restored home that happens to be one of the oldest in the area. A good wine list accompanies dishes like charred octopus, clams, and shrimp on house-made pasta; coriander-crusted grouper; and some excellent calamari.

A community institution you should check out is the **Crab Shack** (146 Headen Ln., Salter Path, 252/247-3444, www.thecrabshacksalterpath.com, 11am-late daily, $16-38), a small waterfront restaurant tucked away behind Salter Path United Methodist Church. Operated by the Guthries—a family name that dates back to the early colonists in this area—the restaurant was wiped out in 2005 by Hurricane Ophelia but was rebuilt, much to the joy of loyal diners of the local and vacationer variety.

It can get crowded at **Amos Mosquito's Restaurant & Bar** (703 E. Ft. Macon Rd., Atlantic Beach, 252/247-6222, www.amosmosquitos.com, 5pm-9:30pm Sun.-Wed., 5pm-10pm Thurs.-Sat., $12-32). That's because the atmosphere is lively, the food is very good, and you can get s'mores to make at your table. That's right, after feasting on seafood, sushi, and maybe a killer burger, you can make s'mores at your table thanks to a handy little portable grill. It's pretty fun for kids and folks like me who think they're children.

Accommodations
The Inn at Pine Knoll Shores (511 Salter Path Rd., Atlantic Beach, 252/247-4155 or 800/338-1533, http://clamdiggerinn.com, $150-255) is another reliable option with

all-oceanfront guest rooms. You'll find beach chairs and umbrellas to use as well as a game room, a poolside bar, and wireless internet. Pets are not allowed. The **Atlantis Lodge** (123 Salter Path Rd., Atlantic Beach, 252/726-5168 or 800/682-7057, www.atlantislodge.com, $69-289) is an established family-run motel. It has simple and reasonably priced efficiencies in a great beachfront location; the hotel's private boardwalk puts you on the beach in two minutes. Well-behaved pets are welcome for an additional fee. The **Windjammer Inn** (103 Salter Path Rd., Atlantic Beach, 252/247-7123 or 800/233-6466, www.windjammerinn.com, $169-205) is another simple, comfortable motel with decent rates through the high season and great rates (under $100) in the off-season.

VACATION RENTALS

In beach towns like these, many vacationers opt for a whole house or a condo rather than a hotel room. I think this is the way to go, as it gives you the chance to dig into that local seafood and cook for yourself or hire a personal chef, like Chef Patrick Hogan of Carlton's Catering Company (910/381-4846, www.carlotonscateringcompany.com), to cook for you. If you're looking for a house, **Emerald Isle Realty** (7501 Emerald Dr., Emerald Isle, 855/324-9856, www.emeraldislerealty.com) is one of the largest rental companies in the region and has a broad portfolio of homes and accommodations in a variety of sizes, configurations, locations, and prices. **Sun-Surf Realty** (7701 Emerald Dr., Emerald Isle, 800/553-7873, www.sunsurfrealty.com) has a smaller selection of homes and condos, but their list is loaded with great places to stay.

GETTING THERE AND AROUND

The Bogue Banks extend from the Bogue Inlet in the west to Fort Macon to the east. Morehead City and Beaufort sit across the sound a short drive away. Along the length of the Banks are several small towns, anchored by Emerald Isle and Atlantic Beach. One road, N.C. 58, runs the length of the island and goes through several name changes as it does, so whether you find yourself on Ft. Macon Rd., Salter Path Rd., or Emerald Drive, it's all the same. Emerald Isle is 24 minutes from Morehead City, a testimony of the length of the Bogue Banks, but with summer traffic, that drive can stretch to 34 or even 44 minutes, so leave in plenty of time if you've made reservations for dinner or an excursion. The B. Cameron Langston Bridge enters Bogue Banks (from Cape Carteret on the mainland) at the west, and the Atlantic Beach-Morehead City Bridge crosses the Bogue Sound from Morehead City on the east side of the island.

Wilmington and Cape Fear

In 1524, the first known European explorer arrived on these shores of North Carolina at the mouth of the Cape Fear River.

Giovanni da Verrazzano wrote to the king of France that the land here was "as pleasant and delectable to behold as is possible to imagine."

The southeastern corner of North Carolina is indeed a natural beauty: Barrier islands here contain the largest intact piece of maritime forest in the state. There are stunning beaches and miles of river, marsh, and creek to explore, plus, as you move inland, the gentle rising of the Sandhills and hardwood forests. Pleasant and delectable indeed.

As enthusiasm for the New World built in Europe, the influence of England, Spain, and France profoundly changed the cultural and

Highlights

Look for ★ to find recommended sights, activities, dining, and lodging.

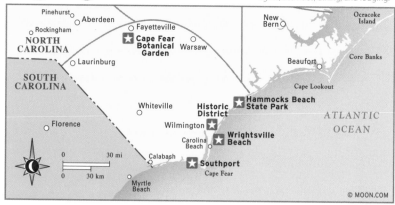

© MOON.COM

★ **Wilmington's Historic District:** Downtown reflects its glory days of commerce and high society in the state's largest 19th-century historic district, a gorgeous collection of antebellum and late-Victorian townhouses and commercial buildings (page 125).

★ **Wrightsville Beach:** North Carolina has many wonderful beaches, but few can compare with Wrightsville for its pretty sand, easy public access, clear waters, and overall beauty (page 127).

★ **Hammocks Beach State Park:** One of the wildest and least disturbed Atlantic coast

beaches, accessible only by boat, Bear Island is a popular stopover for migrating waterfowl and turtles (page 146).

★ **Southport:** From this picturesque fishing town you can see the oldest and newest lighthouses in North Carolina, enjoy dinner on the water, and celebrate your independence on the Fourth of July (page 151).

★ **Cape Fear Botanical Garden:** This gorgeous botanical garden in Fayetteville provides a place for locals and visitors to stretch their legs while admiring the flora of the region (page 164).

physical landscapes of the Caribbean and the southern Atlantic coast of North America. Towns and forts sprung up where Native Americans once lived. Then came plantations built by enslaved Africans for their European masters. Wilmington shares this legacy with other cities in the Atlantic-Caribbean region such as Havana, Nassau, New Orleans, Savannah, and Charleston. The architecture of these cities shows European influence, and the culture—language, food, and folkways—shows the influence of Africans.

The Lumbee people, Native Americans historically and spiritually tied to the blackwater Lumber River, now make their home in Pembroke. They are the largest indigenous community east of the Mississippi River, though their name is not widely known. This is due in part to the fact that they've been denied federal status, a complex and contentious issue that continues to cast a shadow for members of the community. They don't have a reservation and for centuries have lived a rural existence and practiced deeply rooted Christianity. Their little-known history can be explored in and around Pembroke.

Between Wilmington and Lumberton the landscape of the state's southeast corner becomes a waterscape comprising blackwater creeks and seductive, even eerie swamps, bays, marshes, and rivers. It's the world's only native habitat of the Venus flytrap. Many visitors wrinkle their noses at the marsh's distinctive smell as the tide recedes and the mudflats are exposed, but to locals the mingled scent of marsh and salt water is the scent of home. The cypress knees, tannic creeks, marsh birds, and occasional alligator make this region worth staying a little longer.

The greatest draw is the water: the beautiful beaches of Brunswick, New Hanover, Pender, and Onslow Counties and the well-known Wrightsville and Topsail beaches as well as other hidden gems just north of bustling Myrtle Beach, South Carolina. You can find the same mini golf and beach-towel vendors peppering the beach towns of North Carolina, but the state's coast mostly seems downright bucolic compared to its southern neighbor.

Inland, the landscape changes but the water is no less important. At the edge of this region is Fayetteville, with a long history that includes Revolutionary War standoffs, Civil War battles, and ties to the Cape Fear River. At Fayetteville the marshes give way to rolling hills with a mix of pines and hardwoods. Home to Fort Bragg, Fayetteville has a long-standing military presence and history, dating to the colonial era when immigrant Scots called these hills home.

PLANNING YOUR TIME

There's a lot to do in the Cape Fear region and, depending on your interests, a wide range of choices for a home base. Wilmington is the obvious choice: Centrally located on the coast, it's minutes from Wrightsville, Kure, and Carolina Beaches and only a little farther from Topsail and the beaches of Brunswick County. Fayetteville and Raleigh are only a couple of hours away, making day trips a possibility. The town of Wilmington is full of activities and sights, and you'll want a day or two to explore this historic river city. For inland adventures in the region, Fayetteville offers a good selection of motels, and it's still a reasonable drive to the coast for a day at the beach.

Weather across the region is mostly mild, with a short winter on the coast and a slightly longer winter around Fayetteville. Spring is a beautiful time to visit, when the Southern gardens fill with azaleas. Summer starts early, with warm waters (courtesy of the Gulf Stream) and sunny days growing warmer throughout summer months and sticking around until October or later. Fall is short along the coast, and there are few fall leaves to see, however, the hills around Fayetteville see a true autumn color show. Hurricanes are a concern along the coast of the Carolinas, and

---

Previous: stand-up paddleboarders going out for a morning session; pier in morning light; beach access.

Wilmington and Cape Fear

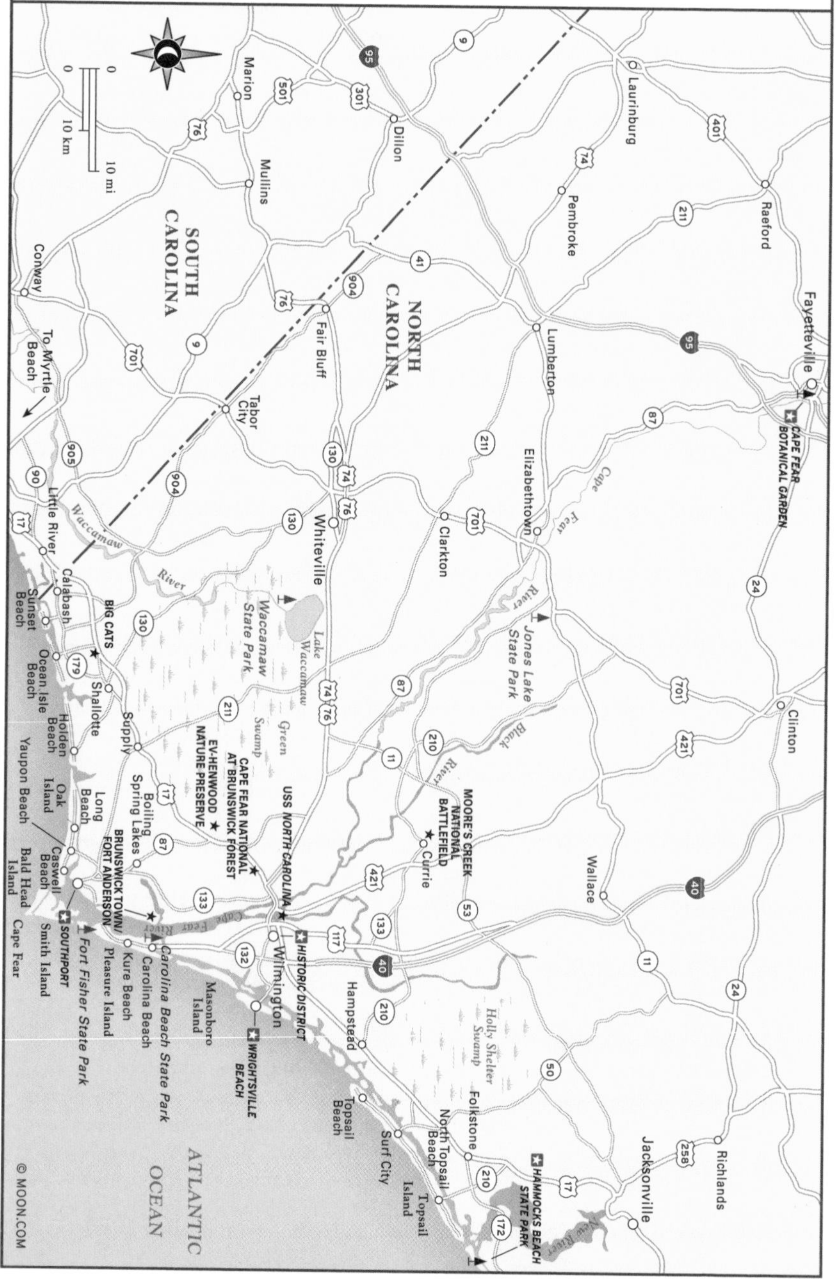

although hurricane season runs from June to November, the biggest threat is during the latter months of the season, usually September and October. On the coast, the dangers are the expected rain, wind, and strong surf and tide, but inland, wind, rain, and flooding are a concern. Keep an eye on the long-range forecast when planning a trip during hurricane season, and be sure to follow the instructions of local authorities if one pops up while you're here.

HISTORY

Giovanni da Verrazzano's 1524 visit started a land race that took two centuries to take off. Lucas Vásquez de Ayllón and his crew, which possibly included the first enslaved Africans brought to what is now the United States, walked the shores here in 1526 scouting for resources and settlement sites before their shipwreck in South Carolina. A number of other colonial parties were warded off, likely by the frightening name given to the river and shoals here: Cape Fear. The shoals and currents at the mouth of the Cape Fear River gave Sir Richard Greenville fits in 1585, and he nearly wrecked; consequently, he gave it the name it has today. Perhaps the name is why it took 140 years for someone to settle here. A couple of failed settlements appeared on the banks of the river, but colonists cited the humidity, hurricanes, and bugs, among other things, as reason to abandon these attempts.

It wasn't until 1726 that European settlement finally took hold in the region. Maurice Moore and his brother Roger established their family's domain at Brunswick Town and Orton Plantation, a half-mile north. Today, only ruins remain at Brunswick Town in the form of ballast-stone house foundations and the brick walls of an Anglican church, but Orton Plantation still stands and is once again owned by Moore descendants. The machinations of the Moores and Brunswick Town residents led to the demise of the indigenous Cape Fear people. Many of them were driven off, and the remainder were rounded up and later murdered.

Brunswick Town was an important port, as the only inland deepwater access on the river,

but it was soon eclipsed by Wilmington to the north once dredging technology allowed the shoals between the two towns to be cleared. As Brunswick Town declined, the American Revolution heated up, and the small port town played important roles in defying George III's taxes and harrying General Cornwallis and his troops as they raided the area. At the same time, the large population of Scottish immigrants around Fayetteville grew even larger, making their living in the forests preparing tar, pitch, and turpentine for naval stores.

In the lower Cape Fear Region, especially present-day Brunswick, New Hanover, Bladen, and Onslow Counties, the concentration of enslaved laborers was significantly larger than in many other parts of the state. The naval stores industry demanded workers, as did the large rice and indigo plantations—including Orton—that once dominated the local agricultural industry. The same was true along the coasts of South Carolina, Georgia, and parts of northern Florida, where many of the slaves had been taken from the same part of Africa. These large communities of African-born and first-generation American-born people shared ideas, memories, and culture, which became what is known today as Gullah or Geechee culture. Most prominent around Charleston and Savannah, the Gullah dialect and cultural influence still exist in and around Wilmington. The dialect is reminiscent of English as spoken in the Caribbean, and cultural traditions still in evidence include the cuisine, heavy with gumbo, peanuts, and okra, and folklore, in which houses are painted bright blue to keep bad luck away and bottle trees are used to capture evil spirits.

Another cultural group in the Cape Fear region is the indigenous Lumbee people. Also called the Croatan Indians, Pembroke Indians, and Indians of Robeson County, they're the largest indigenous community in the eastern United States. During the time of slavery and the Civil War they were called "free people of color," and they had no right to vote or to bear arms. The Lumbee people have a long history of resistance and defending their land. Most famously, in the 19th century the Lowry (sometimes spelled Lowrie) Band of outlaws defined the Lumbee cause for future generations. Another transformative moment in Lumbee history was a 1958 armed conflict near Maxton. Ku Klux Klan grand wizard "Catfish" Cole and about 40 other armed Klansmen held a rally at Hayes Pond. Fed up with a recent wave of vicious intimidation, 1,500 armed Lumbee showed up at the rally and shot out the lone electric light. Although no one was killed in the exchange of gunfire, the Klansmen fled. The confrontation was reported around the country, energizing the cause of Native American civil rights.

In the late 20th and early 21st century, southeastern North Carolina's role as a military center expanded. Fort Bragg in Fayetteville is one of the country's largest army installations and home to thousands of the soldiers who were stationed in Iraq and Afghanistan; the base continues to grow. Nearby Pope Air Field is the home of the 440th Airlift Wing, and there is a major Marine Corps presence nearby at Camp Lejeune in Jacksonville. Numerous museums in Fayetteville and Jacksonville tell the history of the military in southeastern North Carolina.

One of the most important developments in the region's recent history is the arrival of the film industry. Wilmington's EUE/Screen Gems Studios' 50-acre studio lot is the largest outside Los Angeles, and on this lot, more than 350 film, television, and commercial projects have come to life. Productions like *Iron Man 3*, *Dawson's Creek*, *One Tree Hill*, *Under the Dome*, *Eastbound and Down*, and *Firestarter*, which started the film craze, have shot here. Although the film industry was once thriving, today it's a shell of its former self as decisions by state legislators forced productions to shoot elsewhere.

INFORMATION AND SERVICES

Area hospitals include two in Wilmington, **New Hanover Regional Medical Center Orthopedic Hospital** (formerly Cape Fear Hospital, 5301 Wrightsville Ave., Wilmington, 910/667-8100, www.nhrmc.org) and the **New Hanover Regional Medical Center** (2131 S. 17th St., Wilmington, 910/667-7000, www.nhrmc.org); two in Brunswick County, **Brunswick Novant Medical Center** (240 Hospital Dr. NE, Lockwoods Folly, 910/721-1000, www.novanthealth.org) and **Dosher Memorial Hospital** (924 N. Howe St., Southport, 910/457-3800, www.dosher.org); in Onslow County, **Onslow Memorial Hospital** (317 Western Blvd., Jacksonville, 910/577-2345, www.onslow.org); in Pender County, **Pender Memorial Hospital** (507 E. Fremont St., Burgaw, 910/259-5451, www.nhrmc.org); and Fayetteville's **Cape Fear Valley Medical Center** (1638 Owen Dr., Fayetteville, 910/615-4000, www.capefearvalley.com). Myrtle Beach, South Carolina, has the **Grand Strand Regional Medical Center** (809 82nd Pkwy., Myrtle Beach, SC, 843/692-1000, www.mygrandstrandhealth.com), not far from the southernmost communities in Brunswick County. In an emergency, of course, call 911.

More information on dining, attractions, and lodging is available through local convention and visitors bureaus: the **Wilmington, NC River District & Island Beaches** (505 Nutt St., Unit A, Wilmington, 877/406-2356, www.wilmingtonandbeaches.com, 8:30am-5pm Mon.-Fri., 9am-4pm Sat., 1pm-4pm Sun.), **North Carolina's Brunswick Islands** (712 Village Rd. SW, 910/755-5517, www.ncbrunswick.com), and the **Fayetteville Area CVB** (245 Person St., Fayetteville, 910/483-5311, www.visitfayettevillenc.com, 8am-5pm Mon.-Fri.).

Wilmington

In some ways, Wilmington is a town where time has stood still. During the Civil War, General Sherman's fiery march that razed so many Southern towns missed Wilmington. For most of the 20th century the economy moved in fits and starts, with long slumps and standstills punctuated by short boom periods. Surviving the Civil War combined with a slow economy provided Wilmington's architecture with an unexpected benefit: historic preservation. Much of the downtown remains a museum of beautiful buildings dating to the town's first heyday, and that historic appeal accounts for much of its popularity as a destination today.

HISTORY

Founded in the early 1730s, Wilmington went through a short identity crisis as New Carthage, New Liverpool, and New Town before settling on Wilmington in 1739. Early on it was a deepwater port and quickly became a bustling shipping center for the export of lumber, rice, and naval stores, including turpentine and tar tapped from longleaf pine trees, lumber for ships' keels, and ribbing from live oak branches. By 1769, the town had grown from a collection of wharves, warehouses, and homes into a respectable colonial city, included on a map drawn by acclaimed French cartographer C. J. Sauthier. By 1840 the city was booming and positioned as the southern terminus of the Wilmington and Weldon Railroad (the 161-mile track was the longest in the world at the time).

During the Civil War the Wilmington and Weldon Railroad line was an essential Confederate artery for trade and troop transport. The Union navy attempted a blockade of the Cape Fear River and inlets up and down the coast, but Wilmington's port was a hive of blockade runners bringing in arms, food, medicine, and materials from Europe and the Caribbean. In January 1865 the Union took nearby Fort Fisher, the key gun emplacement guarding the river's mouth, and Wilmington soon fell. It was a crushing blow to the failing Confederacy. Continued commerce at the port allowed Wilmington to thrive during the Civil War and Reconstruction, unlike many towns in the South; by 1890 the population hit 20,000, making it the largest city in North Carolina.

Political tensions ran high during Reconstruction, and there were conflicts between whites and blacks, Democrats and Republicans, and staunch Confederate supporters and carpetbaggers (Northerners who came to the South for economic opportunities) and copperheads (their Southern supporters). In 1898 the only successful coup d'état on American soil took place in the Wilmington Race Riot. White Democrats loyal to the long-dead Confederacy threatened to overthrow the city government if their candidate lost. He did, and two days after the election, a mob of white Democrats and their supporters overthrew the city's Republican government, destroyed the city's African American newspaper, the *Daily Record,* and killed at least 22 African American citizens.

In the early 20th century, North Carolina's power center shifted from the agriculture and shipping at coastal towns like Wilmington to the textile mills and manufacturing of the Piedmont region. Charlotte surpassed Wilmington in population, interstate highways joined larger cities to the rest of the nation, and economically Wilmington stood still. In 1960 the Atlantic Coast Line Railroad relocated its headquarters to Florida, and the city experienced several decades of decline. After I-40 was completed, connecting Wilmington to the rest of the country, the tourism industry began to rise. Wilmington and surrounding towns had a real estate boom in the late 1990s that lasted for several years. At the same time, the film industry

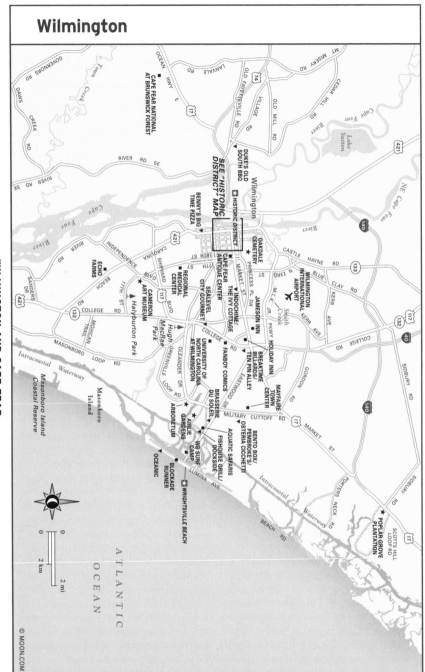

Wilmington

SEE "HISTORIC DISTRICT" MAP

HISTORIC DISTRICT

CAPE FEAR NATIONAL AT BRUNSWICK FOREST

DUKE'S OLD SOUTH BBQ

BENNY'S BIG TIME PIZZA

OAKDALE CEMETERY

ECHO FARMS

CAPE FEAR ANTIQUE CENTER

WILMINGTON INTERNATIONAL AIRPORT

REGIONAL MEDICAL CENTER

SEALEVEL CITY GOURMET

INDOCHINE

THE IVY COTTAGE

CAMERON ART MUSEUM

Halyburton Park

JAMESON INN

HOLIDAY INN

MacRae

Hugh MacRae Park

UNIVERSITY OF NORTH CAROLINA AT WILMINGTON

TANBOY COMICS

BREAKTIME BILLARDS/ TEN PIN ALLEY

MAYFAIRE TOWN CENTER

BRASSERIE DU SOLEIL

ARBORETUM

AIRLIE GARDENS

WB SURF CAMP

FISHOUSE GRILL/ DOCKSIDE

AQUATIC SAFARIS

BENTO BOX/ PEMBROKE'S/ OSTERIA CICCHETTI

OCEANIC

BLOCKADE RUNNER

WRIGHTSVILLE BEACH

POPLAR GROVE PLANTATION

ATLANTIC OCEAN

Masonboro Island Coastal Reserve

Intracoastal Waterway

Masonboro Island

0 2 km
0 2 mi

© MOON.COM

grew, boosting the local economy and influencing local culture. Like most of the country, Wilmington was hit hard by the end of the real estate bubble in 2006, and the city is still climbing out from under the wreckage of that widespread economic collapse. Of late, the film industry is in decline, although there is growth in Wilmington—in high-tech and industrial sectors—and the city continues to make strides in terms of identity and economy, thanks, largely, to the resilience of its people.

SIGHTS
★ Historic District

Wilmington's historic district, which includes some 200 blocks, is among the largest in North Carolina. You'll find shady tree-lined streets and a gorgeous collection of antebellum and late Victorian homes, mansions, and commercial buildings. Wilmington is home to the state's largest 19th-century historic district, which includes beautiful examples of pre-Civil War Italianate architecture as well as influences from the French and English Caribbean. Until 1910, Wilmington was the state's most populous city; the earlier boom and subsequent decline are reflected in the architecture, as the city lacks the fine examples of early-20th-century buildings found in cities like Asheville and Charlotte.

The **Bellamy Mansion** (503 Market St., 910/251-3700, www.bellamymansion.org, tours hourly 10am-5pm Mon.-Sat., 1pm-5pm Sun., $12 adults, $10 seniors, military and college students, $6 ages 6-18) is a superb example of Wilmington's late-antebellum mansions. This porticoed, four-story, 22-room home shows both Greek Revival and Italianate architectural influences and stands as one of the most beautiful Southern city homes of its era. Just two months before North Carolina seceded from the Union in 1861, planter and physician John Bellamy and his family moved into their city home, where they lived until the fall of Fort Fisher and the ensuing fall of Wilmington to the Union. After the war, Bellamy traveled to Washington to ask

President Andrew Johnson, a fellow North Carolinian, for a pardon, and used his pardon to recover the home from federal ownership.

In addition to the mansion, another significant building stands on the property: the slave quarters. This two-story brick building is a rare surviving example of urban dwellings for enslaved people, and the interior, which remained largely unchanged through the years, is an important part of the historical record of slavery in the South.

The **Burgwin-Wright House** (224 Market St., 910/762-0570, www.burgwinwrighthouse.com, tours 10am-4pm Mon.-Sat., final tour at 3pm, $12 adults, $10 military and students, $6 ages 5-12) is older than the Bellamy Mansion by nearly a century, but it has an oddly similar history. John Burgwin ("ber-GWIN"), a planter and treasurer of the North Carolina colony, built the home in 1770 atop the city's early jail. Soon after, British forces commandeered the home as their headquarters during the Revolutionary War. In 1781, General Cornwallis took the house as his headquarters. Joshua Grainger Wright purchased the house in 1799, and it served as a residence until 1937, when the National Society of the Colonial Dames of America purchased the home because of its historic significance.

Like the Bellamy Mansion, the Burgwin-Wright House is a version of the classic white-columned, magnolia-shaded Southern home of the wealthy merchant-planter class, but it's not overly ostentatious. Seven terraced gardens filled with native plants and those grown in the 18th century surround the house; through the years, restoration efforts have helped preserve many original garden structures, including walls, paths, steps, and gates.

Another beautiful home in Wilmington's historic district is the **Zebulon Latimer House** (126 S. 3rd St., 910/762-0492, www.lcfhs.org, tours hourly 10am-3pm daily, $12 adults, $10 military, $6 students). Merchant Zebulon Latimer built this home in 1852, and it housed three generations of Latimers until 1963, when it became a museum and the headquarters of the Lower Cape Fear Historical

Historic District

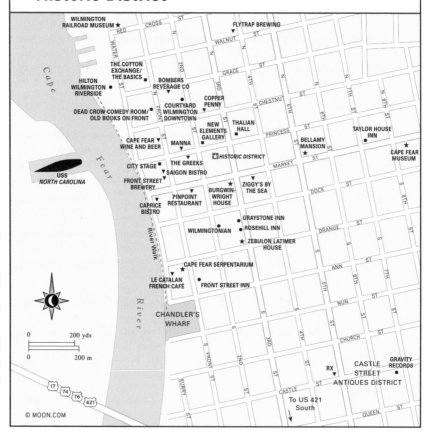

Society. In its day the Latimer House was a little more fashion-forward, architecturally speaking, than its neighbors; delicate cast-iron cornices and porch railings speak to both the Italianate and emerging Victorian influences. Also located on the grounds are a two-story brick dwelling for slaves and gardens planted with period-authentic plants.

A **three-house ticket** ($30) to tour the Bellamy Mansion, the Latimer House, and the Burgwin-Wright House is available at the first house you visit; it will save you several dollars if you plan to spend the day touring the historic district. Join the **Historic Wilmington Guided Walking Tour** (910/762-0492, 10am

Sat., reservations recommended, $12 adults, $6 students), departing from the Latimer House.

Just three blocks from the Latimer House is the **Wilmington Riverwalk,** a mile-long riverside promenade that stretches the length of downtown Wilmington, overlooking the Cape Fear River and the battleship USS *North Carolina*. Most of the boutiques, dining, and nightlife in Wilmington are on the Riverwalk or a block from it. A **Visitors Information Booth** (Market and Water St., 9am-4:30pm April-May, Sept.-Oct., 9:30am-5pm June-Aug., closed Nov.-Mar.) or friendly locals can steer you in the right direction.

★ Wrightsville Beach

A few miles east of Wilmington is one of the nicest beaches on the Carolina coast: **Wrightsville Beach.** Wide and easily accessible, it is one of the most visitor- and family-friendly beaches you'll find. Wrightsville benefits from proximity of the Gulf Stream; here the warm ocean current sweeping up the Atlantic seaboard lies only 30-40 miles offshore, which means warmer waters that are colored more like the Caribbean. Getting to Wrightsville Beach is easy from downtown Wilmington. Simply take Third Street north out of downtown; it will soon turn into Martin Luther King Parkway. Martin Luther King becomes Eastwood Road when it crosses Market Street and leads you straight to Wrightsville Beach, a journey of 11.4 miles.

A number of lodging and rental choices along the beach make it an easy place to stay, and numerous public beach access points (www.towb.org), some of which are disabled-accessible and some with showers or restrooms, line Lumina Avenue. The largest public parking lot, with 99 spaces, disabled access, showers, and restrooms, is at Beach Access 4 (2398 N. Lumina Ave.). Beach Access 36 (650 S. Lumina Ave.) has 86 parking spaces, disabled access, showers, and restrooms. On busy days the parking lots can fill up, but trekking from one access point to the next will often yield a spot. To avoid the rush, plan to arrive before 9am.

Historic Sights
POPLAR GROVE PLANTATION

North of the city, about halfway between Wilmington and Topsail Island, is **Poplar Grove Plantation** (10200 U.S. 17 N., 910/686-9518, www.poplargrove.org, 9:30am-4:30pm Mon.-Sat., noon-4:30pm Sun., closed Easter, Memorial Day, July 4, Labor Day, Mon. following Halloween Festival, Thanksgiving Day, and Black Friday, $12 adults, $10 seniors and military, $6 ages 6-15, $9 self-guided tour, $5 animal sanctuary). This antebellum peanut plantation preserves the homestead of a successful farming family, including the beautiful main house, a restored tenant farmer's cabin, a blacksmith's shop, and a barn. The 67-acre Abbey Nature Preserve maintains an extensive network of hiking trails winding through coastal forests and wetlands adjacent to the house; a **Farmers Market** (8am-1pm Wed. Apr.-Nov.) shows off the bounty of the area's agriculture.

MOORE'S CREEK NATIONAL BATTLEFIELD

In Wilmington and the surrounding area are a number of significant military sites, most dating to the Revolutionary War and the Civil War. About 20 miles northwest of Wilmington, outside the town of Currie, near Burgaw, is the **Moore's Creek National Battlefield** (40 Patriots Hall Dr., Currie, 910/283-5591, www.nps.gov/mocr, grounds 9am-5pm daily, visitors center 9am-5pm Wed.-Sun., closed for all federal holidays, free). The site commemorates the brief but bloody battle of February 1776 between Loyalist Scottish highlanders, kilted and piping and brandishing broadswords, and Patriot colonists. The Patriots fired on the Scotsmen with cannons and muskets as they crossed a bridge over Moore's Creek. Some 30 Loyalists died in the attack, and the remainder scattered into the surrounding swamps and woods. The battle marked an important moment in the Revolutionary War, as the Scottish Loyalists were unable to join General Cornwallis's army in Southport and mount an attack on Patriots nearby. It also marks an important moment in Scottish military history, as the battle was the last major broadsword charge in Scottish history, led by the last Scottish clan army.

USS *NORTH CAROLINA*

Don't be alarmed if you notice a battleship across the Cape Fear River from Wilmington; it's the **USS *North Carolina*** (1 Battleship Rd., Eagles Island, 910/399-9100, www. battleshipnc.com, 8am-8pm daily late May-early Sept., 8am-5pm daily early Sept.-late May, $14 adults, $10 seniors and active or retired military, $6 ages 6-11, free under 5), a decommissioned World War II warship that now serves as a museum and memorial to North Carolinians who died in the war. This hulking gray colossus participated in every major naval offensive in the Pacific, earning 15 battle stars, and was falsely reported to have sunk six times.

Tours are self-guided and start with a short film providing an overview of the museum, then proceed onto the one-acre deck of the battleship. Nine levels of the battleship are open to explore, including the 16-inch gun turrets on the deck, the bridge, crew quarters, ship's hospital, and kitchens, and the magazine, where munitions were stored. It gets tight belowdecks, and stairways are quite steep, so visitors prone to claustrophobia and those unable to traverse steep steps may want to stay topside. A walkway and coffer dam now encircles the ship, allowing you to see it from all angles.

The USS *North Carolina* is also one of North Carolina's most famous haunted houses—reputedly home to several ghosts, seen and heard by staff and visitors alike. The SyFy Channel has featured the ship on various ghost-hunting and paranormal shows, and it has been the subject of extensive investigations. Check out **Haunted NC** (www. hauntednc.com) to hear some chilling and unexplained voices recorded by investigators.

OAKDALE CEMETERY

By the mid-19th century, Wilmington was experiencing growing pains as the bustling shipping and railroad center of North Carolina. The city's old cemeteries were becoming overcrowded with former residents, and **Oakdale Cemetery** (520 N. 15th St., 910/762-5682, www.oakdalecemetery.org, 8am-5pm daily year-round) was founded some distance from downtown to ease the graveyard congestion. Designed in the parklike style of graveyards popular at the time, it was soon filled with superb examples of funerary art—weeping angels, obelisks, willow trees—set off against the natural beauty of the place. Separate sections were reserved for Jewish burials and for

victims of the 1862 yellow fever epidemic. Oakdale's website has an interesting guide to Victorian grave art symbolism.

Museums

CAPE FEAR MUSEUM

The **Cape Fear Museum** (814 Market St., 910/798-4370, www.capefearmuseum.com, 9am-5pm Mon.-Wed. and Fri.-Sat., 9am-7pm Thurs., 1pm-5pm Sun., $8 adults, $7 seniors, military, and college students, $5 ages 6-17) has exhibits showing the history and ecology of Wilmington and the region, including locally important historical perspectives and the fossil skeleton of a giant ground sloth unearthed in town.

CAMERON ART MUSEUM

The **Cameron Art Museum** (3201 S. 17th St., 910/395-5999, www.cameronartmuseum. com, 10am-5pm Tues.-Sun., open until 9pm Thurs., closed July 4, Thanksgiving, Dec. 25, and Jan. 1, $10 adults, $8 seniors, military, and students, free ages 16 and under and for military) is one of the major art museums in North Carolina. This 42,000-square-foot facility includes a permanent collection in a range of styles and media, but with an emphasis on North Carolina artists. Classes and event are held. There's also a delightful café.

WILMINGTON RAILROAD MUSEUM

The **Wilmington Railroad Museum** (505 Nutt St., 910/763-2634, www.wrrm.org, hours vary, generally 10am-4pm Mon.-Sat., $9.50 adults, $8.50 seniors and military, $5.50 ages 2-12) sheds light on a largely forgotten part of Wilmington's history: its role as a railroad town. In 1840, Wilmington became the southern terminus for the world's longest continuous rail line, The Wilmington and Weldon (W&W) Railroad; in 1900 the Atlantic Coast Line Railroad absorbed W&W and kept its headquarters in Wilmington until the 1960s.

1: Wilmington Riverwalk; 2: Bellamy Mansion; 3: USS *North Carolina*; 4: quiet Sunday on Wrightsville Beach

Anoles of Carolina

anole, dewlap extended

While you're in the Wilmington area, you'll almost certainly run across a few anoles. These tiny bright-green lizards skitter up and down trees and walls and dash along railings—impossibly fast and improbably green. You may hear locals call them "chameleons" because anoles can change their color from bright green to dirt brown as a way to camouflage themselves against the background and guard against predators. If you watch them long enough, you'll see a fascinating courtship and territorial dominance ritual: A male anole will spread his forelegs wide, do several "push-ups," and then puff out his little crescent-shaped dewlap, the scarlet pouch beneath the chin. When you see one do this, keep still and keep watching; they often repeat the act several times.

On display at the museum are a number of railroad artifacts, including timetables, tools, and locomotives.

Gardens and Parks
AIRLIE GARDENS
Airlie Gardens (300 Airlie Rd., 910/798-7700, www.airliegardens.org, 9am-5pm daily, closed Thanksgiving Day, Dec. 24-25, and Jan. 1, $9 adults, $5 military and New Hanover County residents, $3 ages 4-12), a formal garden park dating to 1901, features more than 50,000 azaleas, several miles of walking trails, and grassy areas perfect for picnics and park concerts, including the Summer Concert Series (1st and 3rd Fri. May-Sept., call for hours). Highlights of Airlie Gardens include the Airlie Oak, a massive live oak believed to be 500 years old, and the Minnie Evans Sculpture Garden and Bottle Chapel. Evans, a visionary African American artist whose mystical work is among the best examples of outsider art, was the gatekeeper here for 25 of her 95 years; examples of her work can also be seen at the Cameron Art Museum. Most of the paths and walkways comply with federal disabled-access rules, but for visitors not mobile enough to walk the gardens, trams are available; the tram schedule is listed on the website.

BLUETHENTHAL WILDFLOWER PRESERVE
On the campus of the University of North Carolina Wilmington, you'll find the

Bluethenthal Wildflower Preserve (601 S. College Rd., located behind the Fisher University Union on Price Dr., 910/962-3000, http://uncw.edu, dawn-dusk daily, free), a small nature preserve with a rich bed of wildflowers and, more importantly, carnivorous plants like the Venus flytrap. It's a lovely walk any time of year, though a little buggy if the wind is still.

HUGH MACRAE PARK

There are a number of parks in and around Wilmington, but locals and visitors stop by **Hugh MacRae Park** (314 Pine Grove Dr., 910/798-7620, www.parks.nhcgov.com, 8am-10pm daily) for the playground, the splash pad, tennis courts and baseball fields, and the 1.55-mile walking trail. Centrally located, loaded with facilities like picnic areas and the aforementioned playground, it's a big draw. You're just as likely to find someone lounging in a hammock strung between two longleaf pines as you are to find them playing tennis or watching the action on the kids' ball fields.

NEW HANOVER COUNTY ARBORETUM

The **New Hanover County Arboretum** (6206 Oleander Dr., 910/798-7660, www. arboretum.nhcgov.com, dawn-dusk daily) is another popular spot for a stroll or a picnic. The five-acre gardens are also home to a Cooperative Extension horticulture laboratory. Most of the gardens use native plants and showcase the floral variety of the area.

SPORTS AND RECREATION
Land Tours

There are a number of land-based tours of Wilmington that dive into the history, food and brewery scene. **Wilmington Tours** (www.wilmington.tours, tours from $25/person) offers walking tours of downtown that cover the town's history, Civil War happenings, African-American history and more; they also offer tours via smartphone app. Taste Carolina (919/237-2254, www.

tastecarolina.net) offers tasting tours ($67) of five to six restaurants on Friday and Saturday afternoons and a Farmers Market Tour and Cooking Class ($77); they also offer tours in eight other cities across the state. Beer lovers should hop on the Port City Brew Bus (www.portcitybrewbus.com, $55-60); their tours visit breweries in different areas of Wilmington and the beach towns and even include a beer and brunch tour. Guides are brewers, bartenders and members of the Cape Fear Craft Beer Alliance (www.capefearcraft. org), so they know their way around a pint. Most pickups are at **Bomber's Beverage Co.** (108 Grace St., 910/833-5107, www. bombersbevco.com), a bottle shop downtown.

Masonboro Island

Just a few minutes' boat ride or a 30-minute paddleboard or kayak ride from Wrightsville Beach brings you to Masonboro Island. Masonboro is an 8.5-mile-long undeveloped barrier island that is fantastic for shelling, birding, surfing, and camping. Get here via your own boat, kayak, or paddleboard, or catch a lift with **Wrightsville Beach Scenic Tours** (275 Waynick Blvd., Wrightsville Beach, 910/200-4002, www.wrightsvillebeachscenictours.com, Masonboro Island Shuttle $25), docking across the street from the Blockade Runner and offering a shuttle to and from the island three times daily Monday-Saturday during summer. The boat leaves Wrightsville Beach at 9am, 12:30pm, and 2pm and departs Masonboro at 11:30am, 2:30pm, and 5pm. If you go over, you'll be there for a while, so pack a cooler with plenty of water, and remember your sunscreen and bug spray. Wrightsville Beach Scenic Tours also offers a number of other tours for adults and for families, including birding tours ($45) in and around Masonboro Island, a Masonboro Island Safari ($75), shelling tours ($45 adults, $30 kids), pirate tours ($30 adults, $25 kids), sunset tours ($35) and more.

In Wilmington you can tour the Cape Fear River with **Wilmington Water Tours** (212

S. Water St., Cape Fear Riverwalk, 910/338-3134, www.wilmingtonwatertours.net, $12-50 adults, $6-25 kids). From the comfort of the 46-foot catamaran *Wilmington* you can learn more about the Cape Fear River, its tributaries, and the history of the surrounding land. Tours take you by the Wilmington waterfront, multiple branches of the Cape Fear River and the Black River. Bring your binoculars and a zoom lens for your camera because you'll spot ospreys, eagles, and other birds on your trip.

Surfing

East Coast surfers love Wrightsville Beach because the waves are consistent and the surf is fun year-round. If you've never tried hanging 10, join one of the many surf camps in the area. **WB Surf Camp** (222 Causeway Dr., 910/256-7873, www.wbsurfcamp.com, $349-590) is one of the largest surfing schools in the area, including one-day, week-long, kids-only, teens-only, women-only, and family camps, even overnight and international surf camps (international camps range from $1,700-3,600). **Crystal South Surf Camp** (Public Access 39, Wrightsville Beach, 910/465-9638, www.crystalsouthsurfcamp.com) offers individual and group lessons ($85 individual 90-minute lesson, $65 group 2-hour lesson). **Tony Silvagni Surf School** (101 G Cape Fear Blvd., Carolina Beach, 910/232-1592, www.surfschoolnc.com, private lessons $50/one-hour lesson, group lessons $40/person/hour, surf camps $330) receives rave reviews, and he's well respected in the local surf community, and his private and group lessons and camps in Carolina Beach are geared toward helping new surfers catch their first wave and advanced surfers refine their techniques.

Kayaking and Stand-Up Paddleboarding

With miles of winding marsh creeks around Masonboro Island and lining the shores of the Intracoastal Waterway, there's no shortage of areas to explore by kayak or stand-up paddleboard. Several outfitters lead tours, provide lessons, and rent out all the gear you'll need to get on the water. **Hook, Line and Paddle** (435 Eastwood Rd., 910/792-6945, www.hooklineandpaddle.com, fishing kayaks $60/half-day to $225/week, single kayaks $50/half-day to $180/week, double kayaks $70/half-day to $210/week, tours from $65, fishing guide $250 for 5 hours) leads group tours around Wrightsville Beach and Masonboro Island and has a variety of kayaks for rent, including fishing kayaks, sit-in and sit-on kayaks, and double kayaks. **Mahanaim Adventures** (910/547-8252, www.mahanaimadventures.com, from $55/half-day and $65/full day, $150 and up for overnight trips) offers kayak trips on the rivers and in the swamps and creeks inland from the area's beaches. **Town Creek, Three Sisters Swamp,** and **Black River** expeditions are fun and take you into parts of the coastal landscape you'd otherwise never see.

For a different type of paddling experience, **Wrightsville SUP** (96 W. Salisbury St., 910/378-9283, www.wrightsvillesup.com, lessons from $65) rents and provides tours on paddleboards ($35/2 hours, $75/day), kayaks (tours $65, rental from $20/hour), and outrigger canoes ($50), and provides lessons, as does Hook, Line and Paddle (rentals $50/half-day to $180/week). It looks difficult at first, but once you get the hang of it, you'll gain confidence quickly. You can also get a stand-up paddleboard or kayak from **Wrightsville Beach Kayak Company** (910/599-0076, www.wrightsvillebeachkayak.com, kayak or paddleboard rentals $40/2 hours, $80/day, $180/week, tandem and fishing kayaks $50/2 hours, $90/day, $225/week); they deliver to beach houses or meet you at one of the area kayak launches and rend beach supplies (chairs $10/day or $30/week, umbrella $15/day or $45/week, beach tent $30/day or $100/week).

1: cruising near Masonboro Island, watching for dolphins; **2:** kayaking marsh creeks; **3:** Town Creek; **4:** Wrightsville SUP has the gear for watery adventure.

Diving

The warm, clear water along North Carolina's coast beckons divers from the world over, and the abundance of shipwrecks, ledges, and natural formations off the coast of Wrightsville Beach make it an ideal location for diving. **Aquatic Safaris** (7220 Wrightsville Ave., Suite A, 910/392-4386, www.aquaticsafaris. com, 9am-7pm Mon.-Fri., 6:30am-6pm Sat., 6:30am-5pm Sun. summer, 10am-6pm Mon.-Fri., 10am-5pm Sat., noon-4pm Sun. off-season, discover scuba diving program $40, beginner open water classes $330, rental gear $10-66, charters $50-165) has been getting divers in the water since 1988, visiting sites from 3 to 59 miles offshore in water as shallow as 25 feet or as deep as 130 feet. They rent out gear, give classes that will have beginners in open water in as few as three days, and provide charter services to two-dozen offshore sites.

Front Line Dive Charters (349 Military Cutoff Rd., Suite A, 910/338-1600, www. frontlinefreediving.com, charters from $120) offers SCUBA and freediving (diving without gear, just holding your breath for an incredibly long time) training, spearfishing expeditions, dives on the shipwrecks just offshore, as well as excursions searching for megalodon teeth Dive charters include breakfast and lunch.

Golf

One of the best things about the Wilmington region is the weather, perfect for both the beach and the golf course. In the winter the weather is mild enough to play anytime; in the summer the courses are immaculate, and it doesn't get all that hot on the greens. Hit the links at **Beau Rivage** (649 Rivage Promenade, 800/628-7080, www. beaurivagegolf.com, 18 holes, par 72, greens fees $33-60), just south of Wilmington, halfway to Kure Beach; it's a lovely and reasonably priced course with challenging holes. Risk-taking players will enjoy taking shots over water hazards on several holes, including one par 3 that will put your ball in the drink if you don't land it just right.

The Donald Ross-designed **Wilmington**

Municipal Golf Course (311 S. Wallace Ave., 910/791-0558, 18 holes, par 71, greens fees $25-42) features forgiving fairways and on more than one hole raises the classic question "Can I carry that bunker?" North of Wilmington, **Castle Bay** (107 Links Court, 910/270-1978, www.castlebaycc.com, 18 holes, par 72, greens fees $30-49 Mon.-Wed., $36-55 Thurs.-Sun., seniors play for $37 Mon.-Wed. and $42 Thurs.-Sat., includes cart) offers a different round of golf. As a Scottish links-style course, it's level, open, and full of deep bunkers, water, and waste areas. The wind can be a factor here, but it's a beautiful course where you can play a round unlike any other in the area.

Spectator Sports

Most spectator sports in Wilmington revolve around cheering on your friend who's running one of the many marathons and road races in town, watching your kids play softball, baseball, soccer or another youth sport, or cheering on the **University of North Carolina Wilmington Seahawks** (www. uncwsports.com). UNCW fields 18 varsity sports from baseball and softball to basketball, diving and soccer. Always popular here in town, after the men's basketball team have made a few NCAA tournament appearances in the last few years, it seems everyone has become a fan. The local baseball team, the **Wilmington Sharks** (910/343-5621, www. wilmingtonsharks.com, reserved seats $9-11 adults, $8 seniors, military, and ages 1-12, general admission $7, free under age 5) play in the Coastal Plain League. Home games are played at Legion Sports Complex (2131 Carolina Beach Rd.).

Each summer in early July, rugby teams from around the world descend on Wilmington for the **Cape Fear Sevens Tournament** (http://fear7s.com), a stripped-down, fast-paced form of rugby that showcases the best in speed, tackles, and ball handling. It's a fun, free event that serves to introduce newcomers to the sport and give rugby fans a charge. In the past it has been held at Ogden Park (7069 Market St.), but check the website for the date and location of this two-day tournament.

ENTERTAINMENT AND EVENTS
Performing Arts

Thalian Hall (310 Chestnut St., 910/632-2285, www.thalianhall.com), the only surviving theater designed by prominent architect John Montague Trimble, has been in near-continuous operation since it opened in 1858. Once serving as the city hall, a library, and an opera house, at the time of its construction it could seat one-tenth of the population of Wilmington, North Carolina's largest city. In its heyday, Thalian Hall was an important stop for theater troupes, productions, and artists touring the country, and today it serves as a major arts venue in the region, hosting a variety of musical acts, ballet, children's theater, and art-house and limited-release films. The resident theatre company, the **Thalian Association** (910/251-1788, www.thalian. org), can trace its roots back to 1788 and is North Carolina's official community theater company.

A number of other theater groups call Thalian Hall home: the **Opera House Theatre Company** (910/762-4234, www. operahouse.squarespace.com). Opera House has produced annual big-name musicals and dramas as well as works by important North Carolinians and other Southern playwrights at Thalian Hall. **Cape Fear Shakespeare on the Green** (910/399-2878, www. capefearshakespeare.com) puts on free plays by the Bard at Thalian Hall and at Greenfield Lake Amphitheater.

Wilmington being an artsy town with a flair for stage and screen performances, it's no surprise to learn that a lot of theater is produced "off Thalian," as it were. **Big Dawg Productions** (910/367-5237, www. bigdawgproductions.org) puts on several plays each year at their 50-seat Cape Fear Playhouse (613 Castle St.). Plays range from classical to contemporary works. They also host the **New Play Festival** each year, a celebration of first-time productions authored by playwrights under the age of 18. The festival is approaching its 20th anniversary and has seen many works that premiered here go on to wider audiences and acclaim.

The **Wilson Center** (703 N. 3rd St., 910/362-7999, www.cfcc.edu, tickets at www. capefearstage.com), a Cape Fear Community College performing arts venue, sits at the north end of downtown Wilmington and hosts dozens of concerts, plays and stage productions throughout the year. Past performers include Brian Wilson, Lily Tomblin, Chris Isaak, Frankie Valli, Monty Python's Spamalot and Jersey Boys. Another place to catch a concert is **Greenfield Lake Amphitheater** (1941 Amphitheater Dr., 910/343-3614, www. greenfieldlakeamphitheater.com) where they host a bevy of concerts spring through fall. Shows are improv-rock heavy, and past performers include Bob Weir and Ratdog, Tedeschi Trucks Band, Les Claypool, G. Love & Special Sauce, Marcus King Band and more. Seating around 750, it's an intimate venue with great sound and awesome sightlines.

Festivals

Wilmington plays host to a number of small festivals throughout the year, but the crown jewel is the **Azalea Festival** (910/794-4650, www.ncazaleafestival.org), held at venues around the city each April and hopefully co-inciding with the blooming of the namesake flowering shrubs. Tours of azalea-laden historic and contemporary homes and gardens draw many visitors, but the street fair, which takes over much of Water Street and a good portion of Front Street, draws many more. With more than 200 arts and crafts vendors, countless food vendors, a dedicated children's area, and four stages of entertainment from national and local acts, the street fair is quite a party. But garden tours and the street fair are just a small part of what the Azalea Festival has to offer: a parade, a circus, dance competitions, gospel concerts, boxing matches, and fireworks round out Azalea Festival events. Like any self-respecting Southern town, it crowns royalty—in this case, the North Carolina Azalea Festival Queen, a Princess, the Queen's Court, a phalanx of cadets from The Citadel, and 100 Azalea Belles. The Azalea Festival draws more than 300,000 visitors annually, so if you decide to visit the area on a weekend trip in early April, be prepared to find Wilmington far more bustling than normal.

Each October, **Riverfest** (www.wilmingtonriverfest.com) takes over part of downtown for a street fair that includes art shows; art, crafts, and food vendors; and car shows. It's smaller than the Azalea Festival, but many downtown venues coordinate concerts and events with Riverfest, making downtown more vibrant for the weekend.

What would a film town be without a film festival? The **Cucalorus Film Festival** (910/343-5995, www.cucalorus.org) celebrates independent films and filmmakers each November. About 150 films from national and international indie filmmakers are shown, along with panels featuring filmmakers, writers, and actors, at Thalian Hall and other venues around town. In a short time Cucalorus has garnered the attention of major film-industry publications.

Burgaw, a tiny town 30 minutes north of Wilmington, is home to the **North Carolina Blueberry Festival** (www.ncblueberryfestival.com) each June. Live music, food vendors, and loads of products featuring blueberries—soap, barbecue sauce, ice cream, muffins—make up this festival.

April is North Carolina Craft Beer Month and the breweries in Wilmington get in on the action, thanks to the **Cape Fear Craft Beer Alliance** (www.capefearcraft.org). The last week of March is **Cape Fear Craft Beer Week** (www.capefearcraftbeerweek.com), when local breweries host tastings and events, brew celebratory beers and get into the spirit. On the last Saturday in March, they put on **Cape Fear Craft and Cuisine** (www.capefearcraftandcuisine.com), a one-evening event pairing local breweries and restaurants that's become one of the best food events in town.

Nightlife

Craft beer fans will want to pull up a barstool at **Cape Fear Wine and Beer** (139 N. Front St., 910/763-3377, www.capefearwineandbeer.net, 4pm-2am Mon.-Wed., 1pm-2am Thurs.-Sun.), a spot that's more punk than trendy, but one that welcomes beer lovers of any ilk. The bartenders are beer experts and can guide even the choosiest of drinkers to a bottle or draft they'll love. You'll find rare microbrews, meads, and barley wines from around the world, but you'll also find a strong emphasis on the best North Carolina beers. Throughout the week, Cape Fear Wine and Beer runs specials on beer flights, chair massages, and North Carolina brews, among others.

Just down the street, **Front Street Brewery** (9 N. Front St., 910/251-1935, www.frontstreetbrewery.com, 11:30am-midnight daily) serves lunch and dinner ($9-16). As good as the pulled-chicken nachos are, the best part about Front Street Brewery is the IPAs, pilsners, and seasonal beers brewed on-site; you can tour the brewery and get a sample to wet your whistle 3pm-5pm every afternoon. And if that's not enough, take a look at their selection of bourbon—it's tremendous.

There is no shortage of breweries or bottle shops in Wilmington. At **Flytrap Brewing** (319 Walnut St., 910/769-2881, www.flytrapbrewing.com, 3pm-10pm Mon.-Thurs., noon-midnight Fri.-Sat., noon-10pm Sun.) they have a small operation but make some delicious American- and Belgian-style ales. Wilmington's food trucks (of which there are precious few) make this a regular stop, so check their calendar to see if there will be a bite to eat when you get there.

Waterline Brewing Co. (721 Surrey St., 910/777-5599, www.waterlinebrewing.com, 2pm-9pm Tues.-Thurs., 2pm-10pm Fri., noon-10pm Sat., noon-8pm Sun.) typically offers a dozen beers in their taproom in a former warehouse under the Cape Fear Memorial Bridge. Their kölsch is exceptional (my second

Craft Brews in Cape Fear

Just a few years ago there was only one brewery in Wilmington, but times have changed and there are nearly two-dozen in town. Wilmington breweries have racked up accolades, awards and stellar writeups and the city's now on the map as one of North Carolina's great beer destinations. Every bartender in town has their favorite brewery and everyone at the bar will have their favorite beer, so ask for a recommendation. But let us do a little of the work for you. Here's a list of some of our favorite breweries in town (and just for good measure, a *kombucha* brewery):

- **Flying Machine Brewing Company** (3130 Randall Pkwy., www.flyingmachine.beer) has a huge taproom and brewhouse where they have live music and plenty of events. Their Patersbier—a light, hoppy Belgain Pale Ale—is not to be missed.

- **New Anthem Beer Project** (116 Dock St., 910/399-4683, www.newanthembeer.com) makes some of the tastiest IPAs in Wilmington. Don't miss Throwing Shade or Kill the Head-lights, two of their hazy IPAs that remain some of the most popular brews in town.

- **Broomtail Craft Brewery** (6404 Amsterdam Way, 910/264-1369, www.broomtailcraft-brewery.com), an equestrian-themed brewery, their Elysium Bier de Garde, a French style, is a great, malty, high gravity brew.

- **The Sour Barn** (7211 Market St., 844/768-7275, www.broomtailcraftbrewery.com), sister to Broomtail, makes sour beers—tart brews that get their sour flavor from special yeasts—and their Galloping Göse is a must-taste.

- **Bill's Front Porch Pub & Brewery** (4238 Market St., 910/762-6333, www.billsfrontporch.com) serves an excellent breakfast stout—coffee laced, a bit of toasted oats, maple syrup—and the kitchen makes some of the best fried chicken in town.

- **Wilmington Brewing Company** (824 S. Kerr Ave., 910/392-3315, www.wilmingtonbrew-ingcompany.com) brews one of the most popular IPAs in town: Tropical Lightning. You'll bring a crowler or two home with you.

- **Waterman's Brewing Company** (1610 Pavilion Place, 910/839-3103, www.waterman-sbrewing.com) brews Brilliant Sunshine, a great, citrus-forward IPA complete with tropical notes and a big alcohol bill.

- **Edward Teach Brewing** (604 N. 4th St., 910/523-5401, www.edwardteachbrewery.com), a Blackbeard-themed brewery, serves Black Spot, an easy-drinking black lager, and Scallywag, a light session IPA.

- **Mad Mole Brewing** (6309 Boathouse Rd., 910/859-8115, www.madmolebrewing.com) has a flavorful saison, Mole Cowbell, and a fun raspberry Kölsch, Raspberry Molay. Oh, and cheeky names for everything on tap.

- **Ironclad Brewery** (115 N. 2nd St., 910/769-0290, www.ironcladbrewery.com) has a huge, beautiful tasting room, and their Peanut Butter Porter that has big flavor to match.

- **Panacea Brewing Company** (102 Old Eastwood Rd, #A5, 910/769-5591, www.panace-abrewingcompany.com) served *kombucha*—fermented, but low alcohol, tea leaves with added herbal and floral flavors; the Pineapple Ginger Turmeric is excellent.

favorite in the world, literally) and their pilsner near perfect. Food trucks and bands frequent the taproom and patio, and a calendar full of events keeps things lively.

Downtown you'll find two great bottle shops. The first, **Palate Bottle Shop & Reserve** (1007 N. 4th St., 910/399-1081, www.palatenc.com, noon-midnight Tues.-Sun.), has a dozen taps of well-curated beer and walls lined with coolers and shelves filled with some hard-to-find beer, including one cooler dedicated to North Carolina beer. Their wine list is equally impressive, with a small but excellent selection. On top of that, Palate is a fun spot to hang out, whether at the bar, outside, or on their covered patio. The second bottle shop is **Bombers Bev Co.** (108 Grace St., 910/833-5107, www.bombersbevco.com, noon-10pm Mon., 10am-10pm Tues.-Wed., 10am-midnight Thurs.-Sat., noon-6pm Sun.), where you'll find a smaller selection of bottled beer that manages to have some elusive finds and remain accessible. They also have a dozen taps, and growler and crowler (think can plus growler) fills.

Dead Crow Comedy Room (265 N. Front St., 910/399-1492, www.deadcrowcomedy.com, doors open at 7pm Tues.-Thurs., at 7pm and 10 pm for early and late shows Fri.-Sat.) is the only full-time comedy club in the region, and they draw some big national acts—think Todd Glass, Big Jay Oakerson, Godfrey—and some crazy-funny regional comedians—Cliff Cash, Matt White. There's also Comedy Bingo (Tues.), improv night (Wed.), and open-mike night (Thurs.).

Battle House (1817 Hall Dr., 910/387-1610, www.battlehouseilm.com, 1:45pm-8pm Mon.-Tues., 2:15pm-9:15pm Wed.-Thurs., 2:15pm-11pm Fri., 10:45am-11pm Sat., 10:45am-7:30pm, from $36) is a high-adrenaline indoor laser tag arena. It's not laser tag like you might've played at home in the 1990s, it's more like paintball, but without the paint (or sing of getting shot). The game arena is a 10,000 square foot warehouse with multiple levels, buildings and structures to use in the various games. Typically, players are divided into teams and they battle to control points in the arena, "kill" opposing players and survive. It's fun for anyone familiar with paintball or first-person-shooter video games.

Port City Escapes (813 S. 16th St., 910/251-7005, www.portcityescape.com, 2pm-10pm Tues.-Thurs., noon-10pm Fri.-Sat., noon-5pm Sun., $26-42) features four escape rooms—"locked room" puzzles where participants race against the clock to solve a series of puzzles that lead from one clue to the next resulting in "escaping" from the room—perfect for teens and adults. Their four rooms rotate themes, but there's a Blackbeard room (escape from the ship before the dreaded pirate Blackbeard sends you to your doom), a murder motel room mystery (figure out the killer and get away before it's too late), as well as a nuclear bomb incident and a Civil War conspiracy to decipher.

SHOPPING
Shopping Centers

The group of buildings known as **The Cotton Exchange** (Front St. and Grace St., 910/343-9896, www.shopcottonexchange.com, 10am-5:30pm Mon.-Sat., noon-4pm Sun.) has housed a variety of businesses in 150 years of continuous operation: the largest flour and hominy mill in the south, a printing company, a Chinese laundry, a "mariners saloon" (where they served more refreshment than just beer), and, of course, a cotton exchange. Today, dozens of boutiques and restaurants call these historic buildings home. **Heart of Carolina** (910/343-0500) carries all sorts of products made by locals, celebrating North Carolina; **Down to Earth** (910/251-0041) carries essential oils and will make custom blends in-house for you; and **Olde Wilmington Toy and Candy Company** (910/399-3594) carries candy, toys and gifts.

Near Wrightsville Beach, the boutique shops and restaurants of **Lumina Station** (1900 Eastwood Rd., 910/256-0900, www.luminastation.com, 10am-6pm Mon.-Sat.) can keep shoppers busy for an afternoon. Some of Wilmington's nicest boutiques call Lumina

Station home, including Ziabird (Suite 9, 910/208-9650, www.ziabird.com), which carries beautiful jewelry and accessories from local designers; **Island Passage** (Suite 8, 910/256-0407, www.islandpassageclothing. com), specializing in women's wear; and **Airlie Moon** (1908 Eastwood Rd., 910/256-0655, www.airliemoon.com), a purveyor of chic coastal home goods.

Mayfaire Town Center (6861 Main St., 910/256-5131, www.mayfairetown.com, 10am-9pm Mon.-Sat., noon-6pm Sun.) is a Main Street-meets-the-mall shopping center, with a familiar range of shops and chain restaurants. The 16-screen movie theater, wide selection of shops to browse, and numerous restaurants in Mayfaire make it an easy place to spend part of a day shopping, dining, and taking in a movie, alone or in a group.

Antiques and Consignment Stores

Just out of downtown on Market Street, **The Ivy Cottage** (3020, 3030, and 3100 Market St., 910/815-0907, www.threecottages.com, 10am-6pm Mon.-Sat., 12am-5pm Sun.) occupies a trio of buildings and an overflow warehouse, all filled with antiques and consignment furniture. In Cottage 2, you'll find antique jewelry as well as an extensive collection of crystal stemware and decanters. At Cottage 3, you'll find more beachy, shabby-chic furniture and home goods, while Cottage 1 carries more armoires, dressers, and knickknacks.

On Castle Street, along the southern edge of the historic district, an expanding group of antique shops, restaurants, and stores, all clustered in a three- or four-block stretch, have emerged in recent years. **Michael Moore Antiques** (539 Castle St., 910/763-0300, 10am-6pm Mon.-Sat., 1pm-6pm Sun.) carries a collection of pristine furniture, as do many of the antiques stores in the area. Be sure to stop in **Maggy's Antiques and Collectibles** (555 Castle St., 910/399-2373, 10am-5pm Tues.-Sat., closed Sun.-Mon.) and take a walk along Castle as there's always a

new antique shop to stop in. Downtown on Front Street, **Antiques of Old Wilmington** (25 S. Front St., 910/763-6011, www. antiquesofoldwilmington.com, 10am-6pm daily in summer, 10am-5pm daily in winter) has a large antique lighting collection, bookcases, and thousands of small collectibles.

Wilmington has a number of good vintage and consignment clothing stores. On Castle Street, **Style Girl Vintage** (511 Castle St., 910/538-5657, www.stylegirljessjames. com, 11am-5pm Tues.-Sat.) carries a curated selection of vintage fashion; owner Jess James is a stylist and fashion writer, and her pieces are always excellent. **Second Street Vintage** (615 Castle St., 910/833-5770, www. secondskinwilmington.com, 11am-6pm daily) is only a block away and has a good array of men's and women's vintage clothing from the '50s on. Downtown, **The Wonder Shop** (22 N. Front St., 910/763-1982, 11am-7pm Mon.-Fri., 10am-8pm Sat., noon-6pm Sun.) has a fun selection of men's and women's clothing and a few accessories for good measure.

Books and Games

Wilmington has an active and vibrant literary culture. The University of North Carolina Wilmington is home to a creative writing program of national renown, with a growing number of authors (including this one) graduating and producing novels, memoirs, screenplays and more, and the town has several good bookstores that carry their works and works by local authors as well as the expected selections. **Old Books on Front Street** (249 N. Front St., 910/762-6657, www. oldbooksonfrontst.com, 10am-6pm Mon.-Sat., noon-6pm Sun.) is a used bookstore with nearly two miles of books on their floor-to-ceiling shelves. Knowledgeable staff and extensive selection make this a must-stop for book lovers. **Pomegranate Books** (4418 Park Ave., 910/452-1107, 9am-5pm Tues.-Sat.) hosts readings by local writers and boasts a good selection of literary work by local and regional authors. **Two Sisters Bookery** (318 Nutt St., Cotton Exchange, 910/762-4444,

10am-5:30pm Mon.-Sat., noon-4pm Sun.) carries books covering all genres and subject matters and is a great place to pick up a best-seller.

Cape Fear Games (4107 Oleander Dr. Ste. D, 910/798-6006, www.capefeargames.com, 10am-11pm Mon.-Sat., noon-10pm Sun.) carries a large selection of board games, card games, and role-playing games. They have a number of games to try out, and they host Magic: The Gathering and Pokemon tournaments as well as adults-only brews and board game nights pairing craft beer with tabletop games.

Galleries and Art Studios

The ArtWorks (200 Willard St., 910/352-1822, www.theartworks.co, 10am-6pm Fri., 10am-3pm Sat.) is a 7,000 square foot "art village" including more than 50 working artists' studios and space for public art classes. Artists include jewelers, oil and acrylic painters, potters, glass artists, sculptors and illustrators; individual artists have their work for sale. Many of the artists open their studios for the monthly Fourth Friday Gallery Nights (6pm-9pm).

Barouke (119 S. Water St. in the Old City Market, 910/762-4999, www.barouke.com, 10am-6pm daily) carries handcrafted works by master woodworkers, including hand-turned pens and vases, clocks, decorative bowls, boxes, games, kitchen accessories, and more. Most everything is finished in such a way as to allow the wood's natural beauty to show through. Barouke is one of several shops in **The Old Wilmington City Market** (www.oldwilmingtoncitymarket.com) that include clothing boutiques, small art galleries and more.

New Elements Art Gallery (271 N. Front St., 910/343-8997, www.newelementsgallery.com, 11am-6pm Tues.-Sat.) has been showcasing works by local and regional artists since 1985. Featuring contemporary art in a wide range of styles and media, New Elements remains an influential gallery today, and openings are well attended. With art that includes the avant-garde, classical plein air oil paintings, and wire or ceramic sculptures, they always have something you'll want to take home.

Between Wilmington and Wrightsville is **Blue Moon Gift Shops** (203 Racine Dr., 910/799-5793, www.bluemoongiftshops.com, 10am-6pm Mon.-Fri., 10am-5pm Sat., noon-5pm Sun.), a huge gallery with works from more than 100 artists and artisans, ranging in style from folk art to fine metalwork.

Music

Since the introduction of digital music, most of Wilmington's music stores have gone, but **Gravity Records** (612 Castle St., 910/343-1000, 9am-6pm Mon.-Sat., noon-6pm Sun.), has held on, carving out a niche for itself by stocking LPs and CDs by the most relevant contemporary artists. They've got a huge stock of vinyl as well as an impressive selection of new and used CDs.

FOOD
French

Wilmington's dining scene is not what you'd expect from a beachy tourist town. Sure, we've got our share of restaurants where you pay for the view instead of the food and we've got the chains every other town has, but our restaurants have grown up and represent cuisines and approaches to food that span the globe.

Downtown, **Caprice Bistro** (10 Market St., 910/815-0810, www.capricebistro.com, 5pm-10pm Sun.-Thurs., 5pm-11pm Fri.-Sat., bar until 2am daily, $14-27) serves delicious traditional French cuisine and has an extensive wine list. Upstairs, an intimate bar lined with sofas and a scattering of tables serves a limited menu but is one of the more relaxed places to grab a quick bite and a drink downtown.

Brasserie du Soleil (1908 Eastwood Rd., 910/256-2226, www.brasseriedusoleil.com, 11:30am-10pm Mon.-Thurs., 11:30am-11pm Fri.-Sat., 5pm-10pm Sun., $12-32) is a brasserie-style French restaurant that utilizes the best ingredients from local, regional, and small-farm sources to create food that will keep you coming back. Personal favorites include the duck or flounder for dinner, the shrimp salad croissant for lunch, and their build-your-own-salad for any meal. Don't forget the oysters; the raw bar here is small, but exceptional.

Italian

★ **Benny's Big Time Pizzeria** (206 Greenfield St., 910/550-2525, www. vivianhoward.com, 4pm-10pm Tues.-Thurs., 4pm-11pm Fri., 11am-11pm Sat., 11am-10pm Sun., $9-17), from chef Vivian Howard and her husband Ben Knight, is their homage to the checked-tablecloth Italian restaurants Ben grew up with. A departure from the exceptional nouveau southern the couple dishes up at Chef & the Farmer in Kinston (about 90 minutes north), Benny's is no less exceptional. House-made pasta, hand-tossed pizza, and hot honey (a tantalizing blend of honey and Calabrian peppers), plus a slate of creative pies (the Talk'in Shiitake is a mushroom and sausage pie to die for and the Clamuel L. Jackson has, well, clams on it) grace the plates. If the wait—an hour or more on the busiest nights— is any sign, they're doing things right.

At **Osteria Cicchetti** (1125-K Military Cutoff Rd., 910/256-7476, www.osteria-cicchetti.com, from 11:30am Mon.-Fri. and from 5pm Sat.-Sun., entrées $11-21), or OC as it's known to regulars, the pizzas are rustic and a perfect starter (try the Soprano or the Parma); for pasta, the linguini with clams or spaghetti cicchetti, with meatballs and sausage, makes a great meal; but the day fish is where it's at. They have a second location in Monkey Junction, midway between Wilmington and Carolina Beach. **OC2** (5104 S. College Rd., 910/392-3490, open for dinner at 5pm Mon.-Sat., 4pm Sun., $11-21) is just as good as the original, and a little less crowded.

Seafood

Near Wrightsville Beach, the **Fish House Grill** (1410 Airlie Rd., 910/256-3693, www. thefishhousegrill.com, 11:30am-9pm daily, $6-20) and **Dockside** (1308 Airlie Rd.,

910/256-2752, www.thedockside.com, 11am-9pm daily, $7-24), two restaurants only steps apart on the Intracoastal Waterway, deliver good food and great views. At the Fish House, the food is a little more casual, with a menu that focuses on burgers and sandwiches; Dockside focuses more on seafood, and their elevated deck gives you a bird's-eye view of passing boats while you dine.

The seafood from **South Beach Grill** (100 Lumina Ave. S, 910/256-4646, www. southbeachgrillwb.com, 11am-10pm Mon.-Sat., 11am-9pm Sun., lunch $11-16, dinner $13-31) may just be the best in Wilmington. It's fresh, perfectly prepared, and the menu has enough variety to keep you coming back every meal for a week. Whether you're in the mood for blackened fish tacos or fried oyster tacos, shrimp and grits or a pulled pork sandwich, the fresh catch or a sweet potato-crusted flounder, you'll go home raving about it.

Southern

Hands down one of the best restaurants in North Carolina is found in downtown Wilmington. ★ **PinPoint Restaurant** (114 Market St., 910/769-2972, www. pinpointrestaurant.com, 5:30pm-9:30pm Mon.-Thurs., 5:30pm-10pm Fri.-Sat., 5:30pm-9pm Sun., brunch 10:30am-2pm Sun., diner $16-38, brunch $7-15) celebrates Southern cuisine in a restrained, refined way that few other restaurants can pull off. Each plate is beautiful and it's evident that chef Dean Neff has surrounded himself with a kitchen brigade and army of servers who care as much about the food as he does. Dishes like fried catfish with grits come out as elegant to look at as they are to taste, and familiar bites like hummus are given a Southern spin by using butter beans rather than chickpeas. The pork chop is exceptional, the steak is divine, but the catfish, grouper (or whatever the fresh catch is that day) and the seasonal vegetable plate are drool-worthy.

If breakfast is what you're craving, look no further than next door to PinPoint restaurant at **The Dixie Grill** (116 Market St.,

910/762-7280, www.thedixiegrillwilmington. wordpress.com, 8am-3pm Mon.-Sat., 8am-2pm Sun., $4-13). This old-fashioned diner is a fixture for locals and visitors alike, and on the weekends there can be a wait; the biscuits make the wait worth it, but that's only one thing on a killer breakfast menu.

Speaking of breakfast, one of the best in town (expect a wait here, too) is **Cast Iron Kitchen** (8024 Market St., 910/821-8461, www.castiron-kitchen.com, 7:30am-3pm Tues.-Sun., $6-15). This is stick-to-your-ribs comfort food done right. Biscuits and gravy that make you want to high five the next table, a burger that makes you want to stop making them yourself because you'll never make one this good, and a chicken biscuit with a runny egg and peppery cheese that landed them a spot on *Diners, Drive-Ins & Dives* are go-to dishes, but considering I've eaten nearly everything on the menu and have yet to find a don't-get-that dish, you can't go wrong here.

For gussied-up Southern food, head to **Rx** (421 Castle St., 910/399-3080, www. rxwilmington.com, 5pm-9pm Tues.-Thurs. and Sun., 5pm-9:30pm Fri.-Sat., brunch 10am-2pm Sun., $10-33). Their cast iron skillet-fried chicken is hard to beat, and their innovative takes on classic Southern dishes (buffalo-style pig ears? Indeed!) will make you look at the region's cuisine in a new light.

Eclectic American

I'm not a vegetarian nor am I a vegan, but one of my favorite restaurants tends that way. ★ **Sealevel City Gourmet** (1015 S. Kerr Ave., 910/833-7196, www.sealevelcitygourmet. com, open for lunch 11am-2pm Wed.-Sun., serving dinner 5pm-9pm Thurs.-Sat., $3-18), or just Sealevel, serves all the sandwiches and burgers you love, just without the meat. The lentil patty melt is a favorite, as is the kimchi tempeh reuben, but their few seafood dishes—fish and shrimp are the only animal proteins on the menu—like the shrimpburger or special-of-the-day taco are excellent choices. The staff is friendly and fun, sometimes you'll get a visit from the owner or kitchen staff, and

you'll find that you're surrounded by locals who know the secret: No matter your meat-eating proclivity, a bite or two from just about anything on the menu here will bring you back again and again.

Wilmington native Keith Rhodes, a James Beard Award semifinalist and a *Top Chef* contender, owns one of the top restaurants in town, **Catch** (6623 Market St., 910/799-3847, www.catchwilmington.com, 5:30pm-9pm Mon.-Sat., $28). At Catch, Rhodes serves his "Viet-South" cuisine, a fusion of Vietnamese flavors with Southern ingredients and techniques that have won fans including celebrities like Gwyneth Paltrow and renowned chefs.

manna (123 Princess St., 910/763-5252, www.mannaavenue.com, 5:30pm-close Tues.-Sun., $28) is an innovative restaurant that also focuses on local seasonal ingredients. Their menu is playful, with dishes like the Wool Street Journal, The Reel Thing, and Iron Chef: Bobby Filet, but the food is seriously good. One of the few bars in Wilmington where making a cocktail is treated as an art, this is definitely a restaurant where you'll want to show up early and enjoy a drink at the bar. Reservations are advised.

To say **The Fork n Cork** (122 Market St., 910/228-5247, www.theforkncork.com, 11am-11pm Mon.-Thurs., 11am-midnight Fri., 10am-midnight Sat., 10am-10pm Sun., $9-16) serves burgers, sandwiches, and bar food is a disservice. It serves some of the best burgers you'll eat and spun-up takes on dishes you expect (like wings) in a bar. Two of my favorites aren't even burgers. The Texas poutine (a pile of fries topped with smoked brisket, cheese, and barbecue sauce), and duck wings (think chicken wings, but from a duck) have never let me down, but for burgers, The Hot Mess—it's got everything on it—is the way to go.

Chef-owner Sam Cahoon made a name for himself at another restaurant in town, but he's making his mark on Wilmington with **Savorez** (402 Chestnut St., 910/833-8894, www.savorez.com, 11:30am-10:30pm Mon.-Fri., noon-10pm Sat., 10am-2pm Sun., lunch and dinner $9-20, brunch $5-10), a restaurant that blends his love for Latin flavors and local ingredients. Everything here is fresh—it has to be when you regularly feature ceviche on the menu—and packed with flavor. Never too spicy, but never dull, the seasoning brings out the best in every ingredient, making a forkful into something special.

One block over, the **Copper Penny** (109 Chestnut St., 910/762-1373, www.copperpennync.com, 11am-10pm Sun.-Wed., 11am-10:30pm Thur., 11am-11:30pm Fri.-Sat., $10-17) serves traditional pub grub in a traditional pub atmosphere. It can get crowded and loud, especially on game days, but the food, especially their cheesesteak, chicken wings, and fish-and-chips, makes any wait worth it.

At **The Greeks** (5120 S. College Rd., Suite 107, 910/313-3000, www.thegreeksnc.weebly.com, 11am-9pm Mon.-Sat., entrées around $9) the menu includes classic Greek dishes and street food. One of their best dishes is The Authentic, a pork gyro made just like the owner used to have growing up in Greece: loaded down with tomato, onion, French fries, and mustard. But if you love falafel, theirs is the best in town, hands down.

One of my favorite bakeries in the state, **Love, Lydia** (1502 S. 3rd St., 7am-2pm Wed.-Fri., 8am-2pm Sat.-Sun., $2-8) is just up the street from Benny's, and the bread, sweets, and treats that come out of the ovens here are to die for.

Asian

Where Catch takes Asian cuisine and blends it with Southern food culture, a number of Asian restaurants in Wilmington stay true to their roots. ★ **Indochine** (7 Wayne Dr., at Market St., 910/251-9229, www.indochinewilmington.com, 11am-2pm Tues.-Fri., noon-3pm Sat., 5pm-10pm daily, $11-20) serves an expansive menu of Thai and Vietnamese dishes as well as a number of vegetarian options. Entrées are huge, so sharing is encouraged, but even then, be prepared for leftovers.

Bento Box (1121-L Military Cutoff Rd., 910/509-0774, www.bentoboxsushi.com,

11:30am-9pm Mon.-Wed., 11:30am-10pm Thurs.-Fri., 5pm-10pm Sat., $5-18) is hands down the best sushi in Wilmington. Chef Lee goes to great lengths to bring in the highest-quality fish he can find, and it pays off. Sit inside where dark, mica-flecked granite tops the bar and the atmosphere is a little cooler, or go to a more chill spot outside on the patio, weather permitting.

ACCOMMODATIONS
Bed-and-Breakfasts

Wilmington's Historic District is large and filled with historic bed-and-breakfasts. Check with the **Wilmington N.C. River District & Island Beaches** (www.wilmingtonandbeaches.com), the visitors bureau for the area, for a comprehensive listing of lodging, shopping, and dining.

★ **Front Street Inn** (215 S. Front St., 800/336-8184, www.frontstreetinn.com, $149-239) is a tiny boutique B&B only a block from the Riverwalk and a short stroll to a number of notable restaurants and charming shops. It occupies an old Salvation Army building and offers bright, airy guest rooms in a great location. The **Rosehill Inn Bed and Breakfast** (114 S. 3rd St., 800/815-0250, www.rosehill.com, $129-169) occupies a gorgeous 1848 home only three blocks from the river. The flowery high-B&B-style decor suits the house.

The **Taylor House Inn** (14 N. 7th St., 910/763-7581, www.taylorhousebb.com, $137-275) is in a newer home that dates to 1905. Despite this relative novelty, it's a pretty but not ostentatious building, unlike some of the homes nearby. The famous **Graystone Inn** (100 S. 3rd St., 888/763-4773, www.graystoneinn.com, $179-379) was built in the same year as the Taylor House Inn but with a very different aesthetic. Solid stone and castle-like, the Graystone has beautiful guest rooms only blocks from good restaurants, shopping, and nightlife.

Hotels

An upscale place to stay is the **Hotel Ballast** (301 N. Water St., 910/763-5900, www.hotelballast.com, from $165), which overlooks the Cape Fear River. Part of the Tapestry Collection by Hilton, Hotel Ballast has 272 rooms that went under a massive renovation and rebranding in 2017. The Riverwalk is right out the door, putting the restaurants and nightlife of downtown Wilmington only a short walk away, along with the on-site Ruth's Chris Steakhouse, a coffee shop and **Board & Barrel Coastal Kitchen** (910/343-6130, breakfast 6:30am-10am Mon.-Fri. and 7am-10:30am Sat.-Sun., lunch 11am-2pm daily, diner 5pm-11pm daily, breakfast $9-16, lunch and dinner $7-25), a bar and restaurant serving breakfast, lunch and dinner.

At Wrightsville Beach, it's hard to beat the **Blockade Runner** (275 Waynick Blvd., 877/684-8009, www.blockade-runner.com, $189-600). From the outside it looks like any other 1960s hotel, but inside it's chic, stylish, and comfortable. Every guest room has a great view—the Atlantic Ocean and sunrise on one side, the Intracoastal Waterway and sunsets on the other—and with several adventure outfitters operating in the hotel, recreation options abound. The hotel restaurant, East Oceanfront Dining (breakfast 7am-10:30am, lunch 11am-5pm, dinner 5pm-9pm, Sunday brunch 10:30am-2pm, breakfast $10-16, lunch $9-18, dinner $15-34), is a hidden gem in Wilmington's dining scene thanks to the vision of chef Jess Cabo.

On the north end of downtown, **Embassy Suites by Hilton Wilmington Riverfront** (9 Estell Lee Place, 910/765-1131, www.embassysuites3.hilton.com, $185-293) serves the city's convention center and other visitors. With a rooftop bar and its proximity to the Riverwalk and a number of planned parks, restaurants, and facilities (coming on line in 2019 and onward), it's in a prime location. The **Courtyard Wilmington Downtown/ Historic District** (229 N. 2nd St., 910/632-2900, www.marriott.com, from $125) sits in a prime downtown location less than a block from shopping and restaurants, which makes it a great place to stay.

There are plenty of more affordable options available just a couple of miles out of downtown. The **Holiday Inn** (5032 Market St., 910/392-1101, www.wilmingtonhi.com, $97) on Market Street is clean, comfortable, close to downtown, and minutes from the beach. The **Hilton Garden Inn Wilmington Mayfaire Town Center** (6745 Rock Spring Rd., 910/509-4046, www.hiltongardeninn3.com, from $114) is an affordable option that's a short drive to both Wrightsville Beach and downtown Wilmington, and walkable to a large shopping center.

Vacation Rentals

As in any good beach town, there are plenty of vacation rental agencies handling beach house and condo rentals at the beaches near Wilmington. Prices vary by season, size, amenity, and proximity to the waves, but you should be able to find a house that suits your travel style. Bryant Real Estate (800/322-3764, www.bryantre.com) and Intracoastal Vacation Rentals (855/346-2463, www.intracoastalrentals.com) are two of the bigger rental agencies, though the smaller companies—Wrightsville Sands Realty (910/679-4082, www.wrightsvillesands.com) and Sea Scape Properties (910/332-7284, www.seascapevacationhomes.com—also have some gems to rent. The beauty of the beaches around Wilmington is this: If you can travel in September or October, the water is perfect, the crowds are somewhere else, and the rental rates go down.

NORTH OF WILMINGTON
Topsail Island

If you want to say it like a local, Topsail is pronounced "TOP-sul," so called because legend has it that pirates once hid behind the island and only their topsails were visible to passing ships. There are three towns on Topsail Island—Topsail Beach, North Topsail Beach, and Surf City. All are popular beach destinations and are less commercial than many beach communities but still have enough beach shops and souvenir shacks to keep that beach town charm. A swing bridge spans the Intracoastal Waterway at Surf City, and it opens on the hour for passing ships (expect traffic backups when it opens). At the north end of the island, a tall bridge between Sneads Ferry and North Topsail Beach eliminates the traffic backups from passing ships and provides an unheralded view of the 26-mile-long island and the marshes around it.

Among Topsail's claims to fame is its importance in the conservation of sea turtles. The **Karen Beasley Sea Turtle Rescue and Rehabilitation Center** (822 Carolina Ave., Topsail Beach, 910/329-0222, www. seaturtlehospital.org, visiting hours noon-4pm, Mon.-Tues. and Thurs.-Sat., tours $5 adults, $4 active military, $3 children 12 and under) treats sea turtles that have been injured by sharks or boats, or that have fallen ill or become stranded. Its 24 enormous tubs, which look something like the vats at a brewery, provide safe places for the animals to recover from their injuries and recoup their strength before being released back into the ocean. Hospital staff also patrol the full shoreline of Topsail Island every morning in the summertime, before the crowds arrive, to identify and protect any new clutches of eggs that were laid overnight. Founder Jean Beasley has been featured as a Hero of the Year on the Animal Planet TV channel. Unlike most wildlife rehabilitation centers, this hospital allows visitors.

Hands down one of the best places to eat in the region, and certainly the best spot on Topsail, is ★ **The Bistro at Topsail** (602-b Roland Ave., Surf City, 910/328-2000, www. topsailbistro.com, 5:30pm-close Tues.-Sat., $14-44). Located just across the bridge onto the island, this is one of those surprise places you'll return to, tell your friends about, and discuss at length in inferior restaurants. They've received recognition in the form of Wine Spectator Awards of Excellence, Top 100 Most Scenic Restaurants in America, Best Bourbon Bar in America 2016, and Best Chef North Carolina. Chef Bud Taylor mans the grill but also operates a 10-acre farm where he grows a significant amount of the produce used by the Bistro. What should you order? Anything from the sea, as Taylor's relationships with local fishermen ensures he has the freshest catch.

Dirty South Bar & Grill (718 S. Anderson Blvd., 910/541-2800, www. dirtysouthbarandgrill.com, 11am-11pm Tues.-Thurs., 11am-1am Fri., noon-1am Sat., noon-11pm Sun., $9-22) has build-your-own burgers (or just order from their burger

beach houses on Topsail Island

menu) as well as chicken and waffles, hot dogs topped with mac-and-cheese (and, of course, bacon), and "mile high" nachos that have so much stuff on them they're really a nacho tower, not a plate. They have entertainment several times a week, like the steel drummer who shows up on Thursday nights throughout summer, karaoke on Fridays, and live music on the weekends.

Jacksonville

Jacksonville, only 62 miles northeast of Wilmington on Highway 17, is best known as the home of **Camp Lejeune,** a massive Marine Corps installation that dates to 1941. Lejeune is the home base of the II Marine Expeditionary Force and MARSOC, the Marine Corps division of U.S. Special Operations Command. The base's nearly 250 square miles include extensive beaches where service members receive training in amphibious assault skills.

Camp Johnson, a satellite installation of Camp Lejeune, used to be known as Montford Point and was the home of the famous Montford Point Marines, the first African Americans to serve in the United States Marine Corps. Their history, a crucial chapter in the integration of the U.S. Armed Forces, is paid tribute at the **Montford Point Marine Museum** (Bldg. 101, East Wing, Camp Gilbert Johnson, 910/554-0808, www.montfordpointmarines.org, 11am-4pm Tues. and Thurs., other times by appointment, free, donations accepted).

★ Hammocks Beach State Park

At the appealing little fishing town of Swansboro you'll find the mainland side of **Hammocks Beach State Park** (1572 Hammocks Beach Rd., 910/326-4881, http://ncparks.gov, 8am-6pm daily Sept.-May, 8am-7pm daily June-Aug., park office 8am-5pm daily Sept-May, 8am-6pm daily June-Aug.). Most of the park lies on the other side of a maze of marshes on Bear and Huggins Islands. These wild, totally undeveloped islands are important havens for migratory waterfowl and nesting loggerhead sea turtles. Bear Island is 3.5 miles long and less than 1 mile wide, surrounded by the Atlantic Ocean, Intracoastal Waterway, Bogue and Bear Inlets, and wild salt marshes. A great place to swim, Bear Island has a bathhouse complex with a snack bar, restrooms, and outdoor showers. Huggins Island, by contrast, is significantly smaller and covered in ecologically significant maritime forest and lowland marshes. Two paddle trails, one just over 2.5 miles long and the other 6 miles long, weave through the marshes that surround the islands. **Paddle NC** (910/612-3297, www.paddlenc.com) leads kayak and stand-up paddleboard tours ($50-60) of the islands, even circumnavigating Huggins Island ($80). Camping is permitted on Bear Island in reserved and first-come, first-served sites near the beach and inlet, with restrooms and showers available nearby ($10/day).

A private boat or **passenger ferry** (910/326-4881, http://ncparks.gov, $5 ages 13 and up roundtrip, $3 seniors and children) are the only ways to reach the islands. The ferry's schedule varies by the day of the week and the season, but it generally departs from the mainland and the islands every 30 to 60 minutes from mid-morning until late afternoon; ferries don't run every day in the off-season and there's no ferry service to Bear Island Dec.-Mar. Check the website for current ferry times.

GETTING THERE AND AROUND

Wilmington is the eastern terminus of I-40, more than 300 miles east of Asheville and approximately 120 miles south and east of Raleigh. The Cape Fear region is also crossed by a major north-south route, U.S. 17, the old Kings Highway of colonial times. Wilmington is roughly equidistant along U.S. 17 between Jacksonville to the north and Myrtle Beach, South Carolina, to the south; both cities are about an hour's drive away.

Wilmington International Airport (ILM, 1740 Airport Blvd., Wilmington, 910/341-4125, www.flyilm.com) serves the region with flight service from American Airlines and Delta. It's a small airport and flight selections can be limited, but flying into the two nearest airports—RDU in Raleigh, North Carolina, and MYR in Myrtle Beach, South Carolina—will add anywhere from 2 to 2.25 hours to your trip, plus the expense of a rental car.

Wave Transit (910/343-0106, www.wavetransit.com), Wilmington's public transportation system, operates buses throughout the metropolitan area and trolleys in the historic district. Fares are a low $2 one way. If you're planning on exploring outside the city, you'll need a car.

The Southern Coast

From the beaches of Brunswick and New Hanover County to the swampy subtropical fringes of land behind the dunes, this little corner of the state is special. South of Wrightsville Beach, a series of barrier islands and quiet low-key beaches extends to the South Carolina border. Starting with Pleasure Island, which includes Kure and Carolina Beach, and ending with the Brunswick Islands, including Oak Island, Holden Beach, Sunset Beach, and Ocean Isle, these beaches are family-friendly places where you're more likely to find rental homes than high-rise hotels.

You'll see some distinctive wildlife here, including the ubiquitous green anole, called "chameleons" by many locals. These tiny lizards, normally bright lime green, are able to fade to brown. They're everywhere—skittering up porch columns and along balcony railings, peering around corners, and hiding in the fronds of palmetto trees. The males put on a big show by puffing out their strawberry-colored dewlaps.

This part of the state has the largest population of the anole's distant cousin: alligators. Unlike their tiny cousins, alligators have the potential to be deadly. All along river and creek banks and in bays and swamps, you'll see their scaly hulks basking in the sun. If you're in a kayak or canoe or on a paddleboard, you may mistake them for a log until you see their eyes and nostrils poking out of the water. Be aware of where you, children, and pets step when hiking, and avoid swimming in fresh water in places where alligators are prone to lurk. All that said, alligators are thrilling to see and generally will vacate the area if you come too close.

If you're in the area during the early part of summer, you could see a sea turtle dragging herself into the dunes to lay a clutch of eggs. Huge loggerhead sea turtles, tiny Kemp's ridley sea turtles, greens, and even the occasional leatherback make their nests along the beaches here. Nesting season runs from mid-May through August, and they hatch between 60 and 90 days later, depending on the species. Organizations such as the Bald Head Island Conservancy (700 Federal Rd., Bald Head Island, 910/457-0089, www.bhic.org) help protect nests and educate area residents and visitors on issues relevant to protecting sea turtles.

In certain highly specialized environments, mainly in and around Carolina bays, which have both moist and nutrient-poor soil, the Venus flytrap and other carnivorous plants thrive. The flytrap and some of its cousins are endangered, but in this region—and nowhere else in the world—you'll have plenty of opportunities to see them growing wild.

KURE BEACH AND CAROLINA BEACH

Kure is a two-syllable name, pronounced "KYUR-ee" like the physicist Marie Curie, not like "curry." This is a small beach community without the neon lights and towel shops of larger beaches. Kure abuts Carolina Beach, where the boardwalk and beach shops are part of the charm. This island is known as Pleasure Island, and it's a mix of full-time residences and vacation homes—ome second homes, many rentals. You'll find a few motels scattered throughout, a state park and state historic site (like a lot of coastal towns, there's a Confederate gun emplacement here), as well as an excellent aquarium. Kure and Carolina Beaches are classic beach towns, the likes of which you don't see often today. A short drive from Wilmington—only 30 minutes—and you've stepped back in time.

Carolina Beach State Park

Just to the north of Kure is **Carolina Beach State Park** (1010 State Park Rd., off U.S. 421, Carolina Beach, 910/458-8206, http://ncparks.gov, office and visitor center 8am-5pm daily, park 7am-10pm May-Sept., 7am-9pm Mar.-Apr. and Oct., 7am-7pm Feb. and Nov., 7am-6pm Dec.-Jan.). Of all the state parks in the coastal region, this may be the one with the greatest ecological diversity. Within its boundaries are coastal pine and oak forests, pocosins between the dunes, saltwater marshes, a 50-foot sand dune known as Sugarloaf Dune, and limesink ponds. Of the ponds, one is a deep cypress swamp, one is a natural garden of water lilies, and one is an ephemeral pond that dries into a swampy field every year, an ideal home for carnivorous plants. You'll see Venus flytraps and their ferocious cousins, but resist the urge to dig them up, pick them, or tempt them with your fingertips. Sort of like stinging insects that die after delivering their payload, the flytraps' traps can wither and fall off once they're sprung.

The park has 83 drive-in and walk-in campsites (year-round except Dec. 24-25, $20, $15 over age 62), each with a grill and a picnic table. Two are wheelchair-accessible, and restrooms and hot showers are nearby. **Paddle NC** (910/612-3297, www.paddlenc.com) offers kayak and stand-up paddleboard tours ($55-80) departing from the marina.

Fort Fisher State Park

At the southern end of Kure Beach is **Fort Fisher State Recreation Area** (1000 Loggerhead Rd., off U.S. 421, 910/458-5798, http://ncparks.gov, 8am-9pm daily June-Aug., 8am-8pm daily Apr.-May and Sept., 8am-7pm Mar. and Oct., 8am-6pm daily Nov.-Feb.), with six miles of beautiful beach; it's a less crowded and less commercial alternative to the other beaches of the area. A lifeguard is on duty 10am-5:45pm daily late May-early Sept. The park also includes a 1.1-mile hiking trail that winds through marshes and along the sound, ending at an observation deck where visitors can watch wildlife.

Fort Fisher is also a significant historic site, a Civil War earthwork stronghold designed to withstand massive assault. Modeled in part on the Crimean War's Malakhoff Tower, Fort Fisher's construction was an epic saga as hundreds of Confederate soldiers, enslaved African Americans, and conscripted indigenous Lumbee people were brought here to build what became the Confederacy's largest fort. After the fall of Norfolk in 1862, Wilmington became the most important open port in the South, a vital harbor for blockade-runners and military vessels. Fort Fisher held until nearly the end of the war. On December 24, 1864, U.S. General Benjamin "The Beast" Butler attacked the fort with 1,000 troops but was repulsed; his retreat led to him being relieved of his command. A few weeks later, in January 1865, Fort Fisher was finally taken, but it required a Union force of 9,000 troops and 56 ships in what was the largest amphibious assault by Americans until World War II. Without its defenses at Fort Fisher, Wilmington soon fell, hastening the end of the war, which came just three months later. Due to the final assault by the Union forces and 150 years of wind, tides, and hurricanes, not much of the massive earthworks survive, but the remains of this vital Civil War site are preserved in an oddly peaceful and pretty seaside park that contains a restored gun emplacement and a visitors center with interpretive exhibits.

The **North Carolina Aquarium at Fort Fisher** (900 Loggerhead Rd., 910/772-0500, www.ncaquariums.com, 9am-5pm daily year-round except Thanksgiving and Dec. 25, $13 adults, $12 military and seniors, $11 ages 3-12) is one of three aquariums operated by the state; this is a beautiful facility that shows all manner of marine life native to North Carolina waters. The aquarium follows the path of the Cape Fear River from its headwaters to the ocean. Along the way you'll meet Luna, an albino alligator; have the opportunity to touch horseshoe crabs, sea stars, and even bamboo sharks; and see a variety of sharks, fish, eels, and rays in a two-story 235,000-gallon aquarium. Dive shows and daily feedings complement the exhibits. It's hard to miss the Megalodon exhibit, dedicated to the huge prehistoric shark—it was bigger than a school bus—with teeth the size of dinner plates and a jaw eight feet across. Fortunately, all that remains are fossil relics of this two-million-year-old animal, many of which are found at dive sites nearby in less than 100 feet of water. Pose for a picture behind the massive set of jaws as proof of the ultimate fish story.

Food

Seafood is a staple all along Kure and Carolina Beaches. **Shuckin' Shack Oyster Bar** (6 N. Lake Park Blvd., 910/458-7380, www.theshuckinshack.com, 11am-midnight Sun.-Thurs., 11am-2am Fri.-Sat., $9-50) is a friendly oyster bar that serves fresh seafood, including oysters by the bucket. You can shuck your own (don't be ashamed to ask for a tutorial if you've never used a shucking knife) or enjoy oysters on the half shell. The menu at ★ **Surf House** (604 N. Lake Park Blvd., 910/707-0422, www.surfhousenc.com, 5pm-9pm Tues.-Sun., $15-28) may be small, but everything on it is packed with flavor and as local as they can make it. Oysters are particularly good here, whether you get them on the half shell, roasted or fried, and no matter if you hear the shrimp and grits, fresh catch or veggie-friendly dish calling, you're in for a treat. The cocktails here are some of the best in town.

Freddie's Restaurant (111 K Ave., Kure Beach, 910/458-5979, www.freddiesrestaurant. com, 5pm-close daily, $12-25) in Kure Beach has a big menu and serves even bigger portions. With seafood, pasta, and an exceptional specialty pork chop menu, it's not hard to find something to eat. **Pop's Diner** (104 N. Lake Park Blvd., 910/458-7377, 11am-10pm Sun.-Wed., 11am-11pm Thurs., 11am-3am Fri. and Sat., $1-10) serves classics in a 1950s-style diner. The checkerboard tiles, stainless steel storefront, and red vinyl booths, keep a piece of the golden age of beach towns alive.

After dinner or for breakfast or for a snack, stop by **Britt's Donuts** (11 Boardwalk, 910/707-0755, www.brittsdonutshop.com, 8:30am-10pm daily, open April-Oct.), a Carolina Beach institution since 1939. They use a secret recipe for their doughnut batter, and they come out salty, sweet, airy, crispy, and perfect in every way. Pull up a seat at the bar and order half a dozen to enjoy (and if you don't like them, find me and I'll gladly take any leftovers off your hands).

Accommodations

The beaches of the Carolinas used to be lined with boardinghouses, the old-time choice in lodging for generations. Hurricane Hazel razed countless boardinghouses when it pummeled the coast in 1954, ushering in the epoch of the family motel. The **Beacon House** (715 Carolina Beach Ave. N., 877/232-2666 or 910/458-6244, www.beaconhouseinnb-b.com, some pets allowed in cottages, rooms $169-219, cottages $225-299) at Carolina Beach, just north of Kure, is a rare survivor. The early-1950s boardinghouse has the typical upstairs and downstairs porches and dark wood paneling indoors; nearby cottages have a similar aesthetic. You'll be treated to a lodging experience from a long-gone era.

Vacation rentals make up the best

accommodations here, and through rental agencies like **Carolina Beach Realty** (877/456-4311, www.carolinabeachrealty.net), **Victory Beach Vacations** (888/256-4804, www.victorybeachvacations.com), and **Sea Coast Rentals** (800/334-5806, www.seacoastrentals.com) you'll be able to find a house or condo that fits your needs.

★ SOUTHPORT

Without a doubt, Southport is one of North Carolina's most picturesque coastal towns; it's been named America's Happiest Seaside Town and is constantly in the running for best small town, best small coastal town, and best small seaside town from magazines and blogs across the country. The Cape Fear River, Intracoastal Waterway, and Atlantic Ocean meet here, and the water is almost always crowded with watercraft of all sizes and shapes. Wilmington is 45 minutes north by highway, (along N.C. 133 and Hwy. 17) but you can reach this charming town via the Southport-Fort Fisher Ferry if you want to admire the water a little as you travel.

The town's history is rooted in the water, and there are still several multigenerational fishing and shrimping families around. River pilots who know the shoals and tides like no one else operate out of Southport, heading offshore in speedy boats to the container ships and tankers making their way to Wilmington; they help navigate the cumbersome ships safely to the port and back out to sea, just as people from local families have for 200-plus years. Throughout the town, historic buildings, including Fort Johnson, a British fort built in 1745, line the oak-shaded streets. The Old Smithville Burying Ground, a community cemetery dating to before the founding of the town, is a beautiful spot, and many of the headstones are inscribed with epitaphs for sea captains and their widows. Stop in at the **Fort Johnston-Southport Museum and**

Visitors Center (203 E. Bay St., 910/457-7927, www.southportnc.org, 10am-4pm Mon.-Sat., 1pm-4pm Sun., free) for more information on the town, although Southport is small enough to explore and discover on your own. While you're at the visitors center, ask about the history of four of the town's street names: Lord, Howe, Dry, and I Am.

Sights

The **North Carolina Maritime Museum at Southport** (204 E. Moore St., 910/457-5150, www.ncmaritimemuseumsouthport.com, 9am-5pm Tues.-Sat., free) tells the story of Southport as a maritime town in some detail. The pirate Blackbeard and his compatriot Stede Bonnet prowled these waters, and Stede Bonnet was captured on the river about a mile from the museum, then sent to Charleston, where he was hanged for his crimes. Other subjects include a 2,000-year-old Native American canoe fragment, information on the blockade of the river during the Civil War, and many artifacts brought up from nearby shipwrecks.

Given the beauty of the town and its proximity to Wilmington, it's no surprise that Southport has been the setting of several television shows and films. *Safe Haven,* an adaptation of North Carolina literary son Nicholas Sparks's novel of the same name, takes place here; one reviewer called the movie "an extended infomercial for the lulling charms of Southport," and comedian Paul Scheer said Southport was the "star of *Safe Haven.*" Since the movie's 2012 debut, a steady stream of fans has been touring the town. **Southport Tours** (910/750-1951, www.southporttours.com, $10) and **Southport Fun Tours** (910/713-3373, www.southportfuntours.com, tours begin at 10:30am Tues.-Sat. and 11:30am Sun., $10 adults, $5 seniors and under age 12) both offer film and town-history tours.

Golf

In the vicinity of Southport, golfers will find several courses that are both challenging and beautiful. The **Oak Island Golf Club** (928

1: kayaking around the marsh; **2:** dining waterside at Yacht Basin Provision Company; **3:** on the dock after a day of fishing; **4:** Kure Beach boardwalk and pier

Caswell Beach Rd., Oak Island, 910/278-5275, www.oakislandgolf.com, 18 holes, par 72, greens fees from $52) is a 6,720-yard George Cobb-designed course that provides serenity with occasional ocean views and ocean breezes. In Boiling Spring Lakes, you can walk or ride **The Lakes Country Club** (591 S. Shore Dr., Boiling Spring Lakes, 910/845-2625, www.thelakescountryclub.com, 18 holes, par 72, greens fees from $21 walking, from $28 with cart), the oldest golf course in Brunswick County.

Kayaking

The Adventure Kayak Company (807 N. Howe St., 910/454-0607, www.theadventurecompany.net, kayak tours from $49, bike tours from $20, kayak rentals from $45/day, bike rentals $18/day) does tours of the Intracoastal Waterway, blackwater creeks around Southport, sunset and full moon tours, and even trips to some of the uninhabited islands in the river and waterway.

Festivals

Southport has its share of fairs and festivals throughout the year, but they all pale in comparison to the **North Carolina 4th of July Festival** (910/457-5578, www.nc4thofjuly.com), the official Independence Day celebration for the state. Some 50,000 people attend the parade, the festival park and street fair, and the fireworks in the evening. Launched from a barge on the river, the fireworks are a special treat as they reflect on the water. Perhaps the most moving of the events is the naturalization ceremony for new Americans as they declare their loyalty and enjoy their first 4th of July celebration.

Shopping

There are a number of cute boutiques, antiques stores, and kids' shops in Southport, and the local business alliance, **Downtown Southport, Inc.** (www.downtownsouthport.com) works to keep storefronts full and visitors shopping. A few of my favorites are **Ocean Outfitters** (121 E. Moore St.,

910/457-0433, www.oceanoutfitters.com, 10am-5:30pm Mon.-Fri., 10am-6pm Sat., 11am-4pm Sun. summer, 10am-5pm Mon.-Sat., 11am-4pm Sun. winter), a sportswear outfitter that carries clothing and gear perfect for enjoying and exploring the area; **Cat on a Whisk** (600-C N. Howe St., 910/454-4451, 10am-5pm Mon.-Sat.), a kitchen store with knowledgeable staff, a fantastic selection of gadgets and cookware, and always a friendly cat or two; and **Bullfrog Corner** (101 E. Moore St., 910/454-9300, 9am-6pm daily), where you'll find penny candy, games and goofy gifts for the kids, kites, shirts, and a load of fun tourist stuff.

Food

For a town this size, Southport has a surprising number of good restaurants. I love to dine on the water at ★ **Yacht Basin Provision Company** (130 Yacht Basin Dr., 910/457-0654, www.provisioncompany.com, 11am-9pm daily mid-March-late-Oct., $6-18), to enjoy a plate of peel-and-eat shrimp or a grouper sandwich. **Frying Pan** (319 W. Bay St., 910/363-4382, www.fryingpansouthport.com, 11am-9pm Mon.-Sat., 11am-8pm Sun., $12-30) serves fried seafood and local delicacies from a dining room elevated 18 feet off the ground, offering commanding water views. Both restaurants get very crowded in summer, with two-hour waits at Provision for lunch around July 4; you can wait for your table at **Old American Fish Factory** (150 Yacht Basin Dr., 910/457-9870, www.americanfishco.com, 4pm-9pm Mon.-Thurs., 4pm-11pm Fri., 2pm-11pm Sat., 2pm-8pm Sun.), an open-air bar featured in *Safe Haven* and other films and TV shows shot in Southport. The views are incredible, as the deck extends out over the water. During the highest tides, your feet can get wet. Try not to drop anything; it may fall through the cracks in the deck into the river below.

Moore Street Market (130 E. Moore St., 910/363-4203, 7am-4pm Mon.-Sat., $1-10), a small coffee shop and deli that makes a good lunch and serves the best cup of coffee in town. Its central location is steps from antiques shops and historic sites in Southport. Dinner is always good at **Ports of Call Bistro and Market** (116 N. Howe St., 910/457-4544, www.portsofcallbistro.com, 11:30am-3pm and 5pm-9pm Tues.-Sat., 10am-2pm Sun., lunch $8-21, dinner $15-31, brunch $11-18), a Mediterranean-inspired restaurant serving both tapas and entrées. Their menu changes seasonally and always features local seafood.

In South Harbor Marina, between Southport and Oak Island, are a trio of eateries that always deliver great food. **Joseph's Italian Bistro** (5003 O'Quinn Blvd., 910/454-4440, www.josephsitalianbistro.com, 5pm-9pm Mon.-Thurs., 5pm-9:30pm Fri.-Sat., 5pm-9:30pm Sun. Memorial Day-Labor Day, $13-30) serves classic pasta dishes, some of the best veal around, and an excellent array of local and regional seafood; it's perfect for date night or an evening when all the grown-ups have secured a babysitter and need a night out. Across the way is **Dead End Saloon** (4907 Fish Factory Rd. SE, 910/454-4002, www.thedeadendsaloon.com, 11am-late daily, $10-22), a considerably more relaxed spot where the Carolina Bloody Mary is a drink, a meal, and—piled high with bacon, pickled okra, and olives—a sight to behold. Their fresh catch, whether made into a BLT or served over a salad, is always good. Dead End has a great view and selection enough to make the kids and adults happy, so it's certainly worth a meal or two. If you can't tell, **Castucci's, An Italian Joint** (4332 Long Beach Rd., 910/477-6755, 4pm-9pm Tues.-Sun., closed Mon., $14-23) serves excellent Italian food; the owner, originally from Naples, Italy, ensures every plate is as authentic as possible.

Beer lovers will need to stop by the only brewery in town, **Check Six Brewery** (5130 Southport Supply Rd. SE, 910/477-9280, www.checksixbeer.com, 1pm-7pm Sun.-Mon., noon-10pm Tues., noon-11pm Wed.-Thurs., noon-midnight Fri.-Sat.). This aviation-themed brewery has a dozen beers on draft at any given time, all of them brewed right here. Their beers are named for everything aeronautical, from World War I pilots to anti-aircraft weapons. Their Harley Pope Imperial Porter is a good beer with a local history tie, but to find out the story, order a pint for yourself. If you're hungry, bring your own food, as Check Six serves only suds.

Accommodations

Lois Jane's Riverview Inn (106 W. Bay St., 910/457-6701, www.loisjanes.com, $170-195) is a Victorian waterfront home built by the innkeeper's grandfather. The guest rooms are comfortably furnished, bright, and not froufrou; the Queen Deluxe Street, a cottage behind the inn, has its own kitchen and separate entrance. The front porch of the inn has a wonderful view of the harbor. At the same location the **Riverside Motel** (106 W. Bay St., 910/457-6701, $95-130) has a front porch with a fantastic panorama of the shipping channel. Another lovely bed and breakfast in Southport is **Captain Newton's Inn** (120 W. Moore St., 910/477-2743, www.captiannewtonsinn.com, $195-225), in the heart of Southport's historic district and walkable to the river, restaurants and shops. Another affordable option is the **Inn at River Oaks** (512 N. Howe St., 910/457-1100, www.theinnatriveroaks.com, $80-110), a motel-style inn with very simple suites and low off-season rates.

At Oak Island, west of Southport, **Oak Island Inn** (8101 E. Oak Island Dr., Oak Island, 910/278-1689, www.oakisalandinnnc.net, $109-139) is only two blocks from the beach. The **Ocean Crest Motel** (1417 E. Beach Dr., Oak Island, 910/278-3333, www.oceancrestmotel.com, $130-190), a large condo-style motel, is also right on the beach.

As with most seaside towns, vacation rentals are the norm. On Oak Island and Caswell Beach, the two beach towns near Southport, **Oak Island Accommodations** (800/243-8132, www.rentalsatthebeach.com) and **Coastal Vacation Resorts at Oak Island** (8118 East Oak Island Dr., 888/703-5469, www.coastalvacationresortsoakisland.com) have houses and condos all along the island, from beachfront castles to cozy cottages, that are pet friendly, kid friendly, and more.

BALD HEAD ISLAND

Two miles off the coast of Southport is Bald Head Island. From the mainland you can see the most prominent feature, Old Baldy, the oldest lighthouse in North Carolina, poking above the trees. Accessible only by a 20-minute ferry ride or private boat, the island is limited to golf carts, bicycles, and pedestrians; the only larger vehicles permitted are for emergency services, deliveries, or construction. Combined with the largest intact section of maritime forest in North Carolina, Bald Head Island seems like it's a world away.

Sights

Old Baldy was commissioned by Thomas Jefferson and built in 1817. You can climb to the top of the 109-foot lighthouse with admission to the **Smith Island Museum** (101 Lighthouse Wynd, 910/457-7481 www. oldbaldy.org, 9am-5pm Mon.-Sat., 11am-5pm Sun., $6 adults, $3 ages 3-12). The museum, housed in the former lighthouse keeper's cottage, tells the story of Old Baldy and the other lighthouses that have stood on the island. The **Old Baldy Foundation** (910/457-7481, tours

10:30am Tues, Fri., and Sat., $25 ages 13 and up, $15 ages 3-12) also conducts historic tours that reveal the island's long and surprising past.

Sports and Recreation

There are 14 miles of beaches to explore on Bald Head Island, several hundred acres of maritime forest with marked trails, miles of creeks that wind through the marsh behind the island, and ample opportunities to explore with one of the island's outfitters. You won't be able to see much of it on foot, so unless you brought a bike over, you'll need to rent a ride; fortunately, it's easy to get a golf cart or bike.

At **Cary Cart Company** (261 Edward Teach Wynd, 910/457-7333, www.carycartco. com, 8:30am-8pm daily, four-passenger cart $72/day and $350/week, six-passenger cart $102/day and $500/week) you can rent golf carts by the day or additional carts (they're included in nearly every rental on the island) for the week.

Riverside Adventure Company (910/457-4944, www.riversideadventure. com, 8:30am-9pm daily, rentals from $20, tours $25/adults and $12/ages 12 and younger, camps from $50) offers bike rentals, morning archery camps and a frightening but

relaxing beachside on Bald Head Island

family-fun-focused ghost walk. Their sister outfitter, **The Sail Shop** (96 Keelson Row, 910/451-6844, www.thesailshop.com, 8:30am-5pm Sun.-Thurs., 8:30am-6pm Fri.-Sat.) provides rentals and lessons for surfing ($40/day, lessons $75) and sailing ($75/person, lessons from $150/person), and offers kayak rentals (from $50/day) and tours (from $65 guided, from $50 self-guided). If you want to try stand-up paddleboarding on the marsh or ocean, **Coastal Urge** (12-B Maritime Way, 800/383-4443, www.rentals.coastalurge.com, 9am-5pm daily, SUP rentals $60/day, tours $30-60; bike rentals $25-45/day) supplies all the gear and lessons you need to get on the water.

The **Bald Head Island Conservancy** (700 Federal Rd., 910/457-0089, www.bhic. org, tours around $50 for off-island guests and $20 for on island guests, off-island ticket includes round-trip ferry fare, dates and times vary, call or check the website for weekly schedule), a group dedicated to preserving the flora and fauna of the island, leads kayak tours, birding walks, kids camps, and, in the summer, turtle walks, giving Conservancy members (you can join while you're here) the chance to see a sea turtle make her nest.

Exploring Bald Head Island with one of the outfitters is a must-do, but most folks come for the beach. The island has three distinct beaches: West Beach, South Beach, and East Beach. Seeing how the island has east- and west-facing beaches, it's one of a few spots where you can watch the sun both rise and set over the ocean from your beach house. Along West Beach, the Cape Fear River and Intracoastal Waterway meet the Atlantic Ocean, so it's more of a strolling or fishing beach than a swimming one, as currents here can get a little gnarly. Often-secluded South Beach is excellent for surfing, swimming, shelling, sunning, and strolling. East Beach is likewise perfect for swimming, playing in the waves, and soaking up some sun.

Food

There are only a few places to eat on the island, but fortunately they're good. In the harbor, **Delphina Cantina** (8 Marina Wynd, 910/457-1226, www.delphinacantina.webs. com, 11:30am-9:15pm daily, $6-37) serves some good Latin American food. Inside Delphina you'll find **Sandpiper Sweets and Ice Cream** (located inside Delphina, 7:30am-11am daily, under $10) and **Marina Pizza to Go** ($12-22), which are great options for families. **Will O' the Wisp** (8:30am-10pm Mon.-Sat., 8:30am-6pm Sun., under 10), from the same owners, provides a great outdoor space to enjoy your pizza or a dish from Delphina, to sip a drink, or to play games with your family, because they do have activities like family bingo night, trivia night, and concerts on Fridays during summer.

The **Maritime Market Café** (8 Maritime Way, 910/457-7450, www.maritimemarketbhi. com, breakfast 8am-11am daily, lunch and dinner 11:30am-9pm daily, hours vary by season, breakfast $4-10, lunch and dinner $5-11, pizza $3/slice, pies $16-19), attached to a full-service grocery store, serves breakfast and lunch that includes standard options and daily specials. Monthly they hold **Howl at the Moon** parties on East Beach. These community-wide gatherings bring locals and vacationers together to celebrate the full moon with a potluck feast; details and a schedule are available on their website.

MoJo's on the Harbor (10 Marina Wynd, 910/457-7217, www.mojosontheharbor.com, 11:30am-4pm and 4:30pm-10pm daily, limited hours in winter, $15-38) has killer views and a wide-ranging menu that includes some traditional Coastal Carolina seafood dishes like steam pots and fried fish, Italian specialties, sandwiches, and more. There's also a sushi bar ($7-21).

Accommodations

Most of the houses on Bald Head Island are rental homes, ranging from one-bedroom cottages to massive beachside homes ideal for family reunions. Rentals are available through **Bald Head Island Limited** (www. baldheadisland.com) and **Tiffany's Rentals** (910/457-0544, www.tiffanysrentals.com);

rates range from $2,000 to $12,000 per week. One bed-and-breakfast, **The Marsh Harbour Inn** (21 Keelson Row, 910/454-0451, www. marshharbourinn.com, $275-575), operates here. With beautiful harbor and marsh views, free use of golf carts for guests, and membership privileges to the private Bald Head Island Club, this is a great option for visitors not in a large group.

OCEAN ISLE AND SUNSET BEACH

Ocean Isle is one of the most southerly beaches in North Carolina, separated from South Carolina only by Sunset Beach, Bird Island, and the town of Calabash. It's midway between Wilmington and Myrtle Beach, South Carolina, about an hour drive from each. In October, Ocean Isle is the site of the **North Carolina Oyster Festival** (www. ncoysterfestival.com), a huge event that's been happening for nearly 30 years. In addition to an oyster stew cook-off, a surfing competition, and entertainment, this event features the North Carolina Oyster Shucking Competition.

Once, Sunset Beach and Bird Island were separated by a narrow, tidal inlet; this has since filled in, creating one contiguous island. At Sunset Beach, stay at **The Sunset Inn** (9 N. Shore Dr., Sunset Beach, 910/575-1000, www. thesunsetinn.net, $209-360), a 14-room inn where every room has a king bed, a wet bar, and a screened porch facing the marsh—and it's only a 5-minute walk to the beach.

While you're here, you should pay a visit to the **Kindred Spirits Mailbox** (www. thekindredspirit.net), a touching, but odd attraction—a mailbox set in the dunes where people come from all over the world to leave letters for the cosmos. Sometimes these letters and notes are fond memories of a visit to the shore, other times they're prayers or dreams, wishes, reflections, or sorrows, but almost every one is intriguing. And, yes, you can read them. In the mailbox are several notebooks that are distributed, collected, and catalogued by volunteers. Write your own note or simply reflect on the thoughts of others. To get here, you'll park at West 40th St. on Sunset Beach, take the beach access, and walk southwest (away from the pier) about 1.5 miles; you'll see an American flag waving in the dunes, marking the mailbox.

There are several places to dine on Sunset Beach, Ocean Isle, and nearby Holden Beach, but one place in particular stands out as excellent: **The Isles Restaurant** (417 W. 2nd St., Ocean Isle Beach, 910/575-5988, www. islesrestaurant.com, 5pm-9pm Mon. and Wed., 11am-9pm Thurs. and Sun., 11am-10pm Fri.-Sat. Memorial Day-Labor Day, limited hours spring and fall, closed winter, $12-25). At The Isles, you'll find some inventive takes on local seafood, including an incredible smoked wahoo (it's a type of fish) dip and some notable crab-stuffed flounder. Take your dinner at one of the tables on the deck and dine looking out at the ocean; if they're all taken, a window seat will do. One other place to dine is **Provision Company** (1343 Cedar Landing Rd. SW, Holden Beach, 910/842-7205, 11am-8pm daily, $6-20) in Holden Beach. Yes, it shares a name with the restaurant in Southport, and yes, the menu is markedly similar—steamed shrimp; crab cakes; quick, greasy, and delicious burgers—but it has different owners and a different vibe. The view of the Intracoastal Waterway is great, and the food—especially the grouper or tuna steak sandwiches—holds its own.

Makai Brewing Company (5850 Ocean Hwy. W., 910/579-2739, www.makaibrewing. com, noon-8pm Sun.-Thurs., 11am-9pm Fri.-Sat.) has more than a dozen taps featuring their own beer as well as guest taps featuring other area breweries. They keep at least a pair of IPAs on draft, including their popular Carolina Tropical IPA, and those guest taps feature the best of Wilmington breweries.

SOUTH ALONG U.S. 17

U.S. 17 is an old colonial road; its original name, still used in some places, is the King's Highway. George Washington passed this way on his 1791 Southern tour, staying with the prominent planters in the area and leaving in his wake the proverbial legends about where he lay his head of an evening. Today, the King's Highway, following roughly its original course, is still the main thoroughfare through Brunswick County into South Carolina.

Brunswick Town and Fort Anderson

Near Orton is the **Brunswick Town-Fort Anderson State Historic Site** (8884 St. Philip's Rd. SE, Winnabow, 910/371-6613, www.nchistoricsites.org, 9am-5pm Tues.-Sat., free, donations accepted), the site of what was a bustling little port town in the early and mid-1700s. In its brief life, Brunswick saw quite a bit of action. It was attacked in 1748 by a Spanish ship that, to residents' delight, blew up in the river. One of that ship's cannons was dragged out of the river and is on display. In 1765, the town's refusal to observe royal tax stamps was a successful precursor to the Boston Tea Party eight years later. But by the end of the Revolutionary War, Brunswick Town was gone, burned by the British but also made obsolete by the growth of Wilmington.

Today, nothing remains of the colonial port except the lovely ruins of the 1754 **St. Philip's Anglican Church** and some building foundations uncovered by archaeologists. During the Civil War, Fort Anderson was built on this site; some of its walls also survive. It was a series of sand earthworks that were part of the crucial defenses of the Cape Fear, protecting the blockade-runners who came and went from Wilmington. A visitors center at the historic site tells the story of this significant stretch of riverbank, and the grounds, with the town's foundations exposed and interpreted, are an intriguing vestige of a forgotten community.

Perhaps the most interesting artifact on display at the visitors center at Brunswick Town is the Fort Anderson battle flag that Confederate soldiers flew over the fort during their final battle. Once the fort fell, the flag was captured by a regiment from Illinois. They gave it to their commander, who gave it to the Illinois governor, who gave it to Abraham Lincoln in a ceremony at the National Hotel where John Wilkes Booth lived, which was reportedly witnessed by Booth. A number of Civil War and Lincoln scholars believe that this moment was when Booth's plan changed from kidnapping to assassinating the president.

Nature Preserves

The Nature Conservancy's **Green Swamp Preserve** (Hwy. 211, 5.5 miles north of Supply, 910/395-5000, www.nature.org) contains more than 17,000 acres of some of North Carolina's most precious coastal ecosystems, the longleaf pine savanna and evergreen shrub pocosin. Hiking is allowed in the preserve, but the paths are primitive. It's important to stay on the trails and not dive into the wilds because this is an intensely fragile ecosystem. In this preserve are communities of rare carnivorous plants, including the monstrous little pink-mawed Venus flytrap, four kinds of pitcher plant, and sticky-fingered sundew. It's also a habitat for the rare red-cockaded woodpecker, which is partial to diseased old-growth longleaf pines.

The Nature Conservancy maintains another nature preserve nearby, the **Boiling Spring Lakes Preserve** (Hwy. 87, Boiling Spring Lakes, 910/395-5000, www.nature. org), with a trail that begins at the community center. Brunswick County contains the state's greatest concentration of rare plant species and the most diverse plant communities anywhere on the East Coast north of Florida. This preserve is owned by the Plant Conservation Program and includes over half the acreage of the town of Boiling Spring Lakes. The ecosystem is made up of Carolina bays, pocosins, and longleaf pine forests.

The University of North Carolina Wilmington maintains a 174-acre nature preserve in Brunswick County, the **Ev-Henwood Nature Preserve** (6150 Rock Creek Road NE, near Town Creek, www. uncw.edu, dawn-dusk daily). Ev-Henwood (pronounced like "heaven wood" without the initial "h") is named after the surnames of the former owner's grandparents: Evans and Henry. The property had been owned by the family since 1799 and was the site of turpentine stills, tar kilns, and a working farm. Now several miles of hiking trails wind through the property past barns and home sites, across fields, beside the beautiful and eerie blackwater Town Creek, and through longleaf pine woods. Pick up a trail map at the parking lot and head out for a few hours in the woods. Bring water, bug spray, and your camera; if you're quiet enough, you may see otters playing in Town Creek or deer in the woods at the edge of a field.

Outdoor Adventure

Shallotte River Swamp Park (5550 Watts Road, Ocean Isle Beach, 910/687-6100, www.shallotteriverswamppark.com, 9am-5pm Thurs.-Mon. off-season, 9am-7pm Fri.-Mon., 9am-11pm Tues.-Thurs.) is a high-adventure wonderland. A 90-foot tower is your starting point for a cypress canopy tour ($79) and a three-zip zip-line course ($32), each of which takes you through the trees and over sections of swamp; there's a swamp boat tour ($30) and an adventure park ($42/adults, $32 ages 7-13, $22 ages 4-6), which challenges your strength, agility, and nerve in an elevated obstacle course.

Another option for adventure is **Cape Fearless Extreme** (1571 Neils Eddy Rd., Rieglewood, 910/655-2555, www.capefearless.com), an aerial adventure course that sits in the middle of 25 acres of pine forest. Cape Fearless has two challenging courses, one for adults (ages 10 and up, $39 Mon.-Fri., $50 Sat.-Sun.) and one for kids (ages 7-11, $20). The obstacles on the courses here are suited for experienced and novice climbers.

Golf

Brunswick County is a golf mecca, where more than 30 championship courses appeal to all skill levels and playing styles. The website **Brunswick Islands** (www.ncbrunswick.com) maintains a list of golf courses, among

them the notable **Cape Fear National at Brunswick Forest** (1281 Cape Fear National Dr., Brunswick Forest, 910/383-3283, www.brunswickforest.com, greens fees $44-60), named one of the "Top 18 Course Openings in the World 2010" by *Links* magazine when it opened. The course is beautifully maintained and fun to play from any tee. **Crow Creek** (240 Hickman Rd. NW, Calabash, 910/287-3081, www.crowcreek.com, greens fees from $70), is almost on the South Carolina state line. About 45 minutes south of Wilmington, the **Big Cats** (351 Ocean Ridge Pkwy. SW, 800/233-1801, www.bigcatsgolf.com, greens fees $43-85) is at Ocean Ridge Plantation with five stunning courses—Tiger's Eye, Leopard's Chase, Panther's Run, Lion's Paw, and Jaguar's Lair.

Calabash and Vicinity

The tiny fishing village of Calabash, just above the South Carolina state line and only 15 minutes from Ocean Isle, was founded in the early 18th century as Pea Landing, a shipping point for the local peanut crop. Local legend holds that calabash gourds were used as dippers in the town drinking water supply, explaining the town's 1873 renaming. Others hold that the crooked marsh creek that leads to the sea inspired the name. Either way, Calabash is home to some world-famous seafood.

In the early 1940s, Lucy High Coleman began frying fish for the local fisheries workers in a kettle of oil by the dock. Later she used a tent, which in turn became a lean-to and eventually a full-fledged restaurant, The Original, which was, well, the original Calabash-style seafood restaurant. Calabash-style seafood is marked by its light, crispy batter and the freshness of the seafood, and Coleman's descendants carry on the family tradition at several restaurants in town. Locals like to say that like champagne, which can only come from one region in France, or bourbon, only distilled in a single Kentucky county, you can only get Calabash seafood in Calabash; everything else is just an imitation.

For a long while Coleman's descendants ran restaurants just like their mother's, and now there are fewer, but still there are a good number of places where you can get Calabash seafood. **Beck's Restaurant** (1014 River Road, 910/579-6776, www.becksrestaurant. com, 11am-9pm daily, $5-19) is one of the original Calabash restaurants run by the descendants of Lucy High Coleman, and they do a great job of capturing a down-home vibe in the restaurant and on the plate. But another spot, ★ **Waterfront Seafood Shack** (9945 Nance St., 910/575-0017, www. calabashfishingfleet.com, 11am-9pm Mon.-Sat., $4-22), is one of my favorites. Here, you can sit outside and watch the fishing fleet if they're working or just gaze at the river, and order local, freshly caught seafood to be fried—Calabash style—grilled or broiled; don't miss their grilled pound cake for dessert, with a scoop of ice cream it's nearly perfect.

The Oyster Rock (9931 Nance St., 910/579-6875, www.theoysterrock.com, 4pm-10pm Wed.-Mon., $13-64) takes a playful approach to fine dining, Southern cuisine, and local seafood. They serve Calabash fried seafood, iced seafood towers, oysters on the half-shell, smoked oysters, fresh catch, pork chops, and excellent soups. Cheeky names to dishes—The Hummus Dinger (a hummus sampler), Certified Nut Cases (coconut fried shrimp), and Slip Slidin' Away (pork barbecue sliders)—and a fun selection of craft beer make dinner that much better.

Indigo Farms (1542 Hickman Rd. NW, 910/287-6794, www.indigofarmsmarket. com, 8:30am-5:30pm Mon.-Sat., longer hours in summer), three miles north of the South Carolina line in Calabash, is a superb farm market, selling all manner of produce,

preserves, and baked goods. They also have corn mazes and farm activities in the fall.

In the nearby town of Shallotte (pronounced "shuh-LOTE"), **Holden Brothers Farm Market** (5600 Ocean Hwy. W., 910/579-4500, 8am-6pm daily March, 8am-7pm daily Apr.-Labor Day, 8am-6pm daily Labor Day-Oct., 8:30am-5:30pm daily Nov.-Dec., closed Dec. 26-Mar.) is a popular source for local produce. The peaches in season are wonderful, and the homemade canned goods and pickles are worth the trip.

GETTING THERE AND AROUND

The Brunswick County beaches like Holden, Ocean Isle, and Sunset are easily accessed on U.S. 17. The beaches and islands along the cape, due south of Wilmington, can be reached by taking U.S. 76 south from Wilmington, then turning onto Highway 133 (closest to Wilmington), Highway 87, or Highway 211 (closer to the South Carolina border), or by ferry from Southport.

The **Southport-Fort Fisher Ferry** (Ferry Rd. SE, Southport, 800/368-8969 or 800/293-3779, www.ncdot.gov, ferries depart from Southport and Fort Fisher 5:30am-7pm year-round, $1 pedestrians, $2 bicycles, $3 motorcycles, cars $5, longer vehicles $10-15) is popular as a sightseeing jaunt as well as a means to get across the river. It's a 30-minute crossing; most departures are 45 minutes apart. Pets are permitted if leashed or in a vehicle, and there are restrooms on all ferries.

A small airport near Oak Island, **Cape Fear Regional Jetport** (4019 Long Beach Rd., Oak Island, 910/457-6483, www. capefearjetport.com) has no scheduled passenger service but is suitable for small private aircraft.

Inland from Wilmington

Driving inland from the Wilmington area, you first pass through a lush world of wetlands distinguished by the peculiar Carolina bays. Not necessarily bodies of water, as the name would suggest, bays are actually ovoid depressions in the earth of unknown and much-debated origin. They are often water-filled but by definition are fed by rainwater rather than creeks or groundwater. They create unique environments and are often surrounded by bay laurel trees (hence the name) and home to a variety of carnivorous plants.

The next zone, bounded by the Waccamaw and Lumber Rivers, largely comprises farmland and small towns. For generations this was prime tobacco country, and that heritage is still very much evident in towns like Whiteville, where old tobacco warehouses line the railroad tracks. Culturally, this area—mostly in Columbus County and extending into Robeson County to the west and Brunswick County to the east—is linked with Horry, Marion, and Dillon Counties in South Carolina, with many of the same family names still found on both sides of the state line.

The area around the Lumber River, especially in Robeson County, is home to the Lumbee people, Native Americans with a long history of steadfast resistance to oppression and a heritage of devotion to faith and family. If you turn on the radio while driving through the area, you'll hear Lumbee gospel programming and get a sense of the cadences of Lumbee English. The characteristics that distinguish it from the speech of local whites and African Americans are subtle, but idiosyncratic pronunciation and grammar, which include subvariations among different Lumbee families and towns, make it one of the state's most distinctive dialects.

At the edge of the region is Fayetteville. From its early days as the center of Cape Fear Scottish settlement to its current role as one of the most important military communities in the United States, Fayetteville has always been a significant city.

ALONG U.S. 74

A short distance inland from Calabash, the countryside is threaded by the Waccamaw River, a gorgeous dark channel full of cypress knees and dangerous reptiles. The name is pronounced "WAW-cuh-MAW," with more emphasis on the first syllable than on the third. It winds its way down from Lake Waccamaw through a swampy portion of North Carolina and crossing Horry County, South Carolina (unofficial motto: "The *H* is Silent"), before joining the Pee Dee and Lumber Rivers in South Carolina. The Waccamaw crosses through this little fringe of North Carolina, paralleling the much longer Lumber River, surrounding rural Columbus County and part of Robeson County in an environment of deep subtropical wetlands. From Wilmington it's at least an hour drive west to the heart of this area.

Sights

Pembroke is the principal town of the Lumbee people, and at the center of life here is the University of North Carolina at Pembroke (UNCP). Founded in 1887 as the Indian Normal School, UNCP's population is now only about one-quarter Native American, but it's still an important site in the history of North Carolina's indigenous people. The **Museum of the Southeast American Indian** (Old Main, UNCP, University Rd., Pembroke, 910/521-6262, www.uncp.edu, 9am-5pm Mon.-Sat., free) is on campus, occupying Old Main, a 1923 building that's a source of pride for Pembroke. The Resource Center has a small but very good collection of artifacts and contemporary Native American art.

Laurinburg's **John Blue House** (13040 X-Way Rd., Laurinburg, 910/277-2456, www.johnbluehouse.com, grounds open daily, house and grounds tours 10am-4pm Sat., 1pm-4pm Sun., by appointment Mon.-Fri., free, donations accepted) is a spectacle of Victorian design, a polygonal house built entirely of heart pine harvested from the surrounding property and done up like a wedding cake with endless decorative devices. John Blue, the builder and original owner, was an inventor of machinery used in the processing of cotton. A pre-Civil War cotton gin stands on the property, used today for educational demonstrations throughout the year. In October this is the site of the **John Blue Cotton Festival** (www.johnbluecottonfestival.com), which showcases not only the ingenuity of the home's famous resident and the process of ginning cotton but also lots of local and regional musicians and other artists.

Sports and Recreation

Several beautiful state parks line the Waccamaw and Lumber Rivers. **Lake Waccamaw State Park** (1866 State Park Dr., Lake Waccamaw, 910/646-4748, http://ncparks.gov, office 8am-5pm daily, park 7am-7pm Dec.-Feb., 7am-9pm Mar.-April and Oct., 7am-10pm May-Sept., 7am-8pm Nov.) encompasses the 9,000-acre lake. The lake is technically a Carolina bay. Carolina bays are large, oval depressions in the ground, many of which are boggy and filled with water but which are named for the bay trees that typically grow around them. Lake Waccamaw has geological and hydrological characteristics that make it unique even within the odd category of Carolina bays. There are several aquatic creatures that live only in Lake Waccamaw, including the Waccamaw fatmucket and the silverside (a mollusk and a fish, respectively). The park draws boaters and paddlers, but the only launches are outside the grounds. Primitive campsites ($10-32) are available in the park.

North of Whiteville on U.S. 701 is Elizabethtown, home to **Jones Lake State Park** (4117 Hwy. 242, Elizabethtown,

910/588-4550, http://ncparks.gov, office and visitors center 8am-5pm Mon.-Fri., park 8am-6pm Nov.-Feb., 8am-8pm Mar.-May and Sept.-Oct., 8am-9pm June-Aug., closed Dec. 25). You can boat on Jones Lake either in your own craft (no motors over 10 hp) or in canoes or paddleboats ($5/ hour) rented from the park. The lake is also great for swimming ($5 over age 13, $4 ages 3-12) from late May to early September, with shallow, cool water and a sandy beach. A concession stand and a bathhouse are at the beach, and camping ($15-28) is available in a wooded area with drinking water and restrooms nearby.

Singletary Lake State Park (6707 Hwy. 53 E., Kelly, 910/669-2928, http://ncparks.gov, 8am-5pm daily), north of Lake Waccamaw in Kelly, has one of the largest of the Carolina bays, the 572-acre Singletary Lake, which lies within Bladen Lakes State Forest. There is no individual camping allowed, although there are facilities for large groups (including the entrancingly named Camp Ipecac, for the purgative herb that grows here) that date from the Civilian Conservation Corps (CCC) era. There is a nice one-mile hiking trail, the CCC-Carolina Bay Loop Trail, and a 500-foot pier extending over the bay.

Lumber River State Park (2819 Princess Ann Rd., Orrum, 910/628-4564, http://ncparks.gov, Princess Ann Access: 7am-7pm Dec.-Feb., 7am-9pm Mar-April and Oct., 7am-10pm May-Sept., 7am-8pm Nov.; Chalk Banks Access: 8am-6pm Dec.-Feb., 8am-8pm Mar.-April and Oct., 8am-9pm May-Sept., 8am-7pm Nov.) has 115 miles of waterways with numerous put-ins for canoes and kayaks. Referred to as both the Lumber River and Lumbee River, and farther upstream as Drowning Creek, the river traverses both the coastal plain region and the eastern edge of the Sandhills. Camping ($10) is available at unimproved walk-in and canoe-in sites and at group sites.

Yogi Bear's Jellystone Park (626 Richard Wright Rd., Tabor City, 877/668-8586, www.taborcityjellystone.com, RVs $40-84/night, tents $35-70/night, cabins $84-210/

night, yurts $54-120/night) is a popular campground with RV and tent spaces, rental cabins, and yurts. The facilities are clean and well maintained, and there are tons of children's activities on site. Some of the camping is in wooded areas, but for the most part expect direct sun.

Entertainment and Events

Several of the state's big agricultural festivals are held in this area. If you're in the little town of Fair Bluff in late July, you may be lucky enough to witness the coronation of the newest Watermelon Queen. The **North Carolina Watermelon Festival** (www. ncwatermelonfestival.org) began as an annual competition between two friends, local farmers whose watermelons grew to over 100 pounds. The competition expanded into this festival that celebrates watermelon growing throughout the state; a new court of watermelon royalty is crowned every year.

When spring rolls around, Chadbourn holds its annual **Strawberry Festival** (www. ncstrawberryfestival.com), at which the coronation of the Strawberry Queen takes place. If this seems a strange sort of royalty, bear in mind that across the state line in South Carolina, they have a Little Miss Hell Hole Swamp competition.

Food

The Chef & The Frog (607 S. Madison St., Whiteville, 910/640-5550, www.chefnc.com, 11am-2pm Tues.-Fri. for lunch, 5pm-9pm Thurs.-Sat. for dinner, brunch 11:30am-1:30pm Sun., lunch $10-14, dinner $12-25, brunch $8-14) is a bit of a surprise. The chef's family fled Cambodia when the Khmer Rouge took power, settling in France, where she learned to cook French and Cambodian cuisine; she married a French-American and emigrated to the states, eventually landing in Whiteville, where her menu features French dishes, Southern dishes, and a good number of Asian- and Cambodian-inspired plates.

There's a take-out counter in Whiteville that chowhounds will drive an hour out of

their way to reach because it's said to have the best burgers around. Next to the railroad tracks, **Ward's Grill** (706 S. Madison St., Whiteville, 910/642-2004, 7am-2pm Mon.-Fri., under $10) has no seating, just a walk-up counter. The burgers and chili dogs are go-to items here.

In Pembroke, try **Fuller's Old-Fashioned BBQ** (100 East 3rd St., Pembroke, 910/521-4667, www.fullersbbq.com, 11am-9pm Mon.-Sat., 11am-4pm Sun., lunch buffet $9, dinner buffet $11, Sun. buffet $13, entrées $4-14.50, children ages 3-9 are half price). Fuller's has a great reputation for its barbecue, but it also makes all sorts of country specialties like chicken gizzards, chitterlings, and a 12-layer cake.

If barbecue is what you have your heart set on, make the trip to Garland and visit ★ **Southern Smoke BBQ** (29 Warren St., Garland, 910/549-7484, www. southernsmokebbqnc.com, 11:30am until they sell out Thurs. and Fri., $5-18); it's a 1.25-hour drive from Wilmington, but worth every mile. Chef Matthew Register takes an interesting approach to barbecue—which is practically a religion in North Carolina—and provides an array of sauces that represent the state's sauce styles and even reaches beyond our borders for inspiration. Like any good pit master, he has a couple of secret tricks he uses when preparing his pork and ribs, and, of course, he builds sides and desserts off old family recipes. Keep an eye on the website and look out for the **South Supper Series**, a ticketed dinner event (typically $35) held three or four times a year; it features his barbecue, of course, but also dishes reflecting his influences and favorite styles from across the south, and, on special occasions, guest chefs from around the state.

Getting There and Around

This section of southeastern North Carolina is bisected by I-95, the largest highway on the East Coast. I-95 passes near Fayetteville and Lumberton. Major east-west routes include U.S. 74, which crosses Cape Fear at

Wilmington and proceeds through Lake Waccamaw and Whiteville to pass just south of Lumberton and Pembroke to Laurinburg. Highway 87 goes through Elizabethtown, where you can choose to branch off onto Highway 211 to Lumberton, or bear north on Highway 87 to Fayetteville. Highway 87 and Highway 211 are quite rural and beautiful, especially in the spring, when azaleas are in bloom and the country is greening up, as well as in the fall, when cotton fields will make you do a double take, thinking you just sped past a field of snow. Take your time on these roads, and be ready to pull off to take photos of farmhouses, fields, and other pastoral scenes.

FAYETTEVILLE

Fayetteville is North Carolina's sixth-largest city and in its own quiet way has always been one of the state's most powerful engines of growth and change. In the early 1700s it became a hub for settlement by Scottish immigrants, who helped build it into a major commercial center. From the 1818 initiation of steamboat travel between Fayetteville and Wilmington along Cape Fear—initially a voyage of six days—to the building of Plank Road, which was a huge boon to intrastate commerce, Fayetteville was well connected to commercial resources in the Carolinas. Two hours northwest of Wilmington by highway, Fayetteville sits a little higher in elevation in an area that's part Sandhills, part hardwood forest.

Fayetteville serves as the location of two high-level military installations. Fort Bragg is home to the XVIII Airborne Corps, the 82nd Airborne, the Delta Force, and the John F. Kennedy Special Warfare Center and School. It's also home to many military families, and the community has a vibrant international community. Pope Field, home of the 440th Airlift Wing, is nearby.

Sights

The **Museum of the Cape Fear Regional Complex** (801 Arsenal Ave., 910/500-4240, www.musrumofthecapefear.ncdcr.gov,

10am-5pm Tues.-Sat., 1pm-5pm Sun., free) has three components, each telling different stories of Fayetteville's history. The museum has exhibits on the history and prehistory of the region, including its vital role in developing transportation in the state, as well as its military role. There is an 1897 house museum, the **Poe House,** which belonged to an Edgar Allen Poe—not the writer; this one was a brickyard owner. The third section is the 4.5-acre **Arsenal Park,** site of a federal arms magazine built in 1836, claimed by the Confederacy in 1861, and destroyed by General Sherman in 1865.

Market House (intersection of Person, Hay, Green, and Gillespie Streets) is a beautiful and surprisingly important building in downtown Fayetteville. It was in this building that North Carolina ratified the U.S. Constitution in 1789 and chartered the University of North Carolina. The building that stands there now is not the original— that burned in 1831—but was rebuilt in 1865, supposedly by brick mason Thomas Grimes, a free African American known to be one of the best masons in the area.

The **Airborne and Special Operations Museum** (100 Bragg Blvd., 910/643-277876, www.asomf.org, 10am-5pm Tues.-Sat., noon-5pm Sun., free, motion simulator $8.50) is an impressive facility that presents the history of Special Ops paratroopers, from the first jump in 1940 to the divisions' present-day roles abroad in peacekeeping missions and war. In the museum's theater you can watch a film of what it looks like when a paratrooper makes a jump, and the 24-seat Pitch, Roll, and Yaw Vista-Dome Motion Simulator makes the experience even more exciting.

Given Fayetteville's deep and ongoing ties to the military, it's no surprise to learn the first park in the state dedicated to all military veterans is right here beside the Airborne and Special Operations Museum. **North Carolina Veterans Park** (300 Bragg Blvd., 910/433-1547, www.ncveteranspark.org, 10am-4pm Tues.-Sat., noon-4pm Sun. Mar.-Oct., noon-4pm Tues.-Sun. Nov.-Feb., free) is a touching tribute to veterans, living and passed. One of the most moving elements is the Oath of Service Wall, a long, curved wall made of soil from each of the state's 100 counties, with the bronze-casted hands of 100 of North Carolina's veterans raised as if taking their induction oath.

The **JFK Special Warfare Museum** (Ardennes St. and Marion St., Bldg. D-2502, Fort Bragg, 910/432-4272, www.jfkwebstore. com, 11am-4pm Mon.-Fri., free) tells the story of unconventional U.S. military projects, including Special Ops and Psychological Ops. The museum focuses on the Vietnam War era but chronicles warfare from colonial times to the present. Note that ID is required to enter the base.

Looking farther back in time, the **Fayetteville Independent Light Infantry Armory and Museum** (210 Burgess St., 910/433-1457, www.fili1793.com, by appointment, free) displays artifacts from the history of the Fayetteville Independent Light Infantry (FILI). FILI is still dedicated as North Carolina's official historic military command, which is a ceremonial duty. In its active-duty days, which began in 1793, FILI had some exciting times, particularly during the Civil War. In addition to military artifacts, the museum also exhibits a carriage in which the Marquis de Lafayette was shown around Fayetteville—the only one of the towns bearing his name that he actually visited.

Cross Creek Cemetery (N. Cool Spring St. and Grove St., 800/255-8217, dawn-dusk daily) is an attractive and sad spot, the resting place of many Scottish men and women who crossed the ocean to settle Cape Fear. People of other ethnicities and times are buried here, but the oldest section of the cemetery is the most poignant, where one stone after another commemorates early Scots colonists. The cemetery was founded in 1785, and the wall along the southern boundary is believed to be the oldest piece of construction still standing in Fayetteville.

★ **CAPE FEAR BOTANICAL GARDEN**

The 79-acre **Cape Fear Botanical Garden** (536 N. Eastern Blvd., 910/486-0221, www. capefearbg.org, 9am-5pm Mon.-Sat., noon-5pm Sun. Mar.-Nov., 10am-4pm Mon.-Sat., noon-4pm Sun. Nov.-Mar., $10 adults, $9 military and seniors, $5 ages 6-12, free ages 5 and under) is one of the loveliest horticultural sites in North Carolina. The camellia and azalea gardens are spectacular sights in the early spring, but the variety of plantings and environments represented makes the whole park a delight. Along the banks of the Paw Paw River and Cross Creek, visitors will find dozens of garden environments, including lily gardens, hosta gardens, woods, a bog, and an 1880s farmhouse garden. This is the prettiest place in Fayetteville, and a fantastic spot for a picnic lunch on a long road trip down I-95.

Sports and Recreation

In Fayetteville you can attend a dizzying array of sporting events, from drag races to ice hockey. The **Fayetteville Marksmen** (1900 Coliseum Dr., 910/321-0123, www. marksmenhockey.com, $12-$25 adults, $7 children ages 3-12) are an ice hockey team in the Southern Professional Hockey League, unusual for this warm climate. The **Fayetteville Swamp Dogs** (910/426-5900, www.goswampdogs.com, from $8), a baseball team in the Coastal Plains League, play home games at the J. P. Riddle Stadium (2823 Legion Rd.).

The **Rogue Rollergirls** (www. fayettevillerollerderby.com, $10 adults, $6 children ages 9-16) is an up-and-coming all-female flat-track Roller Derby team participating in this fun fringe sport that had its heyday in the 1970s. In basketball, the **Fayetteville Crossover** (910/977-2954, http://crossover.trblproball.com) plays in the Tobacco Road Basketball League. An indoor football team, the **Cape Fear Heroes**

1: North Carolina Veterans Park; 2: Market House in downtown Fayetteville

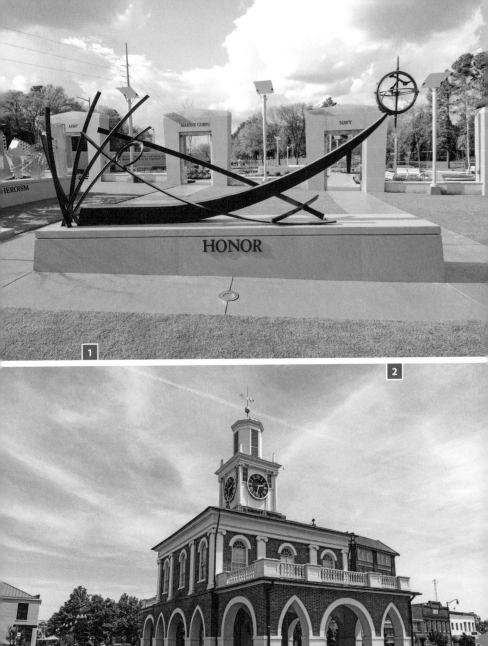

(910/323-1100, www.capefearheroes.com, from $10), play home games at the Crown Center (1960 Coliseum Dr.).

There are two motorsports venues in Fayetteville: **Fayetteville Motor Sports Park** (4480 Doc Bennett Rd., 910/484-3677, www.fayettevillemotorsportspark.com) hosts drag races, and **Fayetteville Motor Speedway** (3704 Doc Bennett Rd., 910/223-7223, www.thenewfayettevillemotorspeedway.com, around $20) hosts a variety of stock car races.

At **Carvers Creek State Park** (2505 Long Valley Rd., Spring Lake, 910/436-4681, www.ncparks.gov, 8am-8pm Mar.-May and Sept.-Oct, 8am-9pm June-Aug., 8am-6pm Nov.-Feb., free) you can fish (with a license) on the 100-acre Millpond, go for an easy hike on the two completed trails in the park, and picnic. One of the newer parks in the North Carolina Parks system, it's still growing, so look for more developments—camping, new trails—as time goes on.

GOLF

The Sandhills of North Carolina are dotted with golf courses, and the countryside around Fayetteville is no exception: **Anderson Creek Golf Club** (125 Whispering Pines Dr., Spring Lake, 910/814-2115, www.andersoncreekclub.com, 18 holes, par 72, greens fees from $40), **Bayonet at Puppy Creek** (349 S. Parker Church Rd., Raeford, 888/229-6638, www.bayonetgolf.com, greens fees from $49), **Cypress Lakes** (2126 Cypress Lakes Rd., Hope Mills, 910/483-0359, www.cypresslakesnc.com, greens fees from $30), and **Gates Four Golf and Country Club** (6775 Irongate Dr., Fayetteville, 910/424-0542, www.gatesfour.com, greens fees from $47) all offer great golf. Call at least 48 hours ahead for the best chance of getting a tee time in summer, although short-notice reservations may be possible.

ZIP LINE

If you want outdoor adventure, **ZipQuest** (533 Carvers Falls Rd., 910/488-8787, www.zipquest.com, 9am-5pm Mon.-Sat., 10am-5pm Sun., $85) gives you a different sort of outdoor experience: flying through the trees on a zip line. The tour takes you one eight zip lines around and over Carver's Creek and even 20-foot Carver's Falls, the only waterfall in the area. There's an abbreviated tour—the Treetop Excursion—which includes only five zip lines and a bevy of platforms, but at $55 it's a great intro to zipping. At the end of the

ZipQuest's gear

run, you have the opportunity to get on the Swingshot, a swing that flies out over a four-story drop into the ravine below. Both the zip line tour and Swingshot are exciting but not for the faint of heart.

INDOOR SKYDIVING

Paraclete XP SkyVenture (190 Paraclete Dr., Raeford, 910/848-2600, www.paracletexp. com, from $64) offers one of the most thrilling experiences you can have in the area: indoor skydiving. After a brief flight school, you'll step into a vertical wind tunnel with an instructor and take your first flight. If you show a little aptitude, they'll let you fly on your own (don't worry, they're never more than a couple of feet away) and even take you soaring to the top of the 51-foot tower and then rushing back down, giving you a real taste of what it's like to free fall. If you're lucky, you'll see the Golden Knights, the U.S. Army's parachute team, practicing aerial maneuvers, or maybe get to fly with world-class and even world-champion competitive skydivers, or see one of Paraclete's teams practice their wild aerial ballet.

Entertainment and Events

The **Cameo Theatre** (225 Hay St., 910/486-6633, www.cameoarthouse.com) is a cool old early-20th-century movie house, originally known as the New Dixie. Today it is "Fayetteville's alternative cinematic experience," a place for independent and art-house movies.

Cape Fear Regional Theatre (1209 Hay St., 910/323-4233, www.cfrt.org) began in 1962 as a tiny company with a bunch of borrowed equipment. Today it is a major regional theater with a wide reputation. Putting on several major productions each season and specializing in popular musicals, it draws actors and directors from around the country but maintains its heart here in the Fayetteville arts community. Its annual summertime **Blue 'N' Brews** is a one-day beer festival featuring some fine blues music

The **Gilbert Theater** (116 Green St., 910/678-7186, www.gilberttheater.com,

around $10) is a small company that puts on a variety of productions throughout the year, with emphasis on classic drama and multicultural offerings.

Fayetteville's late-April **Dogwood Festival** (www.faydogwoodfestival.com) features rock, pop, and beach-music bands; a dog show; a recycled art show; a "hogs and rags spring rally"; and the selection and coronation of Miss, Teen Miss, Young Miss, and Junior Miss Dogwood Festival; there's an October counterpart, the Dogwood Fall Festival, featuring concerts, hay rides, craft beer, and all the festival goodness you expect. In September, the **International Folk Festival** (www.theartscouncil.com) celebrates the many cultures that make up this community through food, music, art, and other cultural expressions.

The Arts Council of Fayetteville/Cumberland County (910/323-1776, www.theartscouncil.com) is in charge of the **4th Friday** celebrations, a downtown celebration of arts and an excuse to get out and get friendly with the community. Various galleries and museums are open late, there are concerts, and everyone has a grand time. At the end of November (check for exact dates), **A Dickens Holiday** takes over downtown. Characters from A Christmas Carol roam downtown, and there are performances and Victorian pubs, a candlelight procession to the Market House, and horse-drawn carriages along with a holiday street fair.

Food and Accommodations

The city's dining choices tend toward the highway chain restaurants, with some exceptions: ★ **Hilltop House** (1240 Fort Bragg Rd., 910/484-6699, www.hilltophousenc. com, 11am-2pm Tues.-Fri., 5pm-9pm Fri.-Sat., 10am-2pm Sun., $24-32) serves hearty fare in an elegant setting and has been recognized with a *Wine Spectator* magazine Award for Excellence—not surprising, given that the Hilltop House has a wine list of more than 100 bottles.

Beer lovers will prefer the **Mash House**

(4150 Sycamore Dairy Rd., 910/867-9223, www.themashhouse.com, 5pm-10pm Mon.-Thurs., 5pm-11pm Fri., noon-11pm Sat., noon-9pm Sun., $8-30), which has a good variety of pizzas and sandwiches as well as heartier entrées and a selection of good homemade brews, or **Huske Hardware House** (405 Hay St., 910/437-9905, www.huskehardware.com, 11am-9pm Mon.-Thurs., 11am-2am Fri.-Sat., noon-9pm Sun., $10-30), a gastropub serving great food and even better beer. Nearby **Dirtbag Ales** (3623 Legion Rd., Hope Mills, 910/426-2537, www.dirtbagales.com, 5pm-10pm Thurs.-Fri., 2pm-10pm Sat., noon-6pm Sun.) is a brewery that's won fans with their Blood Orange Kölsch, and their fresh take on traditional styles. Food trucks show up whenever they're open, so you can grab a bite with your pint.

For a taste of Fayetteville's international cuisine, try **Sherefe** (114 Gillespie St., 910/630-3040, www.sherefe.net, 11am-9pm Mon.-Thurs., 11am-10pm Fri.-Sat., $14-26), a Mediterranean restaurant. The friendly staff can point out something good, and get the Mediterranean Trio (hummus, baba ghanoush, and meze) to share. Don't sleep on **Habana Cuban Restaurant** (5945 Cliffdale Rd., 910/867-7052, www.habanarestaurantnc.com, 11am-2:30pm and 4:30pm-9pm Tues.-Fri., 11am-9pm Sat., closed Sun. and Mon., $12-$24), which serves up fantastic Cuban dishes from the classic El Cubanito sandwich, to grouper sandwiches, to plated seafood and pork dishes that taste so fresh you may even forget you're in North Carolina.

Luigi's (528 N. McPherson Church Rd., 910/864-1810, www.luigisnc.com, 11:30am-2:30pm Mon.-Fri., 5pm-9:30pm Mon.-Wed., 5pm-10pm Thurs.-Fri., noon-10pm Sat., noon-9pm Sun., lunch $9-13, dinner $16-34) is home to some fine Italian food as well as steak. It's old school: wood paneling and a good wine list, the perfect spot for date night.

Fayetteville's lodging options are mostly chain motels, a multitude of which can be found at the Fayetteville exits along I-95. Among the best of the chain offerings are **Embassy Suites Fayetteville** (4760 Lake Valley Dr., 910/826-3600, www.embassysuites.com, from $160), **Hampton Inn Spring Lake** (1050 N. Bragg Blvd., Spring Lake, 910/438-0945, www.hamptoninn3.hilton.com, $117-130), and **Candlewood Suites** (4108 Legend Ave., 910/866-0873, www.ihg.com, $103-135).

Information and Services

Cape Fear Valley Medical Center (1638 Owen Dr., 910/615-4000, www.capefearvalley.com) is a large hospital complex with full services, including acute care and a major cardiac care program.

The website of the **Fayetteville Area Convention and Visitors Bureau** (245 Person St., 910/483-5311, www.visitfayettevillenc.com, 8am-5pm Mon.-Fri.) is an excellent source of visitor information for the city. You'll find not only the basics but also detailed driving tours and extensive historical information.

Getting There and Around

Fayetteville Regional Airport (FAY, 400 Airport Rd., 910/433-1160, www.flyfay.com) has daily flights to Charlotte (US Airways), Atlanta (Delta), and Washington DC (United and US Airways). **Amtrak** (472 Hay St., 800/872-7245, www.amtrak.com, 10am-5:45pm and 10pm-5:45am daily) runs the *Silver Meteor* between New York City and Miami and the *Palmetto* between New York City and Savannah, Georgia; each train stops in Fayetteville once daily in each direction.

Fayetteville is near I-95; it is easily reached via Highway 24 from Jacksonville, Warsaw, and Clinton and via Highway 87 from points south.

Background

The Landscape

GEOGRAPHY

North Carolina's **mountains** and the **Piedmont** descend gradually until the land transforms into the **Coastal Plain.** Though I-95 is commonly regarded as its western boundary, geologically the Sandhills section of the state is part of the Coastal Plain. Wedged between the Piedmont and the wetlands-rich Cape Fear Valley (the delta stretching from Fayetteville to Wilmington), the Sandhills are a zone of transition between the rich soil and rolling topography of the Piedmont and the sandy soil and dune systems of the Coastal Plain. The Sandhills are a

range of sand dunes that mark where the coast was several million years ago. Since then the ocean has retreated a hundred miles or so to the coastline we know today.

The sandy soil, immense freshwater and saltwater wetlands, deep rivers, wide shallow sounds on the northern coast, and chain of barrier islands stretching from Virginia to South Carolina make eastern North Carolina's landscape distinct. Among the wetlands are pocosins and Carolina bays, two distinct types of wetlands. Pocosins are wet, peaty expanses of moist ground that are slightly elevated in the center. Carolina bays are ovoid bodies of water on diagonal axes, unexplained but beautiful; they dot the landscape across the southeastern corner of the state.

The **Outer Banks** make a giant, sweeping arc from Virginia to the north out to the point at Cape Hatteras; they then turn almost due west, forming the Bogue Banks, also known as the **Crystal Coast**. Along this northerly half of the North Carolina coast, the barrier islands work with wide complexes of sounds and marshes to protect the mainland from hurricanes and smaller storms. To the south, the barrier islands are closer to the mainland but also work with marshes, creeks, and rivers to absorb the brunt of a storm's strength. At all points along the coast, from the Outer Banks to the southern border, hurricanes can change the shape and structure of the protective islands in an instant, although the northerly barrier islands, which tend to be longer and thinner than those in the south, are often impacted more dramatically when wind and water join forces to rearrange geography.

CLIMATE

Generalizing about North Carolina's climate is difficult. It's not as hot as at the equator and not as cold as at the poles, but beyond that, each region has its own range of variables and has to be examined separately.

The mountains are much cooler than either the Piedmont or the coast, and winter lasts longer.

The central part of North Carolina, on the other hand, can be brutally hot during the summer and quite warm on spring and fall days. The Piedmont, on the other hand, can be brutally hot during the summer and quite warm on spring and fall days. Cities like Fayetteville, on the edge of the coastal and Piedmont regions, can feel like the hottest places on earth in high summer; the hottest temperature recorded in the state—110°F—was at Fayetteville in 1983.

Along the coast, temperatures are more moderate than in the Piedmont. The warm Gulf Stream washes past not far off shore, influencing air temperatures in all seasons: keeping temperatures from getting too frigid in winter, bringing spring early, keeping water warm near shore and pushing storms farther inland in summer, and extending the fall season, making it a pleasant time to be here. It's windy along the coast, and these breezes help mitigate summer's heat and make the humidity more bearable.

North Carolina gets its fair share of hazardous weather to go along with beautiful summer days and crisp fall nights. Along the Outer Banks, which jut far out into the Atlantic, **hurricanes** are a particular threat. It's not just the Outer Banks that are vulnerable to these powerful storms; the coastline south of the Banks suffers plenty of hits, and even inland, hurricanes that make landfall in South Carolina can curve up through the Lowcountry and into North Carolina's Piedmont, bringing high winds and heavy rains to inland cities and dangerous floodwaters to coastal towns. Hurricane season is June to November, but it's toward the end of summer and the start of fall that the risk becomes greatest. Wind and rain are the first effects of a hurricane, but the storm surge and high waves can cause massive damage to barrier islands, dune systems, and sensitive estuarine

Previous: enjoying the beach in the Outer Banks.

complexes. Flooding from inland rains as well as the coastal deluge can spell disaster. In 1999, Hurricane Floyd killed 35 people in North Carolina, caused billions of dollars of property damage, and permanently altered the landscape in places. During this storm, rivers in eastern North Carolina reached 500-year flood levels, leaving one-third of Rocky Mount under water and causing devastating damage to Tarboro, Kinston, and other towns in the region. Princeville, the oldest African American town in the United States, was nearly destroyed. Today, many towns in eastern North Carolina still carry scars to their infrastructure and economies due to Floyd.

Tornadoes, most common in the spring, can cause trouble any time of year. A rare November twister touched down in 2006, smashing the Columbus County community of Riegelwood, killing eight people and leaving a seven-mile swath of destruction.

Even plain old **thunderstorms** can be dangerous, bringing lightning, flash flooding, difficult driving conditions, and even hail. **Snowstorms** are rare and usually occur in the mountains. The Piedmont sees more snow than the coast, which sees flurries once or twice each winter and the occasional dusting of snow. Outside the mountains, most North Carolinians are woefully inexperienced snow drivers, and the state Department of Transportation doesn't have the equipment in coastal counties to handle much more than a little snow. Along the coast, the humorous rule of thumb is that for every inch of snow that is predicted, banks, schools, and government offices shut down for a day, and for every inch of snow that actually falls, it's two days. As soon as the meteorologists mention flurries, there's a run on the most valuable snowstorm essentials: milk, bread, peanut butter, toilet paper, and magazines.

Plants

In the early 1700s, John Lawson, an English explorer who would soon be one of the first victims of the Tuscarora War, wrote of a magnificent tree house somewhere in the very young colony of North Carolina. "I have been informed of a Tulip-Tree," he wrote, "that was ten Foot Diameter; and another, wherein a lusty Man had his Bed and Household Furniture, and liv'd in it, till his Labour got him a more fashionable Mansion. He afterwards became a noted Man, in his Country, for Wealth and Conduct." Whether or not there was ever a tulip poplar large enough to serve as a furnished bachelor pad, colonial North Carolina's forests must have seemed miraculous to the first Europeans to see them.

FORESTS

Today, after generations of logging and farming across the state, few old-growth forests exist. In the Smoky Mountains, stands of old-growth timber, like the Joyce Kilmer Forest,

are a sight to behold, and some of the trees almost validate Lawson's anecdote. Across the state, scores of specialized ecosystems support a marvelous diversity of plant and animal life. In the east, cypress swamps and a few patches of maritime forest still stand; across the Sandhills are longleaf pine forests; in the mountains are fragrant balsam forests and stands of hardwoods.

Because the state is so geographically and climatically varied, there's a greater diversity in tree species than anywhere in the eastern United States. In terms of land area, more than half of the land is still forested in the Piedmont and eastern North Carolina. Coastal forests are dominated by hardwoods—**oaks** of many varieties, **gum, cypress,** and **cedar**—and the barrier islands have a few remaining patches of maritime forest where the branches of **live oak** trees intertwine to shed storm wind and their roots sink deep to keep islands stable. The best and largest remaining example of a pristine maritime forest is on Bald Head Island, where the Bald Head Island Conservancy provides education and studies the form, function, and future of barrier islands, including these important maritime forest ecosystems. In the Piedmont, **oak** and **hickory** dominate the hardwoods alongside bands of piney woods. In the mountains oak and hickory are also the rule, but a number of conifers, including **pine** and **balsam,** appear.

The science and profession of forestry were born in North Carolina: In the 1880s and 1890s, George W. Vanderbilt, lord of the manor at Biltmore, engaged Fredrick Law Olmstead, who designed New York City's Central Park, to plan a managed forest of the finest, healthiest, and most hardy trees. Vanderbilt hired Gifford Pinchot and later Carl Schenck to be the stewards of the thousands of wooded acres he owned in the Pisgah Forest south of Asheville. The contributions these men made to the nascent field are still felt today and are commemorated at the Cradle of Forestry Museum near Brevard.

Longleaf Pine

Arguably, the most important plant in North Carolina's history is the longleaf pine, sometimes called the pitch pine. This beautiful tree is something of a rare sight today, as the longleaf pines that formerly blanketed the eastern part of the state were used extensively in the naval stores industry in the 18th and 19th centuries, providing valuable turpentine, pitch, tar, and lumber. The overharvesting of this tree has a lot to do with the disappearance of North Carolina's once-legendary pine barrens, but an unanticipated ancillary cause is the efficiency of modern firefighting. Longleaf pines depend on periodic forest fires to clear out competition from the underbrush and provide layers of nutrient-rich singed earth. In the 20th century the rule was to put out forest fires, cutting down on smoke but disturbing the natural growth cycles of these trees. In some nature preserves today, controlled burns keep the longleaf piney

woods alive and healthy as crucial habitats for several endangered species, including the red cockaded woodpecker and the pine barrens tree frog.

A great place to get a feel for this ecosystem that once covered so much of the Southeast is Weymouth Woods-Sandhills Preserve, near Southern Pines. Some of the longleaf pines here are believed to be almost 500 years old. Many of these centuries-old trees bear scars from the days of the naval stores bonanza, when turpentine makers carved deep gashes in the bark to collect the resin that bled out. The tallest and oldest longleaf pine in the state is here, and at over 130 feet tall, it's a sight.

FLOWERS

Some of North Carolina's flora puts on great annual shows, drawing flocks of admirers—the gaudy **azaleas** of springtime in Wilmington, the **wildflowers** of the first warm weather in the hills, the **rhododendrons** and **mountain laurel** of the Appalachian summer. The Ericaceae family, a race of great woody bushes with star-shaped blossoms that includes azaleas, rhododendrons, and laurel, is the headliner in North Carolina's floral fashion show. Spring comes earliest to the southeastern corner of the state, and the Wilmington area is explosively beautiful when the azaleas are in bloom. The **Azalea Festival,** held annually for more than 50 years, draws hundreds of thousands of people to the city in early to mid-April, around the time that public gardens and private yards are spangled with azaleas.

The flame azalea makes a late-spring appearance on the mountainsides of the Blue Ridge and Great Smokies, joined by its cousins the mountain laurel and Catawba rhododendron in May and June. The ways of the rhododendron are a little mysterious; not every plant blooms every year, and there's no sure-fire way of predicting when they'll put on big shows. The area's widely varying elevation also figures into bloom times. If you're interested in timing your trip to coincide with some of these flowering seasons, your best bet is to call ahead and speak with a ranger from the Great Smoky Mountains National Park or the Blue Ridge Parkway to find out how the season is coming along.

Around the end of April and into May, when spring finally arrives in the mountains but the forest floor is not yet sequestered in leafy shade, a profusion of delicate flowers emerges. **Violets** and **chickweed** emerge early on, as do the quintessentially mountainous white **trillium** blossoms and the Wake Robin, also a trillium, which looks something like a small poinsettia. Every year since 1950, around the end of April, the Great Smoky Mountains National Park has hosted the **Spring Wildflower Pilgrimage,** a weeklong festival featuring scores of nature walks that also reveal salamanders, birds, and wild hogs, along with workshops and art exhibits. Visit www.springwildflowerpilgrimage.org for upcoming events.

Surprisingly, one of the best places in North Carolina to view displays of wildflowers is along the major highways. For more than 20 years the state Department of Transportation has carried out a highway beautification project that involves planting large banks of wildflowers along highways and in wide medians. The displays are not landscaped but are allowed to grow up in unkempt profusion, often planted in inspired combinations of wildly contrasting colors that make the flowerbeds a genuinely beautiful addition to the environment. The website of the state's **Department of Transportation** (www.ncdot.org) offers a guide to the locations and seasons of the wildflower beds.

FALL FOLIAGE

Arriving as early as mid-September at the highest elevations and gradually sliding down the mountains through late October, autumn colors bring a late-season wave of visitors to western North Carolina. Along the coast, don't expect much by way of leaf peeping, as leaves tend to go from green to brown to off the tree quite suddenly.

CARNIVOROUS PLANTS

You've probably seen **Venus flytraps** for sale in nurseries, and maybe you've even bought one and brought it home to stuff with kitchen bugs. Venus flytraps grow in the wild only in one tiny corner of the world, a narrow band of counties between Wilmington and Myrtle Beach, South Carolina. The flytraps and their dozens of carnivorous Tar Heel kin, including Seussian sundews and pitcher plants, the abattoirs of the bug world, are fondest of living in places with nutrient-starved soil, like pine savannas and pocosins, where they have little competition for space and sunlight and can feed handsomely on meals that come right to them.

There are many species of **pitcher plants,** a familiar predator of the plant world. Shaped like tubular vases with a graceful elfin flap shading the mouth, pitcher plants attract insects with an irresistible brew. Unsuspecting bugs pile in, thinking they've found a keg party, but instead find themselves paddling in a sticky mess from which they're unable to escape, pinned down by spiny hairs that line the inside of the pitcher. Enterprising frogs and spiders that are either strong or clever enough to come and go safely will often set up shop inside a plant and help themselves to stragglers. Another local character is the **sundew,** perhaps the creepiest of the carnivorous plants. Sundews extend their paddle-shaped leaf-hands up into the air, hairy palms baited with a sticky mess that bugs can't resist. When a fly lands among the hairs, the sundew closes on it like a fist and gorges on it until it's ready for more.

There are several places where you can see wild carnivorous plants in North Carolina. Among the best are the **Bluethenthal Wildflower Preserve** at the University of North Carolina Wilmington, **Carolina Beach State Park,** and the **Green Swamp Preserve** and **Ev-Henwood Nature Preserve** in Brunswick County. There's also a good collection of them on display at Chapel Hill's **North Carolina Botanical Garden.**

Animals

Among the familiar wildlife most commonly seen in the state, **white-tailed deer** are out in force in the countryside and in the woods; they populate suburban areas in large numbers as well. **Raccoons** and **opossums** prowl at night, happy to scavenge from trash cans and the forest floor. **Skunks** are common, particularly in the mountains, and are often smelled rather than seen. They leave an odor something like a cross between grape soda and Sharpie markers. There are also a fair number of **black bears,** not only in the mountains but in swamps and deep woods across the state.

In woods and yards alike, **gray squirrels** and a host of familiar **songbirds** are a daily presence. Different species of **tree frogs** produce beautiful choruses on spring and summer nights, while **fireflies** mount sparkly shows in the trees and grass in the upper Piedmont and mountains. Down along the southeast coast, **alligators** and **turtles** sun themselves on many a golf course and creekside backyard.

The town of Brevard, in the Blue Ridge south of Asheville, is famous for its population of ghostly **white squirrels.** They're regular old gray squirrels that live all over North America, but their fur ranges from speckled gray and white to pure bone-white. They're not albinos; it's thought that Brevard's white squirrels are cousins of a clan that lives in Florida and that their ancestors may have found their way to the Blue Ridge in a circus or with a dealer of exotic pets in the early 20th century.

The Carolina woods harbor colonies of **Southern flying squirrels.** It's very unlikely that you'll see one unless it's at a nature center or wildlife rehabilitation clinic because flying squirrels are both nocturnal and shy. They're also almost unspeakably cute. Fully extended, they're about nine inches long snout to tail, weigh about four ounces, and have super-silky fur and pink noses. Like many nocturnal animals, they have comically long whiskers and huge, wide-set eyes that suggest amphetamine use. When they're flying—gliding, really—they spread their limbs to extend the patagium, a membrane that stretches between their front and hind legs, and glide along like little magic carpets.

While panther sightings are more common in the mountains, big cats have been spotted in coastal areas as well. There are tales of a panther in the inland woods of Brunswick and Columbus Counties on the southeast coast.

WILD PONIES

Small herds of wild ponies have called several barrier islands in the Outer Banks home for more than 400 years. Locally known as **"Banker ponies"** but more properly as feral horses, they're descendants of Spanish horses, a fact established by extensive DNA testing. No one's quite sure how they arrived here, but the consensus is that they've been here since the 1500s. They may have arrived with early English colonists or with even earlier Spanish explorers. Stories passed down here for hundreds of years say they swam ashore from long-ago shipwrecks. Today, the primary herds are on Shackleford Banks in the Cape Lookout National Seashore and in Corolla, at the extreme north end of the Outer Banks, near the Virginia border. Since they roam freely in areas open to public visitation, you may find one staring you down from behind a sand dune or a stand of scrubby cedar trees. Remember to use caution around the Banker ponies; they may resemble domestic horses, but they are wild animals. Feeding them or approaching them only ends up hurting the herd in the long run. They also pose some physical danger; all it takes for them to show you who's boss is one swift kick. You can learn more about the horses and their history at http://shacklefordhorses.org and www.corollawildhorses.com.

REINTRODUCED SPECIES

In the 1990s and early 2000s a federal program to reestablish **red wolf** colonies in the Southeast focused its efforts on parkland in North Carolina. Red wolves, thought to have existed in North Carolina in past centuries, were first reintroduced to the Great Smoky Mountains National Park. They did not thrive, and the colony was moved to the Alligator River National Wildlife Refuge on the northeast coast. The packs have fared better in this corner of the state and now roam several wilderness areas in the sound country.

BIRDS

Bird-watchers flock to North Carolina because of the great diversity of songbirds, raptors, and even hummingbirds across the state—a 2013 count put the number of species at 473—but the state is best known for waterfowl. In the sounds of eastern North Carolina, waterfowl descend en masse as they migrate. Hundreds of thousands of birds crowd the lakes, ponds, trees, marshes, and waterways as they move to and from their winter homes. Many hunters take birds during hunting season, but they're outnumbered by bird-watchers. Birders say that one of the best spots for birding in the state is around large, shallow **Lake Mattamuskeet** on the central coast, with 40,000 acres of water to attract incredible numbers of snow geese and tundra swans, Canada geese, and ducks. Just a few miles away, **Swan Quarter National Wildlife Refuge** is also a haven for ducks, wading birds, shorebirds, and their admirers.

While in eastern North Carolina, bird fanciers should visit the **Sylvan Heights Waterfowl Park and Eco-Center,** a remarkable park in the small town of Scotland Neck that's a conservation center and breeding facility for rare waterfowl from across the globe. Visitors can walk through the grounds, where large aviaries house bird species that, unless you're a world traveler and a very lucky birder, you're unlikely to see elsewhere. There are more than 170 species, and you can get quite close to most of them. Bring your camera; you'll have the chance to take shots you could never get in the field.

There are many books and websites about birding in North Carolina. One of the most helpful is the **North Carolina Birding Trail**, both a website (www.ncbirdingtrail.org) and a series of print guidebooks. Organized by region, these resources list dozens of top sites for bird-watching and favorite bird-watching events throughout the state. Another good resource is the **Carolina Bird Club** (www.carolinabirdclub.org).

AMPHIBIANS

Dozens of species of **salamanders** and their close kin, including **mudpuppies, sirens,** and **amphiuma,** call North Carolina home, and Great Smoky Mountains National Park harbors so many of them that it's known as the Salamander Capital of the World. Throughout the state, **frogs** and **toads** are numerous and vociferous, especially the many species of dainty **tree frogs.** Two species, the gray tree frog and the spring peeper, are found in every part of North Carolina, and beginning in late winter they create the impression that the trees are filled with ringing cell phones.

REPTILES

Turtles and **snakes** are the state's most common reptiles. **Box turtles,** found everywhere, and **bog turtles,** found in the Smokies, are the only land terrapins. A great many freshwater turtles inhabit the swamps and ponds, and on a sunny day every log or branch sticking out of fresh water will become a sunbathing terrace for as many turtles as it can hold. Common water turtles include **cooters, sliders,** and **painted turtles. Snapping turtles** can be found in fresh water throughout the state, so mind your toes. They grow up to a couple of feet long and can weigh more than 50 pounds. Not only will they bite—hard!—if provoked, they will actually initiate hostilities, lunging for you if they so much as disapprove of the fashion of your shoes. Even the tiny hatchlings are vicious, so give them a wide berth. Finally, we are visited often by **sea turtles,** a gentle and painfully dwindling race of seafarers. The most frequent visitor is the **loggerhead,** a reddish-tan living coracle that can weigh up to 500 pounds and nests as far north as Ocracoke. Occasional visitors include the **leatherback,** a 1,500-pound goliath at its largest, **hawksbills, greens,** and **olive ridleys.** The Bald Head Island Conservancy on Bald Head Island has been protecting the turtles and their nests since the mid-1980s, gathering data on birth rates, nest numbers, and the mother turtles. During the nesting season, conservancy members can tag turtles along with ecologists and interns and watch them lay their eggs.

There are not many kinds of **lizards** native to North Carolina, but those that are present make up for their homogeneity with ubiquity. **Anoles,** tiny, scaly dragons that dart along almost any outdoor surface, are found in great numbers in the southeastern part of the state, up the coast, and along the South Carolina state line to west of Charlotte. They put on great shows by puffing their ruby-red dewlaps and by vacillating between drab brown and gray or lime-Slurpee green, depending on the color of the background they hide on. The ranks of lizardkind are rounded out by several varieties of **skinks** and **glass lizards,** also called glass snakes because they look like snakes, although they're not, and **fence lizards.**

There are plenty of real **snakes** in North Carolina. The vast majority are shy, gentle, and totally harmless to anything larger than a rat. There are a few species of venomous snakes that are very dangerous. These include three kinds of **rattlesnake:** the huge diamondback, whose diet of rabbits testifies to its size and strength; the pigmy; and the timber or canebrake rattler. Other venomous species are the beautiful mottled **copperhead** and the **cottonmouth or water moccasin,** famous for flinging its mouth open in hostility and flashing its

brilliant white palate. The **coral snake** is a fantastically beautiful and venomous species.

Most Carolina snakes are entirely benign to humans, including old familiars such as **black racers** and **king snakes** as well as **milk, corn,** and **rat snakes.** One particularly endearing character is the **hognose snake,** which can be found throughout North Carolina but is most common in the east. Colloquially known as a spreading adder, the hognose snake compensates for its total harmlessness with amazing displays of histrionics. If you startle one, it will first flatten and greatly widen its head and neck and hiss most passionately. If it sees that you're not frightened by plan A, it will panic and go straight to plan B: playing dead. The hognose snake won't simply lay inert until you go away, though; it goes to the dramatic lengths of flipping onto its back, exposing its pitiably vulnerable belly, opening its mouth, throwing its head back limply, and sticking out its tongue as if it had just been poisoned. It is such a devoted method actor that should you call its bluff and poke it back onto its belly, it will fling itself energetically back into the mortuary pose and resume being deceased.

Alligators make their reptilian kin look tiny. Tar Heel gators are most abundant in the area south of Wilmington, but they've been seen the full length of the state's coast— note how far north the Alligator River is— and as far inland as Merchants Millpond State Park near the Virginia state line. The biggest ones can reach 1,000 pounds and measure 10-15 feet long. Smaller gators are more common, and the six- and eight-foot females are small in comparison to the massive bull gators. They have approximately a mouthful of sharp teeth, and even hatchlings can pack a nasty bite. These amazing prehistoric-looking amphibious assault machines appear to spend most of their waking hours splayed out in the sun with their eyes closed, or floating motionless in the water. Don't fall for it; it's their fiendishly clever, or perhaps primitively simple, ploy to make you come closer. They can launch themselves at prey as if spring-loaded and are more than capable of catching and eating a dog, cat, or small child. It happens very rarely, but given the chance, large gators can and will eat an adult human. The best course of action, as with most wildlife, is to admire them from a distance.

History

ANCIENT CIVILIZATION

By the time the first colonists arrived and called this place Carolina, the land had already sustained some 20,000 years of human history. We know that Paleo-Indians hunted these lands during the last ice age, when there were probably more mammoths and saber-toothed tigers in North Carolina than people. Civilization came around 4000 BC, when the first inhabitants settled down to farm, make art, and trade goods. By the first century, Southern Woodland and Mississippian Indians were also living in advanced societies with complex religious systems, economic interaction among communities, advanced farming methods, and the creation of art and architecture.

When the Europeans arrived, there were more than a dozen major Native American groups within what is now North Carolina. The Cherokee people ruled the mountains while the Catawba, Pee Dees, Tutelo, and Saura, among others, were their neighbors in the Piedmont. In the east, the Cheraw, Waccamaw, and Tuscarora were some of the larger communities, while many bands occupied land along the Outer Banks and sounds.

CONQUEST

The first Europeans to land here were Spanish. We know conquistador Hernando de Soto and his troops marched around western North Carolina in 1539, but they were just passing through. In 1566, another band of Spanish explorers, led by conquistador Juan Pardo, came for a longer visit. They were making a circuitous trek in the general direction of Mexico, and along the way they established several forts in what are now the Carolinas and Tennessee. One of these forts, called San Juan, has been identified by archaeologists outside present-day Morganton in a community called Worry Crossroads. Although the troops who were garrisoned for a year and a half at Fort San Juan eventually disappeared into the woods or were killed, it's theorized that they may have had a profound impact on the course of history, possibly spreading European diseases among the Native Americans and weakening them so much that, a couple of decades later, the indigenous people would be unable to repel the invasion of English colonists.

The next episode in the European settlement of North Carolina is one of the strangest mysteries in American history: the Lost Colonists of Roanoke. After two previous failed attempts to establish an English stronghold on the island of Roanoke, fraught by poor planning and disastrous diplomacy, a third group of English colonists tried their luck. Sometime between being dropped off in the New World in 1587 and one of their leaders returning three years later to resupply them, all of the colonists—including Virginia Dare, the first English person born in the Americas—had vanished into the woods. To this day, their fate is unknown, although a host of fascinating theories are still debated and probably always will be.

The disappearance of the Roanoke colonists did little to slow the process of the European conquest of North America. After the establishment of the Virginia colony in 1607, new English settlers began to trickle southward into Carolina, while Barbadians and Europeans from Charles Town (in present-day South Carolina) gradually began to populate the area around Wilmington. The town of Bath was established in 1706, and New Bern was settled shortly thereafter. The bloody Tuscarora War followed, and after a crushing defeat near present-day Snow Hill, in which hundreds were killed, the Tuscarora people retreated, opening the land along the Neuse River to European colonization.

COLONIALISM

The conflict between Europeans and Native Americans wasn't the only world-changing cultural encounter going on in the Southern colonies. By the middle of the 18th century, nearly 100,000 enslaved people had been brought to North Carolina from West Africa. By the end of the 18th century, many areas, especially those around Wilmington, had populations where enslaved African Americans outnumbered whites. Although North Carolina did not experience slavery on as vast a scale as South Carolina, there were a handful of plantations with more than 100 slaves, and many smaller plantations and town homes of wealthy planters, merchants, and politicians with smaller numbers of slaves. Africans and African Americans were an early and potent cultural force in the South, influencing the economy, politics, language, religion, music, architecture, and cuisine in ways still seen today.

In the 1730s the Great Wagon Road connected Pennsylvania with Georgia by cutting through the Mid-Atlantic and Southern backcountry of Virginia and North Carolina. Many travelers migrated south from Pennsylvania, among them a good number of German and Scottish-Irish settlers who found the mountains and Piedmont of North Carolina to their liking. Meanwhile, the port of Wilmington, growing into one of the most important in the state, saw a number of Gaelic-speaking Scots move through, following the river north and putting down roots around what is now Fayetteville. Shortly before the American Revolution, a group of German-speaking religious settlers known as the Moravians constructed a beautiful and industrious town, Salem, in the heart of the Piedmont, later to become Winston-Salem. Their pacifist beliefs, Germanic heritage, and artistry set them apart from other communities in colonial North Carolina, and they left an indelible mark on the state's history.

The 18th century brought one conflict after another to the colony, from fights over the Vestry Act in the early 1700s, which attempted to establish the Anglican church as the one official faith of the colony, through various regional conflicts with Native Americans and events that played out at a global level during the French and Indian War. At mid-century the population and economic importance of the Piedmont was growing exponentially, but colonial representation continued to be focused along the coast. Protesting local corruption and lack of governmental concern for the western region, a group of backcountry farmers organized themselves into an armed posse in resistance to colonial corruption. Calling themselves the Regulators, they eventually numbered more than 6,000. Mounting frustrations led to an attack by the Regulators on the Orange County courthouse in Hillsborough. Finally, a colonial militia was dispatched to crush the movement, which it did at the Battle of Alamance in 1771. Six Regulators were captured and hanged at Hillsborough.

REVOLUTION AND STATEHOOD

Many believe the seeds of the American Revolution were sown, tended, and reaped in New England, but the southern colonies, particularly North Carolina, played important roles before and during the rebellion. In 1765, as the War of the Regulation was heating up, the residents of Brunswick Town, the colonial capital and the only deep-water port in the southern half of the colony, revolted in protest of the Stamp Act. They placed the royal governor under house arrest and put an end to taxation in the Cape Fear region, sending a strong message to the crown and to fellow patriots hungry to shake off the yoke of British rule. In the ensuing years, well-documented events like the Boston Tea Party, the Battles of Lexington and Concord, and the signing of the Declaration of Independence occurred, but North Carolina's role in leading the rebellion was far from over.

After the Battles of Lexington and Concord, the colonies were aflame with patriotic fervor, and Mecklenburg County (around Charlotte) passed the first colonial declaration rejecting the crown's authority. By this time, North Carolina, like the other colonies, had formed a provincial government, and it was busy in the tavern at Halifax writing the Halifax Resolves, the first official action in the colonies calling for independence from Britain. On April 12, 1776, the resolves were ratified and delegates carried them to the Second Continental Congress in Philadelphia. Other delegates were so inspired that more such resolves appeared, ultimately the Declaration of Independence was written and ratified, and the revolution was on in earnest.

Although North Carolina may have been the first to call for independence, the state was divided in its loyalties. Among the most noteworthy Loyalists was the community of Highland Scots living in and around modern-day Fayetteville. Men from this community were marching to join General Cornwallis near Brunswick Town and Southport (then Smithville) when Patriots ambushed them at the bloody battle of Moore's Creek, killing 30 Scots and routing the Loyalist force.

North Carolinians fought all over the eastern seaboard during the Revolution, including about 1,000 who were with Washington at Valley Forge. The year 1780 brought fighting back home, particularly in the area around Charlotte, which a daunted General Cornwallis referred to as "the hornets' nest." The battle of Kings Mountain, west of Charlotte, was a pivotal moment in the war and particularly costly to the Loyalist forces. Cornwallis received another blow at the Battle of Guilford Courthouse; although technically a British victory, it weakened his forces

considerably. By the time the war ended, thousands of North Carolinians were dead, and the treasury was far in debt. But North Carolina was now a state with the business of statehood to attend to. The capital was moved inland to Raleigh, and 20 miles away at Chapel Hill, ground was broken for the establishment of the University of North Carolina, the first state university in the country.

THE FEDERAL ERA

The early 19th century in North Carolina was a good deal more peaceful than the previous hundred years had been. The first decade of the 1800s saw a religious awakening in which thousands of North Carolinians became devout Christians. At the same time, the introduction of the cotton gin and bright-leaf tobacco were economic boons in the state, particularly the eastern counties. Railroads and plank roads made trade immeasurably more efficient, bringing new prosperity to the Piedmont.

THE CIVIL WAR

Compared to South Carolina and a few other Southern states, North Carolina was considered politically moderate in the mid-19th century because it was less invested economically and politically in slavery. Combined with the knowledge that if secession became a reality, war would follow and North Carolina's tobacco and cotton fields would quickly become battlefields, secession was on the lips of everyone across the South. As some states voted to remove themselves from the Union, North Carolina's voters rejected a ballot measure authorizing a secession convention. As grand a gesture as that victory may have been, when fighting erupted at Fort Sumpter in Charleston Harbor, North Carolina's hand was forced and its secession was a reality. Secessionist governor John Ellis rejected Lincoln's call to federalize state militias, instead seizing control of the state and all federal military installations within its boundaries as well as the Charlotte Mint. North Carolina officially seceded on May 20, 1861, and a few weeks later Union ships began to blockade the coast. Roanoke Island in the Outer Banks fell, and a freedmen's colony (a home for enslaved people who had been freed or escaped) sprung up. New Bern, which fell in the spring of 1862, became a major focal point of Union military strategy and a thriving political base for freed and escaped African Americans. To the south, Fort Fisher, on the Cape Fear River just south of Wilmington, guarded the river's inlet and was crucial to the success of the blockade runners—smugglers whose speedy boats eluded the Union blockade. Fort Fisher kept Wilmington in Confederate hands until nearly the end of the war. When it finally did fall to Union forces in February 1865, it required what would be the largest amphibious assault in American military history until World War II. Wilmington was the last major port on the Confederacy's eastern seaboard, and its fall severed supply lines and crippled what remained of the Confederate Army in the area.

The varying opinions felt by Southerners about the Civil War, in the South also called the War between the States, was particularly strong in North Carolina, where today you'll still hear whites refer to it as the War of Northern Aggression or the War of Yankee Aggression. More than 5,000 African Americans from North Carolina joined and fought in the Union Army, and there were pockets of strong Union sentiment and support among white North Carolinians, especially in the mountains. Some 10,000 North Carolinians fought for the Union. Zebulon Vance, who won the 1862 gubernatorial election and served as governor through the duration of the war, was a native of Weaverville, near Asheville, and felt acutely the state's ambivalence toward the Confederacy. Much to the consternation of Richmond (the Confederate capital), Governor Vance was adamant in his refusal to put the interests of the Confederacy over those of his own state. Mountain communities suffered tremendously during the war from acts of terrorism by deserters and rogues from both armies.

The latter years of the Civil War were particularly difficult for North Carolina and the rest of the South. Approximately 4,000 North Carolina men died at the Battle of Gettysburg alone. After laying waste to Georgia and South Carolina, General William T. Sherman's army entered North Carolina in the spring of 1865, destroying homes and farms. His march of fire and pillage spared Wilmington, which is one reason the town contains such an incredible collection of Federal architecture. The last major battle of the war was fought in North Carolina, when General Sherman and Confederate General Joseph Johnston engaged at Bentonville. Johnston surrendered to Sherman in Durham in April 1865.

By the end of the war more than 40,000 North Carolina soldiers were dead—a number equivalent to the entire present-day population of the city of Hickory, Apex, or Kannapolis.

RECONSTRUCTION AND THE NEW SOUTH

The years immediately after the war were painful as well, as a vast population of newly free African Americans tried to make new lives for themselves economically and politically in the face of tremendous opposition and violence from whites. The Ku Klux Klan was set up during this time, inaugurating an era of horror for African Americans throughout the country. Federal occupation and domination of the Southern states' political and legal systems also exacerbated resentment toward the North. The state's ratification of the 14th Amendment on July 4, 1868, brought North Carolina back into the Union.

The late 1800s saw large-scale investment in North Carolina's railroad system, launching the industrial boom of the New South. Agriculture changed in this era as the rise of tenancy created a new form of enslavement for many farmers—black, white, and Native American. R. J. Reynolds, Washington Duke, and other entrepreneurs built a massively lucrative empire of tobacco production from field to factory. Textile and furniture mills sprouted throughout the Piedmont, creating a new cultural landscape as rural Southerners migrated to mill towns.

THE 20TH CENTURY AND TODAY

The early decades of the 1900s brought an expanded global perspective to North Carolina, not only through the expanded economy and the coming of radio but as natives of the state scattered across the globe. About 80,000 North Carolinians served in World War I, many of them young men who had never before left the state or perhaps even their home counties. Hundreds of thousands of African Americans migrated north during what became known as the Great Migration. The communities created by black North Carolinians in the Mid-Atlantic and the Northeast are still closely connected by culture and kinship to their cousins whose ancestors remained in the South. The invasion of the boll weevil, an insect that devastated the cotton industry, hastened the departure of Southerners of all races who had farmed cotton. The Great Depression hit hard across all economic sectors of the state in the 1930s, but New Deal employment programs were a boon to North Carolina's infrastructure, with the construction of hydroelectric dams, the Blue Ridge Parkway, and other public works.

North Carolina's modern-day military importance largely dates to the World War II era. Installations at Fort Bragg, Camp Lejeune, and other still-vital bases were constructed or expanded. About 350,000 North Carolinians fought in World War II, and 7,000 of them died.

A few old-timers remember World War II quite vividly because they witnessed it firsthand: German U-boats prowled the waters off the coast, torpedoing ships and sinking them with frightening regularity. These German submarines were often visible from the beach, but more often the evidence of their mission of terror and supply-chain disruption—corpses,

wounded sailors, and the flotsam of exploded ships—washed up on the shore. More than 10,000 German prisoners were interned in prisoner-of-war camps, in some parts of the state becoming forced farm laborers. In Wilmington, just a few blocks from downtown, is an apartment complex that was part of a large prisoner-of-war compound for U-boat officers.

In the 1950s and 1960s, African Americans in North Carolina and throughout the United States struggled against the monolithic system of segregation and racism enshrined in the nation's Jim Crow laws. The Ku Klux Klan stepped up its pro-segregation efforts with political and physical violence against Native Americans as well as African Americans; in the famous 1958 Battle of Maxton, 500 armed Lumbee people foiled a Klan rally and sent the Knights running for their lives. Change arrived slowly. The University of North Carolina accepted its first African American graduate student in 1951 and the first black undergraduates four years later. Sit-ins in 1960 at the Woolworth's lunch counter in Greensboro began with four African American men, students at North Carolina A&T. On the second day of their protest they were joined by 23 other demonstrators; on the third day there were 300, and by day four about 1,000. This was a pivotal moment in the national civil rights movement, sparking sit-ins across the country in which an estimated 50,000 people participated. You can see the counter today at the International Civil Rights Center and Museum in Greensboro. Even as victories were won at the level of Congress and in the federal courts, as in *Brown v. the Board of Education* and the 1964 Civil Rights Act, actual change on the ground was inexorably slow and hard-won. North Carolina's contribution to the civil rights movement continues to be invaluable for the whole nation.

As of the most recent bit of census data, provided in 2014, North Carolina had a population approaching 10 million (9.94 million), a number the state should hit by 2016. The state continues to adapt and contribute to the global community, thanks in large part to larger cities like Charlotte and the university-, research-, and tech-rich Raleigh, Durham, and Chapel Hill area. It is now a place of ethnic diversity, growing especially quickly in Latino residents. In 2014 an estimated 9 percent of North Carolinians were Latino, and that number is still climbing. There are also significant communities of Dega and Hmong people from Southeast Asia as well as Eastern Europeans, among many others.

Government and Economy

POLITICAL LIFE
Liberal Enclaves

Although historically a red state, North Carolina's large population of college students, professors, and artists has created several boisterous enclaves of progressive politics. The outspoken archconservative U.S. Senator Jesse Helms supposedly questioned the need to spend public money on a state zoo in North Carolina "when we can just put up a fence around Chapel Hill." The Chapel Hill area is indeed the epicenter of North Carolina's liberalism, with its smaller neighboring town of Carrboro at its heart. Would-be Democratic presidential candidates and politicians on the campaign trail regularly stop here to bolster support in the state.

Although you'll find a mixture of political views statewide, the Triangle is not the only famously liberal community. In Asheville, lefty politics are part of the community's devotion to all things organic and DIY. Significant pockets of liberalism also exist in Boone, the cities of the Triad, and Wilmington.

Famous Figures

Several major players in modern American politics are from North Carolina. The best-known politician in recent years is former U.S. senator John Edwards, who made two runs for the White House, the first leading to a vice presidential spot on the Democratic ticket. Edwards was born in South Carolina but grew up here in the Sandhills. At the other end of the political spectrum, Monroe native Jesse Helms spent 30 years in the U.S. Senate, becoming one of the most prominent and outspoken conservative Republicans of our times. Upon his retirement, Helms was succeeded in the Senate by Salisbury-born Duke University graduate Elizabeth Dole, who had previously served in Ronald Reagan's cabinet and George H. W. Bush's cabinet. She was also president of the American Red Cross and had a close brush with the White House when her husband, Kansas senator Bob Dole, ran for president in 1996.

MAJOR INDUSTRIES

Over the last 20 years, North Carolina has experienced tremendous shifts in its economy as the industries that once dominated the landscape and brought wealth and development declined. The **tobacco** industry ruled the state's economy for generations, employing innumerable North Carolinians from field to factory and funding a colossal portion of the state's physical and cultural infrastructure. The slow decline of the tobacco industry worldwide from the 1980s changed the state dramatically, especially the rural east, where tobacco fields once went from green to gold every fall. Other agricultural industries, especially **livestock**—chickens and hogs— are still important in the east. The **textile** industry, a giant for most of the 20th century, suffered the same decline as manufacturers sought cheaper labor overseas. Likewise, the **furniture** industry slipped into obscurity. Today, the once-thriving **fishing** industry is in steep decline, largely due to globalization and overfishing.

While these staple industries have fallen off, new industries and fields have sprouted across the state. **Pharmaceutical** and **biotech** companies have set up in the Research Triangle, formed by Raleigh, Durham, and Chapel Hill. The **film industry** has made Wilmington a hub of feature film production, Charlotte is a major production center for television programming and commercials, and Raleigh is home to a number of visual-effects studios that contribute to films and TV. **High-tech** leaders like Apple have set up in North Carolina, and other tech giants have followed, locating database and network centers here. Charlotte is second only to New York City among the country's largest **banking** centers. **Tourism** continues to grow and contribute in a major way to the state's economy. **Agriculture** remains relevant, though it is increasingly becoming more specialized, especially as demand for organic products and locally and regionally sourced products continues.

Tourism

North Carolina has always drawn visitors to its mountains, waters, beaches, and cities. As the economy evolves, the tourism sector has become even more important. Beach landscapes sell themselves, but competition is strong to be the town visitors thing of first. **Heritage tourism** is also enormously important, with a number of guidebooks and driving trails established or under development to promote history, traditional music, folk arts, and literary achievements. The state's Department of Commerce estimates that nearly 46 million people visit North Carolina every year, bringing in more than $19 billion, and that close to 200,000 state residents work in industries directly related to and dependent on tourism.

DISTRIBUTION OF WEALTH

For the most part, North Carolina is basically working-class. Pockets of significant wealth exist in urban areas, and as more and more retirees relocate to North Carolina, there are moneyed people in the mountains and coastal counties. Extensive white-collar job availability makes the Triangle a comparatively prosperous region, with average household incomes in 2010 exceeding $60,000, much higher than the state's median household income of just over $46,000.

The state also experiences significant **poverty.** The proportion of people living in poverty has been rising since 2000, partly due to the ongoing worldwide economic slowdown but also due to the derailment of many of North Carolina's backbone industries. As recently as 15 years ago, a high school graduate in small-town North Carolina could count on making a living wage in a mill or factory; nowadays those opportunities have dried up, and the poverty rate in 2011 was just over 16 percent. Even more distressing, the number of children living in poverty is just over 24 percent, climbing to 28 percent for children under age six.

The northeastern quadrant of North Carolina is the most critically impoverished, which points to **financial inequality** correlating to race, as the region has a significant African American population. Broken down by ethnicity, the data reveal that 10 percent of urban and rural whites live in poverty, while 20-30 percent of rural and urban Latinos, African Americans, and Native Americans live in poverty.

Several hardworking organizations and activists are trying to alleviate the economic hardship found in North Carolina. National organizations like **Habitat for Humanity** (www.habitat.org) and regional groups like the **Southern Coalition for Social Justice** (http://southerncoalition.org) and the **Institute for Southern Studies** (www.southernstudies.org) bring community activism and research to the state. There are also excellent North Carolina-based advocates in groups such as the **North Carolina Rural Economic Development Center** (www.ncruralcenter.org), the **North Carolina Justice Center** (www.ncjustice.org), the **Black Family Land Trust** (www.bflt.org), and **Student Action with Farmworkers** (http://saf-unite.org).

People and Culture

DEMOGRAPHICS

The ninth most populous state in the union, North Carolina's population of 9.94 million residents is slightly more than Michigan and New Jersey and slightly less than Georgia. More than two-thirds of North Carolinians are white, primarily of German and Scottish-Irish descent, and not quite one-quarter are African American. The state is about 9 percent Latino and has the seventh-largest Native American population of any state.

More than 40 percent of North Carolinians are between the ages of 25 and 59, but the older population is steadily rising, due in large part to the state's popularity with retirees. The majority—about 70 percent—of North Carolinians live in family groups, with married couples constituting about half of those and married couples with children making up almost one-quarter of households. Of the remaining one-third of the state's population who live in "nonfamily households"—that is, not with blood relatives or a legally recognized spouse—the vast majority are individuals living on their own. Unmarried couples, both straight and gay, have a much lower rate of cohabitation here than in more urban parts of the United States, but such households are common and accepted in the Triangle, Asheville, Charlotte, and other urban areas.

Native Americans

Many Americans have never heard of the **Lumbee people** despite the fact that they claim to be the largest Native American nation east of the Mississippi. This is in part due to the federal government's refusal to grant them official recognition, although the state of North Carolina does recognize them. The Lumbee are primarily based in and around Robeson County in the swampy southeastern corner of the state, their traditional home. In the Great Smoky Mountains, the town of Cherokee on the Qualla Boundary, which is Cherokee-administered land, is the governmental seat of the **Eastern Band of the Cherokee.** The Eastern Band are largely descended from those Cherokee people who escaped arrest during the deportation of the Southeast's Native Americans on the Trail of Tears in the 19th century, or who made the forced march to Oklahoma but survived and walked home to the mountains again. The Lumbee people and Cherokee people are both important cultural groups in North Carolina. Several other Native American communities are indigenous to the state as well; those recognized by the state are the **Waccamaw-Siouan, Occaneechi Band of the Saponi Nation, Haliwa-Saponi, Coharie, Sappony,** and **Meherrin.**

Latinos

North Carolina has one of the fastest-growing Latino populations in the United States, a community whose ranks have swelled since the 1990s, in particular as hundreds of thousands of **Mexican and Central American laborers** came to work in the agricultural, industrial, and formerly booming construction trades. Their presence in such large numbers makes for some unexpectedly quirky cultural juxtapositions, as in small rural towns that are now majority Latino or in Charlotte, where the Latino population has made Roman Catholicism the most common religion.

Other Immigrants

Significant numbers of non-Latino immigrants also live in North Carolina. Charlotte is a dizzying hodgepodge of ethnicities, where native Southerners live and work alongside **Asians, Africans,** and **Middle Easterners,** where mosques and synagogues and *wats* welcome worshipers just down the street from Baptist churches and Houses of Prayer. Many **Hmong** and other **Southeast Asian** immigrants have settled in the northern foothills and the Piedmont Triad, and the dense thicket of universities in the Triangle attracts academics from around the world.

RELIGION

As early as the 17th century, North Carolina's religious landscape foreshadowed the diversity we enjoy today. The first Christians in North Carolina were Quakers, soon followed by Anglicans, Presbyterians, Baptists, Moravians, Methodists, and Roman Catholics. Native American and African religions, present in the early colonial days, were never totally quashed by European influence, and Barbadian Sephardic Jews were here early on as well. All of these religions remain today, with enrichment by the presence of Muslims, Buddhists, and an amazing mosaic of other Christian groups.

North Carolina claims as its own one of the world's most influential modern religious figures, Billy Graham, who was raised on a dairy farm outside Charlotte and experienced his Christian religious awakening in 1934. After preaching in person to more people around the world than anyone in human history, and being involved with every U.S. president since Harry Truman, Billy Graham is now home in his native state, where he divides his time between Charlotte and Montreat, outside Asheville.

LANGUAGE

Few states can boast the linguistic diversity of North Carolina. North Carolina speech varies widely by region and even from county to county. These variations have to do with the historical patterns of settlement in a given area—whether Scots-Irish or German ancestry is common, how long Native American languages survived after the arrival of the Europeans, the presence or lack of African influence—as well as other historical patterns of trade and communication.

Of our distinct regional accents, the **Outer Banks brogue** is probably the best known. Much like the residents of the Chesapeake islands in Maryland and Virginia, "Hoi Toiders," as Outer Bankers are jokingly called, because of how they pronounce the phrase "high tide," have a striking dialect that resembles certain dialects in the north of England. "I" is rounded into "oi," the r sound is often hard, and many distinctive words survive from long-ago English, Scottish, and Irish dialects. Not dissimilar is the Appalachian dialect heard through much of the mountains. The effect is more subtle than in the Outer Banks, but "oi" replaces "I" in Appalachian English too, and r's are emphasized. A telltale sign of upcountry origins is the pronunciation of the vowel in words like bear and hair, which in the mountains is flattened almost inside-out so that the words are pronounced something like "barr" and "harr." This is similar to mountain accents in Tennessee, West Virginia, Virginia, and Kentucky.

There are a great many smaller linguistic zones peppered throughout the state. Folks from up around the **Virginia border** in eastern North Carolina may have a distinctively Virginian accent. Listen for the classic telltale word *house.* Southside Virginians and their neighbors south of the state line will pronounce it "heause," with a flat vowel. **Cherokee English,** heard in the Smokies, combines the Appalachian sound with a distinctively Cherokee rhythm, while **Lumbee English,** spoken in and around Robeson County in the southeast, combines sounds somewhat like those of the Outer Banks or deep mountains with a wealth of unusual grammatical structures and vocabulary of unknown origin. Oft-cited examples are the Lumbee construction "be's," a present-tense form of "to be," and words like *ellick* for coffee and *juvember* for slingshot: "Get me some more ellick, please, if you be's going to the market." Residents of the **Sandhills** area, bounded by the Uwharries to the west, Sanford to the north, and Southern Pines to the southeast, have a highly unusual rhythm to their speech—a rapid, soft, almost filigreed way of talking, delivered in bursts between halting pauses. Down around Wilmington and south to the South Carolina state line, African American English, and to a lesser extent white English, have some of the inflections of the **Gullah language** of the Lowcountry. These are only a few of the state's dialects, and even these have subvariations. Old-timers can pinpoint geographical differences within these categories—whether a Lumbee speaker is from Prospect or Drowning Creek, for example, or whether a Banker is from Ocracoke or Hatteras.

Of course, English is hardly the only language spoken here. If you visit Cherokee, you'll see that many street and commercial signs bear pretty, twisty symbols in a script that looks like a cross between Khmer or Sanskrit and Cyrillic; **written Cherokee** uses the script famously devised by **Sequoyah** in the early 19th century. Cherokee also survives as a spoken language, mostly among the elders in traditional communities such as Snowbird, near Robbinsville, and many younger Cherokee people are determined to learn and pass on their ancestral tongue, but the small pool of speakers points to the slow death of the language. **Spanish** is widely spoken throughout the state as the Latino population continues to grow rapidly, and within Latino communities here are many national and regional dialects of Spanish. Some Central American immigrants who speak indigenous languages arrive unable to understand English or Spanish. Anyone who doubts that newcomers to this country are dedicated to the task of integrating into American society need only consider the incredibly difficult task faced by such immigrants, who must first learn Spanish before they can enroll in ESL programs to learn English.

The Arts

As much as North Carolinians like to brag about the beaches and mountains and college sports teams, it's the artists across the state who help North Carolina distinguish itself. There is an incredibly rich and complex cultural heritage here that has strong support from the North Carolina Arts Council and a vast network of local and regional arts organizations. These groups have supplied inspiration, financial and emotional support, and sustenance for generations of remarkable musicians, writers, actors, and other artists.

LITERATURE

Storytelling seems to come naturally to Southerners. From the master storytellers of Jack Tales in the Blue Ridge to the distinguished journalists we see every night on television, North Carolinians have a singular gift for communication. Thomas Wolfe was an Asheville native, and O. Henry, whose real name was William Sidney Porter, was born and raised in Greensboro. Tom Robbins (*Even Cowgirls Get the Blues*) was born in Blowing Rock. Charles Frazier (*Cold Mountain*) is from Asheville. Sarah Dessen (*Just Listen*) is from Chapel Hill. Kaye Gibbons, Lee Smith, Fred Chappell, Randal Kenan, and Clyde Edgerton, leading lights in Southern fiction, are all natives or residents of North Carolina. Also closely associated with the state are Carl Sandburg, David Sedaris, Armistead Maupin, and Betsy Byars, who have all lived here at some point in their lives. Arts programs focused on creative writing have sprung up across the state, imbuing the literary scenes in towns like Wilmington, Greensboro, Asheville, and Chapel Hill with talented undergraduate and graduate students and their professors. Notable writers teaching creative writing programs include poet A. Van Jordan, essayist David Gessner, and novelist and short story writer Jill McCorkle.

North Carolina has also given the world some of the giants of 20th-century journalism. Edward R. Murrow, Charles Kuralt,

David Brinkley, and Howard Cosell were all sons of Carolina, and Charlie Rose carries their torch today.

MUSIC

It's hard to know where to begin in describing the importance of music to North Carolinians. With fiddlers conventions, renowned symphony orchestras, busy indie-rock scenes, and a thriving gospel-music industry, there is no escaping good music here. Since the earliest days of recorded country music, North Carolinians have shared their songs with the world. Charlie Poole and Wade Mainer were among the first to record and became influential artists in the 1930s. By 1945 a banjo player named Earl Scruggs was helping create what would become the quintessential sound of **bluegrass** music, particularly his three-fingered picking style. Bluegrass greats like Del McCoury helped further define the sound. Today, bluegrass is alive and well in North Carolina; Steve Martin's collaboration with the Steep Canyon Rangers sells out concerts around the world and garners awards at every turn, and the late Doc Watson's annual **MerleFest** is still going strong. **Country** musicians like Ronnie Milsap, Donna Fargo, Charlie Daniels, and Randy Travis made big names for themselves from the 1970s to the 1990s; more recently, Kellie Pickler and Scottie McCreery (of *American Idol* fame) and Eric Church have made waves on the country charts.

The growth of **jazz** and **funk** would be unimaginably different if not for a number of notable innovators that make North Carolina nearly as important as New Orleans to the development of these genres. John Coltrane was raised in High Point, Thelonious Monk was a native of Rocky Mount, Nina Simone hails from Tryon, and Dizzy Gillespie grew up just over the South Carolina state line but contributed greatly when he studied music in Laurinburg. On the funk side of the coin, what would the genre be without George Clinton, founder of Parliament and Parliament-Funkadelic? Saxophonist Maceo

Parker and his brother, drummer Melvin Parker, played with Clinton and with South Carolina's favorite son and the Godfather of Soul, James Brown. Together they developed the classic funk sound and influenced the groove-driven side of **soul** music.

In North Carolina, you're never far from some good **gospel** music. On the coast, African American choirs blend spirituality and faith with showmanship and serious talent to perform beautiful inspired sets. In the mountains, you're more likely to find gospel quartets and old-time gospel music, which is more inspired by bluegrass and traditional music, at camp meetings and gospel sings on weekend nights. The state's Native American communities also have thriving gospel traditions of their own.

Artists that include James Taylor, Tori Amos, Clay Aiken, the Squirrel Nut Zippers, the Avett Brothers, Fred Durst (from Limp Bizkit), rapper and producer Jermaine Dupri, Corrosion of Conformity, Ben Folds Five, Daughtry, Southern Culture on the Skids, and Megafaun have all had a hand in shaping the state's musical legacy.

THEATER

Regional theater companies such as the venerable Flat Rock Playhouse near Hendersonville make great theater accessible in small towns and rural areas. Wilmington is home to Thalian Hall and the Thalian Association, a group founded in 1788 that was named the Official Community Theatre of North Carolina thanks to their long-running commitment to the arts in Wilmington. The North Carolina School for the Arts in Winston-Salem mints great actors and filmmakers, among other artists. The film and television industries have long recognized North Carolina as a hotbed of talent as well as a place with amazing filming locations.

For some reason, **outdoor historical dramas** have long flourished in North Carolina. The most famous is North Carolina playwright Paul Green's *Lost Colony,* which has been performed every summer since 1937 on Roanoke Island, except during World War II when German U-boats lurked nearby. The Cherokee people depict emblematic episodes in their history in the outdoor drama *Unto These Hills,* in production since 1950. The community of Boone has presented *Horn in the West* since 1952, and it is joined by Valdese and several other communities in North Carolina in turning to performance tableaux to commemorate their heritage. It's especially important to note that among the characteristics of outdoor drama in North Carolina is the fact that the cast, crew, and often the producers and playwrights are members of the communities whose stories the plays tell.

ARTS AND CRAFTS

Folk art and studio crafts show vitality in North Carolina. Several communities are known worldwide for their local traditions, and countless individual artists, studios, and galleries can be found across the state.

As people become more accustomed to a world where almost every object we see and use was mass-produced far away, we develop a deeper appreciation for the depth of skill and aesthetic complexity that went into the production of everyday objects in past generations. North Carolinians have always been great crafters of utilitarian and occupational necessities. As you travel through the state, keep an eye out for objects that you might not immediately recognize as art—barns, fishing nets, woven chair bottoms—but that were made with the skill and artistry of generations-old traditions. In North Carolina, art is everywhere.

Food

You'll probably have heard of North Carolina's most famous specialties—**barbecue, Brunswick stew,** and **hush puppies**—but are you brave enough to venture deeper into the hinterlands of Carolina cooking? Few snacks are more viscerally craved by locals, and more revolting to non-Southerners, than **boiled peanuts.** The recipe is simple: Green peanuts are boiled in their shells in bulk in water as salty as the chef deems necessary. Once they're soft and slimy, the peanuts are dumped into a strainer and are ready to eat. All you need to make them is a big kettle and a fire, so boiled peanuts are often made and sold in small bags at roadside stands, primarily in the Lowcountry and coastal plain, but increasingly in the mountains as well. Often these roadside stands are themselves folk art, with handmade signs reading "Bolit P-Nuts Here," with a collection of carvings or sculptures for sale in the bed of a truck nearby. To eat a boiled peanut, pick it up by the ends with your thumb and forefinger and place it lengthwise between your front teeth. Gently crack open the shell—don't bite through it—and detach the halves. Pry off half of the shell, and nip or slurp the peanuts out as if you're eating an oyster (boiled peanuts often show up at Lowcountry oyster roasts). Toss the shell out the window—chances are you're driving as you eat—and have another. Be sure you have a lot of something to drink close at hand, because you'll soon get thirsty.

Many cultures have a recipe that makes thrifty use of the leftover meat scraps that are too small, too few, or too disgusting to be served alone. For upper Piedmont Carolinians, particularly those of German ancestry raised in the wavy ribbon of towns between Charlotte and Winston-Salem, that delicacy is **livermush.** Some folks say that if you're from the Mid-Atlantic and are familiar with scrapple, you'll have a pretty good idea of what livermush is like. That's not true—livermush is much worse and tastes like some bitter combination of burning hair and pepper. Under North Carolina law (really), livermush must contain at least 30 percent hog liver, which is supplemented with sundry scraps from hog heads, sometimes some skin, and cornmeal. At the factory, it's mashed up and cooked in loaves. In the kitchen, it's sliced and fried. You can eat it at breakfast like sausage, in a sandwich, or even on a stick if you go to the annual livermush festivals in Drexel and Shelby. Should you try it? Yes, at least a bite; plenty of people like it.

In the eastern part of the state, a similar aesthetic underlies the creation of **hog hash,** best made directly after an old-time hog killing, when the animal's organs are pulled steaming hot out of the carcass in the frosty fall morning. The liver, lungs, and a variety of other organs and appendages are dumped in a kettle with potatoes, a liquid base (broth, milk, or just water), and some vegetables and seasonings. Unlike livermush, hog hash is served in bowls or tubs as a dark, musky stew; it's not common.

Another food that you have to look pretty hard for is **dandoodle,** also called **tom thumbs,** seen in far northeastern North Carolina and the bordering Virginia counties. At hog-killing time, the animal's stomach is removed and stuffed with sausage and flavorings. It is then tied shut and hung in the smokehouse for seasons with hickory smoke. Like livermush, dandoodle comes out in a sort of loaf shape, held together by the stomach membrane. Some people toss their tom thumbs in the pot to boil, either alone or with greens, while others slice them and lay them out with sliced boiled eggs.

You can read all about these and other acquired tastes at **NCFOOD** (www.ncfolk.org) or **Our State Eats** by *Our State* magazine (www.ourstate.com), two food blogs devoted to Carolina cooking, or on the **Southern Foodways Alliance** (www.southernfoodways.com) and **Dixie Dining** (www.dixiedining.com) websites.

Vegetarians and devotees of organic food, fear not; North Carolina is an unusually progressive state when it comes to healthy and homegrown grub. Nevertheless, if you want to avoid meat, you have to be cautious when ordering at a restaurant: Make sure the beans are made with vegetable oil rather than lard, ask if the salad dressing contains anchovies, and beware of hidden fish and oyster sauce. Traditional Southern cooking makes liberal use of fatback (cured pork fat) and other animal products; greens are often boiled with a strip of fatback or a hambone, as are most soups and stews. Even pie crusts are still made with lard in many old-time kitchens.

In the major cities, you'll find organic grocery stores. Earth Fare and Whole Foods are the most common chains, but there are also plenty of small independent markets. Farmers markets and roadside stands are so plentiful that they almost have to fight for space. Visit the state Department of Agriculture's **North Carolina Farm Fresh** (www.ncfarmfresh.com) for directories of farmers markets and pick-your-own farms and orchards.

Essentials

Getting There

AIR

The state where air travel began has over 70 public airports, almost 300 privately owned airfields, and about 20 "fly-in" communities where residents share an airstrip and have their own hangar space. Nine airports have regularly scheduled passenger service, and two of them host international flights. The state's Department of Transportation estimates that more than 35 million people fly in and out of North Carolina every year. The main hubs are North Carolina's international airports in

Charlotte, Greensboro, and Raleigh-Durham; Wilmington has more limited service.

To reach the coast by air, your nearest airports are in Wilmington and Raleigh, depending on your end destination. From either airport, you'll need a rental car or a friend. The **Wilmington International Airport** (ILM, 1740 Airport Blvd., Wilmington, 910/341-4125, www.flyilm.com) is only 15 minutes from Wrightsville Beach. **Raleigh-Durham International Airport** (RDU, 2400 W. Terminal Blvd., Morrisville, 919/840-2123, www.rdu.com) is farther from the coast. Located in Wake County about midway between Raleigh and Durham, has flights to most domestic hubs as well as London, Paris, Toronto, and Cancún, Mexico. Hourly and daily parking is available for reasonable rates within walking distance of the terminals and in satellite lots linked by shuttle buses. The nearest beach to Raleigh is Wrightsville Beach, two hours south; drive another 15-20 minutes to reach Carolina Beach and Kure Beach. Topsail Island (north of Wilmington and Wrightsville Beach) is two and a half hours away. To reach central beaches of the Crystal Coast and the southern beaches of Brunswick County, you'll need almost three hours of windshield time from Raleigh. It will take you between three and four hours to reach the Outer Banks, depending on which beach town you're visiting. Ocracoke is a whopping five hours from Raleigh, thanks in large part to a long ferry ride to this one-time pirate haven.

The eighth-busiest airport in the country, **Charlotte Douglas International Airport** (CLT, 5501 Josh Birmingham Pkwy., Charlotte, 704/359-4013, http://cltairport. org) has more than 730 daily departures and is served by dozens of airlines. There are nonstop flights to 140 U.S. cities as well as international flights to Latin America and the Caribbean, London, Frankfurt, Munich, and Toronto. Parking is abundant and inexpensive, with parking shuttle buses operating from 5am. Arriving in Charlotte isn't necessarily ideal for a visit to the beach. By car from Charlotte, it's four hours to Wrightsville Beach, four and a half to Topsail Island, and five hours to the beaches of Brunswick County. The drive is long and isolated, with few spots to stop for gas or food. If you're flying into Charlotte, look into a commuter flight into the Wilmington Airport. It will be worth the money.

In addition to the Wilmington airport, there are several smaller airports around the state with regularly scheduled domestic passenger service. **Fayetteville Regional Airport** (FAY, 400 Airport Rd., Fayetteville, 910/433-1160, www.fayettevillenc.gov), **Pitt-Greenville Airport** (PGV, 400 Airport Rd., Greenville, 252/902-2025, www.flypgv.com), **Coastal Carolina Regional Airport** (EWN, 200 Terminal Dr., New Bern, 252/638-8591, www.newbernairport.com), and the **Albert J. Ellis Airport** (OAJ, 264 Albert Ellis Airport Rd., Richlands, 910/324-1100, www.flyoaj. com) near Jacksonville and Richlands are all on or within a couple hours drive of the coast.

Private aircraft can fly into any of over 75 regional, county, and municipal air strips statewide; **NC Airports Association** (www. ncairports.org) has a full list with phone numbers, website links, navigational information, airstrip specifications, and aerial photos.

CAR

Several major interstate highways run through North Carolina, so if you're driving and would prefer that your trip be efficient rather than scenic, you've got several choices. From anywhere along the eastern seaboard, I-95 slices through the eastern third of the state, providing easy access to the beaches, which are mostly one or two hours east of I-95, and to the Triangle area, under an hour west of I-95 via U.S. 64, U.S. 70, or I-40. From the north, you might choose to veer southwest at

Richmond, Virginia, on I-85; this is an efficient route to Durham and Chapel Hill as well as to the Triad and Charlotte regions.

I-40 starts in Wilmington and runs west to Barstow, California. It's a fast road all the way through North Carolina, although weather—ice in the fall, winter, and spring, and fog any time of year—might slow you down considerably between Knoxville, Tennessee, and Asheville. U.S. 64 and I-77 connect North Carolina to the Midwest. I-77 cuts through the toe of Virginia, in the mountains, straight to Charlotte, while U.S. 64 meanders east through the Triangle all the way to Roanoke Island and the Outer Banks. From the Deep South or Texas, the best bet is probably I-20 to Atlanta, and from there I-85 to Charlotte, or U.S. 19 or U.S. 23 if you're going to the mountains.

There are no checkpoints at the state line to inspect vehicles for produce or animals, but sobriety checkpoints are established and staffed throughout the year.

BUS

Travel around North Carolina can be accomplished easily and cheaply by bus. **Greyhound** (800/231-2222, www.greyhound.com) offers daily service to many towns and cities, with the exception of the Outer Banks and mountain towns other than Asheville, but you can access that region via the Tennessee cities close to the state line, including Knoxville and Johnson City. Before you reserve bus tickets, be sure to check out special discounts on the Greyhound website. There are often regional promotions as well as special "Go Anywhere" fares as low as $29

Driving Trails

The state of North Carolina and a variety of regional organizations have created a wonderful network of automobile "trails"—thematic itineraries showcasing North Carolina's treasures. Check out the destinations on this sampling of trails.

- **Civil War Traveler:**
  www.civilwartraveler.com

- **Core Sound Itinerary:**
  www.ncfolk.org

- **Historic Albemarle Tour:**
  www.historicalbemarletour.org

- **North Carolina Scenic Byways:**
  www.ncdot.gov/travel-maps/traffic-travel/scenic-byways

each way with 14-day advance booking, for example, as well as regular discounts for students and seniors.

These days, the large buses used by Greyhound and its local subsidiaries are clean and comfortable, and if you make a reservation ahead of time, you can choose your seat. One word of caution is that some bus stations are located in seedy parts of town, so make sure taxi service is available at your destination station after dark.

TRAIN

Although it does not currently serve the coast, **Amtrak** (800/872-7245, www.amtrak.com) does have service in Raleigh, Charlotte and Fayetteville, making those cities starting points for coastal exploration.

Getting Around

CAR

North Carolina's highway system, with the largest network of state-maintained roads in the country and a good interstate grid, provides access to the whole state. I-95 crosses north-south, demarcating the eastern third of the state, and I-85 runs northeast-southwest from north of the Triangle area through Charlotte. I-40 is the primary east-west route, from Wilmington through the Smoky Mountains to Knoxville, Tennessee. The highest speed limit, which applies to some rural interstates and four-lane roads, is 70 mph. Highways in developed areas have much lower speed limits, and in residential areas it's a good idea to keep it under 25 mph.

You can take your pick of car-rental agencies at the major airports at Charlotte, Winston-Salem, and Raleigh-Durham; there are fewer choices at smaller regional airports. There are also car-rental pickup and drop-off offices in many towns. Rental car companies in North Carolina include **Alamo** (844/354-6962, www.alamo.com), **Avis** (800/230-4898, www.avis.com), **Budget** (800/218-7992, www.budget.com), **Dollar** (800/800-4000, www.dollar.com), Enterprise (855/266-9289, www.enterprise.com), Hertz (800/654-3131, www.hertz.com), **National** (844/382-6875, www.nationalcar.com) and **Thrifty** (800/3334-1705, www.thrifty.com). To rent a car you must be at least 25 years old and have both a valid driver's license and a credit card, although some companies will accept a cash security deposit in lieu of credit.

For getting around town in every city of a reasonable size, you can always use **Uber** (www.uber.com). Service will be limited in small towns and rural areas, but check the website or the app for available drivers in your destination.

Driving to and through the Outer Banks can be a bit complicated, depending on your destination, because there are not many bridges. The northern banks are linked to the mainland by bridges between Point Harbor and Kitty Hawk and from Manns Harbor over Roanoke Island to just south of Nags Head. There are no bridges to Hatteras and none until you get all the way to the southern end of the banks, where bridges link Morehead City and Cedar Point to the towns along Bogue Banks. The state's excellent ferry system connects the Outer Banks to the mainland; it's a fun way to travel. Detailed information is available from the state Department of Transportation (www.ncdot.gov/ferry). Several ferries link mainland points across sounds and rivers, while ferries from Currituck to Knotts Island, and from both Swan Quarter and Cedar Island to Ocracoke, will carry you to the Outer Banks.

Highway Safety

Write "***HP**" (***47**) on a sticky note and affix it to your dashboard. That's the direct free hotline to the North Carolina Highway Patrol, which will send help if you're trouble. North Carolinians don't hesitate to report aggressive, reckless, or drunk motorists to the highway patrol, and you might be reported by another driver if you're tailgating, speeding, weaving, or driving aggressively. What passes for normal driving in many parts of the United States is regarded as aggressive driving in the South.

Pull well off the road and turn on your hazard lights if you have an accident. If you can't safely pull your vehicle out of traffic, at least get away from the roadway. A distressing number of motorists with disabled vehicles as well as pedestrians are struck and killed by cars every year.

Some rules to remember while driving in North Carolina: Wearing your seat belt is required by law; child safety seats are mandatory for anyone under age 8 or weighing less than 80 pounds; and if it's raining hard enough to need windshield wipers, you must also turn your headlights on.

Weather Considerations

If you're driving in the mountains in the morning or at night, you may run into heavy **fog**. Because the clouds perch on and around mountaintops, you may find yourself in clear weather one moment and only seconds later in a fog with little visibility. It can be dangerous and frightening, but if this happens, slow down, keep an eye on the lines on the road, watch for other cars, and put on your low beams. As in any kind of bad weather, it's always best to find a safe place to pull off the road and wait for the weather to improve. Fog can dissipate as quickly as it appears.

In the winter you might encounter icy roads in any part of the state, and up in the mountains you might hit **ice and snow** three seasons of the year. Many Southerners on the coast and in the Piedmont tend to panic when snow is forecast; folks in the mountains manage to keep their wits about them no matter the weather. In anticipation of a half-inch dusting of snow, coastal schools and businesses may close, fleets of sand and salt trucks hit the highway, and residents mob the grocery stores. This overreaction to snow makes the roads a little safer because many folks are more likely to stay home, but those who do drive in winter weather are less likely to know how to drive on ice than the average Yankee or Midwesterner. That can make the roads hazardous, so even if you are an experienced snow driver, stay alert.

The other weather concern is rain. In spring and fall, you can encounter thunderstorms in all parts of the state, and these are run-of-the-mill storms usually, but heed any weather warnings you hear or see. Late summer and fall is hurricane season, and while most people think of hurricanes as coastal events, the torrential rains brought on by a hurricane (or tropical system of any sort) can cause flash flooding, high winds, and heavy rains as these systems move inland. Whether you're on the coast or in the mountains and you learn there is a hurricane on the way, follow the directions of civil authorities and be safe. If you're on the coast, familiarize yourself with hurricane evacuation routes (they're marked on highways and in local literature) and follow directions.

Wildlife on the Road

A final note about highway travel: Be conscious of wildlife. Deer, rabbits, turtles, foxes, coyotes, raccoons, and opossums litter the highways. Head-on collisions with deer can be fatal to both species, and smaller animals die because drivers are going too fast to avoid them. If you see an injured animal and are able to help it without putting yourself in danger, you'll find a phalanx of wildlife rehabilitators throughout the state to give it the care it needs.

The large number of deer in urban and rural areas makes them frequent victims of highway accidents. In clear weather when there's not much oncoming traffic, use your high beams so that you'll see them from farther away. If you see a deer cross the road in front of you, remember that they usually travel in small herds, and there may be several more waiting to jump out.

Road Etiquette

Certain informal rules of road etiquette apply in North Carolina, and they help make driving less stressful. North Carolina drivers generally let others' vehicles get in front of them, whether merging onto the highway or exiting a parking lot. Wave to say thanks when someone lets you in; positive reinforcement helps keep these habits alive. Folks will often wave at drivers in oncoming traffic on two-lane country roads, and there is an expectation of a quick wave from drivers and pedestrians as well. It's not a big production; simply lift two or three fingers off the steering wheel. A general rule of thumb is that if you're able to discern the facial features of someone outside your car, waving to that person is appropriate.

Drivers are legally obligated to pull over to let emergency vehicles pass. There's also an old tradition of pulling over to allow funeral processions to pass. Very few drivers are willing to merge into or cross a train of cars headed for a funeral, but in rural areas you may still see drivers pulling all the way off the road and waiting for a procession to pass before resuming driving. It's meant as a gesture of respect to the deceased and the mourners.

In all of these situations, safety should be the top priority. You don't need to wave or make eye contact with someone you feel is threatening, and don't pull off the road if there's no safe place to do so. But if you show courtesy to other drivers when you're able, you'll find that traffic karma will work its way back around to you when it's needed.

BUS

Municipal bus services operate in larger towns and some of the more popular tourist areas. The state **Department of Transportation** (www.ncdot.gov/nctransit) maintains an index of information on the state's 99 public transportation systems, including those that serve rural counties.

BICYCLE

Before the Wright brothers made history as the first aviators, they were bicycle men. With its temperate climates, abundance of scenic roads, and full spectrum of terrain, North Carolina is bicycling heaven. There are hundreds of organized bicycling events every year, many of them in support of charities, and they welcome participants from all over. The most popular bike events are held spring to fall, including a six-day Ocracoke Vacation Tour from New Bern to the tip of the Outer Banks, regular scenic rides through wine country, and rides along the Blue Ridge that include a five-day bicycling vacation starting in Blowing Rock.

Each month except December has as many as a dozen public cycling events, including January's New Year's Day Breakfast Ride in Jacksonville, February's Frostbite Tour in Raleigh, and March's Rumba on the Lumber 5K Run and Bike Ride in Lumberton. In April there's the annual Circle-the-Bald Bike Ride, starting in Hayesville, and in May, Wilkesboro's Burn 24 Hour Challenge, a team relay endurance challenge. June has bicycling events as part of the North Carolina Blueberry Festival in Burgaw; July has North Wilkesboro's Hurt, Pain, and Agony Century Race; and August has a Beginner Skills Bicycling Camp in Asheville. In late September is the state-spanning Annual Mountains to the Coast Ride that even goes to the islands of the Outer Banks by ferry; approximately 1,000 cyclists take part. In October there's Rutherfordton's Tour de Pumpkin, and in November, the North Carolina Horse Country Tour takes place. For a full roster of routes, trails, and events, see the **Traveling by Bicycle** page maintained by the North Carolina Department of Transportation (www.ncdot.gov).

Baggage cars on **Amtrak**'s *Piedmont* trains are equipped with bicycle racks; call 800/872-7245 to reserve bike space on a train. You can also take your bicycle on any of the seven **North Carolina Ferries** (800/293-3779, www.ferry.ncdot.gov/).

TRAIN

North Carolina has good rail connections among the major cities in the central part of the state, but lacks service to the coast.

FERRY

For hundreds of years, ferries were a crucial link between points on North Carolina's coast, and they still provide an essential service today. The **North Carolina Department of Transportation's Ferry Division** (877/293-3779, www.ferry.ncdot.gov/) operates seven primary ferry routes along the coast. All ferries have restrooms, and some can accommodate cars and allow pets. Commercial ferries also operate throughout the coastal region.

Vacation Rentals

In addition to hotels and bed and breakfasts in eastern North Carolina, vacation homes are available from a number of rental companies:

THE OUTER BANKS

- **Beach Realty** (800/635-1559, www.beachrealtync.com)
- **Outer Banks Rentals by Southern Shores Realty** (800/334-1000, www.southernshores.com)
- **Rent A Beach** (www.rentabeach.com)
- **Resort Realty Vacations** (800/458-3830, www.resortrealty.com)
- **Seaside Vacations** (866/884-0267, www.outerbanksvacations.com)
- **Sun Rentals** (888/853-7770, www.sunrealtync.com)
- **Twiddy** (866/457-1190, www.twiddy.com)

THE CRYSTAL COAST

- **Bluewater Real Estate and Vacation Rentals** (866/231-5892, www.bluewaternc.com)
- **Emerald Isle Realty** (855/324-9856, www.emeraldislerealty.com)
- **Rent A Beach** (www.rentabeach.com)
- **Spectrum Properties** (252/247-7610, www.spectrumproperties.com)
- **Sun-Surf Realty** (7701 Emerald Dr., Emerald Isle, 800/553-7873, www.sunsurfrealty.com)

Conduct and Customs

GREETINGS

Common courtesy, such as saying "please" and "thank you," being deferential to the elderly, and demonstrating concern for others, is hardly particular to the South. No matter where you're from, chances are your parents raised you to "act like folks," as people say here. The difference is that in North Carolina and elsewhere in the South, manners are somewhat more ritualized.

If you're unfamiliar with Southern ways, the thing you may find strangest is the friendliness of strangers. When passing a stranger on the sidewalk or in a corridor, riding together in an elevator, or even washing hands in the restroom, eye contact and a quick greeting are usually in order. Most common greetings are "Hey," "How you doing," and "How you," spoken as a statement rather than a question. The reply is usually equally casual: "Doing good, how about you," pronounced with just four syllables, "Doin' good, 'bout you," again spoken as a statement rather than a question. Often that's the end of the conversation, although passengers on elevators sometimes wish each other a good day when one gets out. In these encounters, eye contact needn't be lingering, there's no expectation of false pleasantries, and there is certainly no obligation to engage someone who makes you uncomfortable.

WILMINGTON AND THE BRUNSWICK BEACHES

- **Bald Head Island Limited** (800/432-7368, www.baldheadisland.com)
- **Beach Girls Realty** (910/458-5611, www.beachgirlsrealty.com)
- **Better Beach Rentals** (910/278-1147, www.betterbeachrentals.com)
- **Brunswickland Realty** (800/842-6949, www.brunswicklandrealty.com)
- **Bryant Real Estate** (800/322-3764, www.bryantre.com)
- **Carolina Beach Realty** (877/456-4311, www.carolinabeachrealty.net)
- **Coastal Vacation Resorts at Oak Island** (888/703-5469, www.coastalvacationresortsoakisland.com)
- **Intracoastal Vacation Rentals** (855/346-2463, www.intracoastalrentals.com)
- **Oak Island Accommodations** (800/243-8132, www.rentalsathtebeach.com)
- **Rent A Beach** (www.rentabeach.com)
- **Seashore Realty** (910/328-3400, www.seashorerealtync.com)
- **Sea Scape Properties** (910/332-7284, www.seascapevacationhomes.com)
- **Tiffany's Rentals** (910/457-0544, www.tiffanysrentals.com)
- **Wrightsville Sands Realty** (910/679-4082, www.wrightsvillesands.com)
- **Victory Beach Vacations** (888/256-4804, www.victorybeachvacations.com)

It's standard courtesy in a retail or similarly casual transaction to inquire as to the well-being of the person serving you. It takes little time, especially when delivered in the spoken shorthand most Southerners use. For instance, a cashier at McDonalds in another part of the country might greet you with "What would you like?" or simply wait for your order and not speak until asking for your money. The transaction here would more likely start with the "How you," "Doin' good, 'bout you," exchange. With that two- or three-second dialogue, a bit of human warmth and mutual respect is shared.

It's expected that people hold doors open for each other and thank each other for doing so. In addressing someone elderly that you don't know well, the standard courtesy is to use a title, Mr. or Ms., with the last name, or in friendlier situations, Mr. or Ms. with the first name. The South was way ahead of the curve in adopting the "Ms." designation; Southerners have always pronounced both "Mrs." and "Miss" as "miz." North Carolinians will likely address you as ma'am or sir regardless of your age; it doesn't mean they think you're old.

TIPPING

Besides restaurant servers, tip motel and hotel housekeeping staff, bartenders, cab drivers, bellhops, redcaps, valet parking staff, and other service workers. Standard tipping rates are 20 percent for meals, 15 percent for a taxi ride, and $1 per piece of luggage for a redcap or porter, although tipping extra for good service is always gracious and appropriate.

Travel Tips

GAY AND LESBIAN TRAVELERS

North Carolina offers no legal protection against discrimination based on sexual orientation or gender identity, and, like in most states, hate-crimes statutes do not address violence targeting victims because of their sexual orientation or gender identity. Despite all this, don't close the book on North Carolina. While some laws may be retrogressive, the people are not; much of North Carolina is LGBTQ-friendly.

Despite being a red state, North Carolina has a strong purple streak. Metropolitan areas have active and open queer communities with numerous organizations and social groups, publications, human rights advocacy services, and community centers. Like anywhere in the United States, smaller and more rural communities are less likely to be gay-friendly, although there are exceptions and pleasant surprises. As a general rule, a same-sex couple will attract little attention holding hands on Durham's 9th Street, Asheville's Patton Avenue, or Weaver Street in Carrboro, but they may not be received warmly at the Big Al's Shuckin' Shack in Backwards Creek (not a real place, but you get the idea).

Gay, lesbian, bisexual, and transgendered travelers planning to visit North Carolina can learn a great deal about community resources and activities at QNotes (www.go-qnotes.com), North Carolina Pride (www.ncpride.org), and NC Gay Travel (http://nc-gaytravel.com).

SENIOR TRAVELERS

North Carolina has attracted a tremendous number of retirees in recent years, especially in the mountains and coast. It's also an increasingly popular destination for older travelers. For those who want to visit the state through organized programs, Elderhostel (www.roadscholar.org) is a great choice. Tours and classes are available throughout the state; the offerings in the mountains are particularly rich, with a great variety of courses and hands-on workshops about Appalachian culture and crafts. The North Carolina chapter of the AARP (www.local.aarp.org) is a good resource for senior issues and information. VisitNC (800/847-4862, www.visitnc.com) can also answer questions about activities and accessibility.

WOMEN TRAVELERS

Women from other parts of the country might find male strangers' friendliness a little disconcerting, but keep in mind that while some of them may be flirting with you, it's just as likely that they are simply being courteous. When a Southern man holds a door open for you, offers to help you carry something, or even calls you "honey," "darlin'," or "dear heart," it usually implies no ulterior motives and isn't intended to be condescending; he's probably just showing that he was raised up right. Again, manners should never preclude safety, so if some sketchy character is coming on to you in a way that gives you the creeps, trust your instincts.

TRAVELERS WITH DISABILITIES

Access North Carolina (voice and TTY 800/851-6099, Videophone 919/890-0859, www.ncdhhs.gov) is an excellent up-to-date guide on the accessibility of hundreds of cultural, recreational, historical, environmental, and commercial sites of interest and a goldmine for travel planning. Download a copy or phone to ask for the current edition, published by the state Department of Health and Human Services. The guide is set up by region and county, and sites and venues are described and rated in terms of accessibility.

Health and Safety

CRIME

As nice a place as North Carolina is, it's not immune to crime. Common sense about safety applies, particularly for women. Lock your doors immediately when you get into the car, park in well-lit areas as close as possible to your destination, and don't hesitate to ask a security guard or other trustworthy type to see you to your car. Don't carry too much cash on you. Pepper spray might save your life if you're attacked, whether by a person or by a bear.

Note that 911 emergency phone service is available everywhere in the state, but cell phone signals are not dependable everywhere. The deep mountains and more remote parts of western North Carolina and isolated stretches of the coast are more likely to have cell-phone dead zones.

SPECIAL WEATHER CONCERNS

Hurricanes

Hurricanes are a perennial danger, but luckily there tends to be plenty of warning when one is approaching. The Atlantic Hurricane season runs from June 1 to November 30, but North Carolina generally sees the highest hurricane activity late in the season, in September and October. Evacuation orders should always be heeded, even if they are voluntary. It's also a good idea to leave sooner rather than later to avoid being trapped in traffic when the storm hits. The state **Department of Crime Control and Public Safety** (www.ncdps. gov) posts a map online every year showing evacuation routes. You'll also see evacuation routes marked along the highways.

Tornadoes

Tornadoes can happen in any season and have killed people here in recent years. Pay close attention to tornado watches and warnings, and don't take chances: Find a safe place to shelter until the danger is over.

Rip Currents

More than 100 people die every year on U.S. beaches because of rip currents. Also called riptides, these dangerous currents can occur on any beach and can be very difficult to identify by sight. In rip current conditions, channels of water flow swiftly out toward deep water, and even if you are standing in relatively shallow water, you can suddenly be swept under and out into deep water. Rip current safety tips are available on the National Oceanic and Atmospheric Administration's National Weather Service website (www. weather.gov/safety/ripcurrent). Among their advice: "Don't fight the current. Swim out of the current, and then to shore. If you can't escape, float or tread water. If you need help, call or wave for assistance." Heed riptide warnings, and try to swim within sight of a lifeguard. Even good swimmers can drown in a rip current, so if you have any doubts about your swimming abilities or water conditions, play it safe and stay close to shore.

ANIMAL THREATS

There are a handful of dangerous creatures across the state, ranging in size from microscopic to monstrous, that can pose risks to health and safety. Be on the lookout for mean bugs: **Ticks** can carry Lyme disease and Rocky Mountain spotted fever, both serious and lingering conditions. Most likely to climb on you if you are walking through brush or bushes but liable to be lurking about anywhere, ticks come in many sizes and shapes, from barely visible pinpoint-size to that thing that looks like a grape hanging off your dog's neck. Wear insect repellent if you're going to be tramping around outside, and check your body and your travel companions thoroughly—your clothing as well as your skin—for stowaways. They'll attach themselves to any soft surface on your body, but they particularly like people's heads, often latching on to the scalp an inch or so behind the ears. If you find a tick on you or a human or canine companion, don't remove it roughly, no matter how freaked out you are. Yanking can leave the tick's head buried in your skin, increasing the risk of infection. Grasp the tick in a pinching motion, and pull slowly but firmly. You may have to hang on for several moments, but eventually it will decide to let go. Dab the bite with antiseptic, and over the next several weeks be alert for a bull's-eye-shaped irritation around the bite and for flu-like symptoms such as fever, achiness, malaise, and fatigue. If you have any of these signs, visit your doctor for a blood test.

Mosquitoes can carry West Nile virus, La Crosse encephalitis, and eastern equine encephalitis. Wear insect repellent and clothing that covers your arms and legs to avoid bites. Although not disease vectors, **fire ants** are among the state's most feared insects. It's easy to stumble onto one of their nests, and before you realize what you've stepped in, they can be swarming up your legs and biting you. Certainly this is a painful and frightening experience, but it's also potentially dangerous if you're allergic. There have been documented cases of adult humans being swarmed and killed by fire ants. Watch where you step, and keep an eye out for areas of disturbed ground and turned-up soil. Sometimes their nests look like conventional anthills, sometimes like messy piles of dirt, and other times just soft spots on the ground.

Another reason to mind where you tread: snakes. The vast majority of snakes in North Carolina are harmless and shy, but we do have a few pit vipers. **Copperheads** are quite common in every part of the state and in wooded or semiwooded terrain—even in backyards, where they can lurk in bushes and leaf piles, under porches and in storage sheds, and in the walls of a house. They have a gorgeous pattern of light and dark brown splotches, which makes them incredibly difficult to spot against the ground in fall. Copperheads are usually less than three feet long. Their bite is poisonous but usually not fatal.

Found in the eastern half of the state and up into the Sandhills, **cottonmouths**—also called water moccasins—are very dangerous. They range in color from reddish brown to black, can grow up to 5.5 feet long, and are easily mistaken for harmless water snakes (and vice versa). They sometimes venture into the woods and fields, but cottonmouths are most commonly seen on or near water. Be especially careful walking along creek beds or in riverside brush. When threatened, they display the inside of their mouths, which are a startling and beautiful cottony white. Their bite is potentially lethal.

Coral snakes are endangered in North Carolina, but if you're going to be in the woods in the southeastern quarter of the state, keep an eye out. These jewel-toned snakes are generally small and slim, rarely more than a couple of feet long. Like the harmless scarlet king snake and scarlet snake, coral snakes have alternating bands of red, yellow, and black. The way to tell coral snakes from their harmless kin is to note the order of colors. On coral snakes, the yellow bands separate the black and the red, whereas on their imitators, red and black touch. An adage advises, "Red and black, friend of Jack; red and yellow, kill a fellow." Coral snakes can also be identified by their sinister black snouts, making them look like cartoon burglars, whereas scarlet snakes and scarlet king snakes have red clown noses. That's a lot to remember in that instant of panic when you notice a coil of red and yellow and black stripes at your feet looking up at you testily. Rather than stopping to figure out if the snake is friend or foe, it's better just to step away fast. Coral snakes' venom works on its prey's respiratory system, and it can kill humans. They're cousins of cobras and are some of the most beautiful snakes in these parts, but locals fear them more intensely than the huge, lumpy-headed, tusky-fanged vipers that appear more threatening.

There are also three poisonous native rattlesnakes: The **eastern diamondback rattlesnake** is the largest of rattlesnakes and can grow to nearly six feet long and as fat around as an adult human's arm. They are extremely dangerous—powerful enough to catch and eat rabbits, and willing, if provoked, to kill a person. Eastern diamondbacks are rare but can be found in the southeastern sandy swamp counties. Also large are **canebrake rattlers,** more formally known as timber rattlers. They are found throughout the state, including the mountains. Their bite can be fatal to humans. To make them even scarier, they too can grow to nearly six feet in length, and in cold weather they like to congregate in large numbers to hibernate. **Pygmy rattlesnakes** are found along the state's coastline, up into the Sandhills, and around Crowder's Mountain. Generally up to about 1.5 feet long, pygmies are also venomous.

Alligators are incredible creatures, scaly submarines that can exceed 15 feet snout to tail (females generally mature at around 10 feet) and can weigh 1,000 pounds, with a steel-trap maw of 75-80 fangs. They are found through much of eastern North Carolina, as far north as Merchants Millpond State Park near the Virginia border, but they are most common from Wilmington south. You don't have to trek into the depths of a swamp to see gators; they like to sun themselves on golf courses, next to roadside drainage ditches, and even in yards that adjoin fresh water. Their behavior is deceptive: they seem to spend 90 percent of their time in a motionless stupor, but they can awaken and whirl around to grab you before you have time to back away. They also spend much of their time submerged, sometimes entirely underwater, and more often drifting just below the surface with only their nostrils and brow ridges visible. Be aware of floating logs, as they may have teeth attached. Alligators will gladly eat dogs that venture too close, so it goes without saying that small children should never be allowed to wander alone near potential alligator habitats. An adult alligator can kill an adult human, and even the cute little ones will be only too happy to help themselves to your foot, so don't tempt fate for the sake of a photo or a closer look. If

you're determined to get a close-up picture, visit one of the state's aquariums.

Bear attacks are rare and usually defensive, but considering that the creatures can weigh up to 800 pounds, caution would seem to be indicated. They are present in the woods in various parts of the state, especially up in the mountains and in the deep swamps and pocosins along the coast. They're quite shy and apt to gallop into the brush if they see a human coming. They will investigate potential meals, though, so securing your food when camping is crucial. If your car is nearby, lock the food in it; otherwise, hoist it into a tree with a rope, too high to reach from the ground and out of reach from the tree trunk. The National Park Service recommends the following course of action if a bear approaches you. First, try backing away slowly. If the bear follows, stand your ground. If it continues to menace you, try to scare it: Make yourself look bigger and more threatening by standing on a rock or next to your companions. Try waving sticks and throwing rocks. In the extremely unlikely event that you actually find yourself in hand-to-hand combat with a bear, remember the Park Service's advice to "fight back aggressively with any available object." Your chances of seeing a bear in North Carolina, much less being threatened by one, are pretty slim.

DISEASES AND NATURAL THREATS

Among the invisible villains here is **giardia,** a single-celled protozoan parasite that can be contracted by drinking untreated water. Hikers and campers should avoid drinking from streams unless they first boil the water vigorously for at least one minute. Filtering water with a filter of 0.1 to 1 micron absolute pore size or chemically treating it with iodine or chlorine is less reliable than thorough boiling.

There's a fairly high incidence of **rabies** in North Carolina's raccoons, bats, foxes, groundhogs, and skunks. If you're bringing a pet into the state, be sure that its vaccinations are up-to-date. If you plan to go hiking with your dog, it may even be wise to bring a copy of its rabies vaccination certificate in case you have to prove its immunity. If you are bitten by a wild animal, seek medical help immediately, even if you're out in the woods. Rabies is deadly to humans, and it's extremely important to start treatment immediately.

HEALTH PRECAUTIONS
Emergencies

As elsewhere the United States, calling 911 in North Carolina will summon medical help, police, or fire fighters. On the highway, blue road signs marked with an "H" point the way to hospitals, but if you're experiencing a potentially critical emergency, it's best to call 911 and let the ambulance come to you. There are plenty of rural places in the state where cell-phone coverage is spotty to nonexistent, so if you have a medical condition from which an emergency could arise, keep this in mind.

Summer Weather

Heat, humidity, and air pollution often combine in the summer to create dangerous conditions for children, the elderly, and people with severe heart and lung conditions. Even if you're young and healthy, don't take chances in the heat. Carry drinking water with you, avoid exertion and being outside in the hottest part of the day, and stay in the shade. Even young, healthy people can die from the heat. Remember that even if it doesn't feel very warm outside, children and pets are in grave danger when left in cars. Temperatures can rise to fatal levels very quickly inside closed vehicles, even when it's not terribly hot outside.

Information and Services

MONEY

For international travelers, currency-exchange services can be found in the big cities at some major banks and at currency-exchange businesses. Numerous money-transfer services, from old familiars like Western Union to a multitude of overseas companies, are easily accessible. The easiest place to wire or receive money is at a grocery store—most have Western Union or a proprietary wiring service—or at a bank. Banking hours vary by location and chain, but most are closed on Sunday and federal holidays. ATMs are located at most bank branches as well as in many grocery stores and convenience stores.

COMMUNICATIONS AND MEDIA
Newspapers and Radio

North Carolina has several major newspapers, the largest of which is the Pulitzer Prize-winning *Charlotte Observer* (www.charlotteobserver.com). In addition to the print edition, the *Observer* has extensive online-only content for travelers. The Raleigh *News & Observer* (www.newsobserver.com) serves the Triangle area and much of central Carolina. Other prominent newspapers include the Wilmington *Star-News* (www.starnewsonline.com) Among the many local and regional radio stations is a number of NPR affiliates. There are few parts of the state where you won't be able to tune in to a clear NPR signal.

Magazines

Our State magazine (www.ourstate.com) is a widely distributed monthly that tells the stories of the people, places, and history across North Carolina. As a travel resource, it will give you a feel for the people you're likely to encounter, but it will give you an even better idea of places to eat and towns you may not have thought to visit. Their website has an extensive collection of archived stories arranged by topic. In most larger cities in North Carolina it isn't hard to find magazines covering the local arts scene or guiding area parents to the best the town has to offer for kids. Look at news racks outside grocery stores and on street corners to pick up free publications like *North Brunswick Magazine* and *South Brunswick Magazine* in and around Brunswick County; *Salt, Wilma!, Wrightsville Beach Magazine, Wilmington NC Magazine* and *Encore* in Wilmington.

Internet Access

Internet access is widespread. Coffee shops are always a good place to find Wi-Fi, usually free but sometimes for a fee. A few small towns have free municipal wireless access. Most chain motels and major hotels offer free wireless access, and smaller hotels and bed-and-breakfasts often do too. This is true for some remote areas as well. The deep mountains and remote coastal areas are the most difficult places to get a reliable Internet connection, but you'll probably be able to get online at your place of lodging or the coffee shop in town.

Cell Phones

Cell phone coverage is not consistent across North Carolina. You'll get a signal in all of the cities and most areas in between. You may hit dropout spots in central North Carolina, but there aren't many. On the other hand, service can be spotty in the eastern and western parts of the state. Up in the mountains, you may have a good signal on one side of a ridge and none on the other. Driving along the Blue Ridge Parkway, you'll find that signals come and go. This is also true on the coast and in rural eastern North Carolina. Along the sounds, and certainly on the Outer Banks, there are plenty of areas where you could drive 20 miles before finding any reception. Spotty cell-phone coverage is a safety issue; if you're treed by a bear or run out of gas on a backwoods track, 911 may be unreachable.

MAPS AND VISITOR INFORMATION

Among the best sources for travel information in North Carolina is the state's tourism website, **VisitNC** (www.visitnc.com). They maintain an up-to-date list of festivals and events, tours and trails, and almost anything else you might want to know. Also excellent is the magazine *Our State* (www.ourstate.com), available at grocery stores, drugstores, and bookshops. Their website monitors upcoming events as well.

North Carolina Welcome Centers, located at several major highway entry points to the state, are sources for more free brochures and maps than one person could carry. They are located at the Virginia state line on I-77 near Mount Airy, on I-85 in Warren County, and on I-95 in Northampton County; at the Tennessee state line on I-26 in Madison County and on I-40 in Haywood County; and along the South Carolina state line on I-26 in Polk County, I-85 in Cleveland County, I-77 just outside Charlotte, and I-95 in Robeson County.

For basic planning, the maps on the VisitNC website will give you a good sense of the layout of the state and its major destinations. Many areas are experiencing rapid growth, particularly around Charlotte and the Triangle, so if your map is even a little out of date, you may not know about the newest bypass. For features like mountains, rivers, back roads, and small towns that don't change, atlas-style books of state maps are useful. My own favorite is DeLorme's *North Carolina Atlas & Gazetteer*.

Resources

Suggested Reading

TRAVEL

Eubanks, Georgann. *Literary Trails of the North Carolina Mountains: A Guidebook.* Chapel Hill: UNC Press, 2007. This book and its companion books *Literary Trails of the North Carolina Piedmont: A Guidebook,* 2010, and *Literary Trails of Eastern North Carolina: A Guidebook,* 2013, introduce fans of Southern literature to the places that produced and inspired various scribes. Also included are the best bookstores and book events across the state.

North Brunswick Magazine. www.lifein-brunswick.com. A monthly lifestyle magazine covering Brunswick County; along with its sister publication, *South Brunswick Magazine*, it features stories from beach towns like Oak Island and Ocean Isle Beach, as well as Southport. Leland and other towns.

North Carolina Atlas and Gazetteer. Yarmouth, ME: DeLorme, 2012. Since I was in Boy Scouts, I have always been partial to DeLorme's state atlases. This series represents in great detail the topography and other natural features of an area, giving far more useful and comprehensive information than the standard highway map.

Our State. www.ourstate.com. For a lively and informative look at North Carolina destinations and the cultural quirks and treasures you may find in your travels, *Our State* magazine is one of the best resources around. The magazine is easy to find, sold at most bookstores and even on grocery store and drugstore magazine racks. It covers arts, nature, folklore, history, scenery, sports, and lots of food, all from a traveler's perspective.

Salt. www.saltmagazinenc.com. This monthly arts and culture magazine covers Wilmington and the Cape Fear region but occasionally reaches out to other parts of the state. For a focused look at one part of the North Carolina coast, it's hard to find a better magazine.

HISTORY AND CULTURE

Cecelski, David. *The Waterman's Song: Slavery and Freedom in Maritime North Carolina.* Chapel Hill: UNC Press, 2001. A marvelous treatment of the African American heritage of resistance in eastern North Carolina, and how the region's rivers and sounds were passages to freedom for many enslaved individuals.

Powell, William S. *North Carolina: A History.* Chapel Hill: UNC Press, 1988. A readable, concise account of our fascinating and varied past.

Powell, William S., and Jay Mazzocchi, editors. *Encyclopedia of North Carolina.* Chapel Hill: UNC Press, 2006. A fantastic compendium of all sorts of North Carolina history, letters, and politics. If you can lift this mammoth book, you'll learn about everything from Carolina basketball to presidential elections to ghosts.

Setzer, Lynn. *Tar Heel History on Foot: Great Walks through 400 Years of North Carolina's Fascinating Past.* Chapel Hill: UNC Press, 2013. This book sends you on a series of short walks in all parts of the state—coastal and mountain, city and country, historic sites and state parks—to discover the history of the state. The walks are arranged by theme and location, making it simple to find one near you.

Wright, David, and David Zoby. *Fire on the Beach: Recovering the Lost Story of Richard Etheridge and the Pea Island Lifesavers.* New York: Oxford University Press, 2002. The riveting tale of the first African American captain of a U.S. Life Saving Station and his all-African American crew. Spanning the time from just before the Civil War to the turn of the 20th century, it's a fascinating look at life for enslaved people and former slaves on the Outer Banks.

Internet Resources

NEWSPAPERS

North Carolina newspapers have unusually rich online content and are great resources for travel planning.

Fayetteville Observer
http://fayobserver.com
News and culture from Fayetteville and the surrounding towns.

Port City Daily
www.portcitydaily.com
A website devoted to reporting daily and breaking news in Wilmington.

StarNews
www.starnewsonline.com
Daily news coverage of Wilmington and neighboring towns.

Outer Banks Sentinel
www.obsentinel.com
News and events pertinent to Outer Banks towns.

ARTS AND CULTURE

North Carolina's arts and history have an ever-growing online dimension, telling the story of the state in ways that paper and ink simply can't.

North Carolina Folklife Institute
www.ncfolk.org
The website will fill you in on the many organizations across the state that promote traditional music, crafts, and folkways. You'll also find a calendar of folk life-related events in North Carolina and travel itineraries for weekends exploring Core Sound as well as Cherokee heritage in the state.

NC Beer Guys
www.ncbeerguys.com
Two guys who love beer and write about it on the state's biggest beer-centric blog. They're always up to date with brewery and bottle shop openings, and their videos and blog posts get in-depth about beer.

NCFOOD
www.ncfolk.org/category/food
This wonderful food blog, maintained by the Folklife Institute, features articles about the culinary back roads of the state.

North Carolina Arts Council
www.ncarts.org
The Arts Council provides information about performing arts, literature, cultural trails, galleries, and fun happenings.

Our State
www.ourstate.com
The online companion to this print publication provides expanded coverage of the history, people, food, and arts across North Carolina. An extensive archive of stories lets you look back several years for the best the state has to offer.

Visit North Carolina
www.visitnc.com
The state's official tourism portal has great, and regularly updated, content including trip ideas and itineraries, spotlights on regions and cities, and articles on specific elements of North Carolina culture.

OUTDOORS

Great online resources exist for planning outdoor adventures in North Carolina, where rich arts and blockbuster sports are matched by natural resources.

North Carolina Sierra Club
http://sierraclub.org/north-carolina
Find information about upcoming hikes and excursions as well as an overview of the state's natural areas and environmental issues.

North Carolina Birding Trail
www.ncbirdingtrail.org
Covering bird-watching across the state, this site contains information about dozens of pristine locations and active flyways along the coast.

Carolina Canoe Club
www.carolinacanoeclub.org
A clearinghouse of statewide canoeing resources.

Carolina Kayak Club
www.carolinakayakclub.org
A repository for flat-water kayaking information, resources, trails, and activities across the state.

CanoeNC
www.canoenc.org
A nice starting point for planning a flat-water paddling trip in eastern North Carolina.

Carolina Sportsman
www.carolinasportsman.com
Covering hunting and fishing news, destinations, and seasonal trends across North and South Carolina.

Friends of the Mountains to Sea Trail
www.mountainstoseatrail.org
Find details, hike-planning tools, and resources for a day or longer on the 1,000-mile-long Mountains to Sea Trail that crosses North Carolina.

Index

List of Maps

Photo Credits

All photos © Jason Frye except page 6 © (bottom) Eric Sause - Dreamstime.com; page 7 © (top) Bhamms - Dreamstime.com; (bottom left) Bhamms - Dreamstime.com; (bottom right) Kelley Albert - Dreamstime.com; page 8 © (top) Richard Slack - Dreamstime.com; page 9 © (top) Daveallenphoto - Dreamstime.com; (bottom left) Iofoto - Dreamstime.com; (bottom right) Bruceflye - Dreamstime.com; page 10 © Zimmytws - Dreamstime.com; page 12 © Loganban - Dreamstime.com; page 13 © Cvandyke - Dreamstime.com; page 14 © Iofoto - Dreamstime.com; page 15 © Moonborne - Dreamstime.com; page 16 © (bottom) Cvandyke - Dreamstime.com; page 19 © (bottom) Kelley Albert - Dreamstime.com; page 23 © (bottom) Kendallwritings - Dreamstime.com; page 55 © Wangkun jia / 123rf.com; page 58 © (top left) Mark Vandyke | Dreamstime.com; (top right) Cynthia Mccrary | Dreamstime.com; (bottom left) Cynthia Mccrary | Dreamstime.com; (bottom right) Steven Prorak | Dreamstime.com; page 68 © (top) Sergey Kuznetsov | Dreamstime.com; (left middle) Joseph Morelli | Dreamstime.com; (right middle) Joe Sohm | Dreamstime.com; (bottom) Joe Sohm | Dreamstime.com; page 111 © (top left) Keifer | Dreamstime.com; page 129 © (left middle) Marie-claire Lander | Dreamstime.com; (right middle) Elizabeth Paige Brown | Dreamstime.com; page 145 © Patricia Shrout | Dreamstime.com; page 165 © (top) Rex Williams | Dreamstime.com; (bottom) Chris Boswell | Dreamstime.com; page 169 © Jmaentz - Dreamstime.com.

More Guides & Getaways

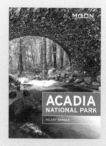

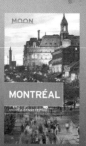